Modelling Engine Sheds
& Motive Power Depots
OF THE STEAM ERA

Modelling Engine Sheds & Motive Power Depots
OF THE STEAM ERA

TERRY BOOKER

THE CROWOOD PRESS

First published in 2016 by
The Crowood Press Ltd
Ramsbury, Marlborough
Wiltshire SN8 2HR

www.crowood.com

British Library Cataloguing-in-Publication Data
A catalogue record for this book is available from the British Library.

ISBN 978 1 78500 114 7

Disclaimer
The author and the publisher do not accept any responsibility in
any manner whatsoever for any error or omission, or any loss,
damage, injury, adverse outcome, or liability of any kind incurred
as a result of the use of any of the information contained in this
book, or reliance upon it. If in doubt about any aspect of railway
modelling skills and techniques, readers are advised to seek
professional advice.

Designed and typeset by Guy Croton
Publishing Services, Tonbridge, Kent

Printed and bound in Malaysia by Times Offset (M) Sdn Bhd

CONTENTS

PREFACE

One of the more difficult tasks facing the railway modeller, or indeed the model railway author, is to try to define the exact time at which the model is set. It's possibly fair to say that this problem is unique to our hobby. Our colleagues who model military subjects certainly have no such difficulties: if their diorama represents the Battle of Hastings, the Battle of the Bulge or the Battle of Gettysburg, then their definitions of time and place are predetermined. Even the Battle of Britain can be pinned down to a matter of weeks and specific locations. The same is true of their single models, where the tank or aircraft belonged to a particular unit or even to a particular officer.

It is not so easy for us who strive to produce realistic models of the steam or early diesel periods. In most cases, though not all, even our locations are hypothetical and our time-span is often defined in years ... if not decades. This is not made any easier by the simple fact that our chosen subjects were in a constant state of evolution. Many engines reached the scrapyards of the 1960s looking much as they did when they left the factories a half-century earlier, but in the intervening years they may well have worn a dozen or more different liveries. This fact is an undoubted boon to ready-to-run (r-t-r) manufacturers, who can produce scores of 'new' models from their original investment.

These anachronisms are almost inevitable and I must admit that on my own layouts, which ostensibly are set in the decade from 1945 to 1955, Southern engines can appear in pre-war Maunsell livery, Bulleid Malachite Green, early BR blue or post-1956 Brunswick Green with the later crest. Nor are things any better with my ex-GWR, LMS, LNER and BR Standards.

Fortunately most engine sheds tended to look pretty much the same throughout their lives, give or take the odd coat of paint. For this book, at least, we can let the description 'Steam Era' span the whole period from the last years of the Big Four up to the last wisps of steam at end of the 1960s. Indeed, we'll go even further by giving our motive power depot (MPD) a new lease of life as a contemporary 'Steam Centre', where you can feature your locomotives in whatever livery you choose.

ACKNOWLEDGEMENTS

It is not long since I was grappling with the problem of what to say in my previous book on modelling goods trains. The difficulty is compounded by the need to avoid repeating myself even while thanking those same kind individuals. However, I must begin by expressing my gratitude to my publishers at The Crowood Press who bravely commissioned this second title almost before the first manuscript had been delivered. Next I cannot allow the immense tolerance, generosity and encouragement of my late parents to pass unacknowledged. Even when times were hard they never failed to foster my love of steam railways and my passion for model-making. How lucky can one get to then have a family of one's own who continued to support 'the old chap' in both these hobbies. My poor wife and my two fine sons have been dragged from one end of the country to another in pursuit of steam. Even our continental holidays meant *dampf* on the Rhine and not loungers on the Riviera.

For this book in particular I must thank those companies who kindly contributed some of the kits and bits for the many projects, notably Dapol, Scalescenes, Langley, Freestone Models, Sankey Scenics and Model Railway Scenery. The assistance of the archivists who have provided the invaluable, and duly credited, images has helped to anchor the work firmly in the long-past steam era. Finally, and as before, I would like pay tribute to the scores of photographers, authors and publishers who keep us engrossed as readers and inspired as modellers.

(All photographs are the Author's unless otherwise credited.)

INTRODUCTION

Engine sheds are often referred to as 'Cathedrals of Steam', usually by romantically inclined authors who never had the dubious pleasure of having to work within their dark, dank and dangerous environments. It is true that the shafts of hazy sunlight filtering through the smoke-begrimed windows, recorded for posterity by talented cameramen, sometimes resemble the heavenly beams glimpsed in our magnificent churches, but there the resemblance ends. Just read a few chapters of any engineman's autobiography and any ecclesiastical images will be quickly dispelled. The sheds were Victorian in their origins, Victorian in their practices and the standards of health and safety were certainly Victorian. Our fathers and grandfathers were as unlike us as a Patriot is to a Pendolino. They didn't just endure these primitive working conditions; they thrived amid them and took enormous and justifiable pride in being a part of that elite community of railway servants.

This is the epitome of the 'Cathedrals of Steam' shot, as a veteran pre-grouping 4-4-0 enjoys its twilight years. BEN BROOKSBANK AND LICENSED FOR REUSE UNDER THIS CREATIVE COMMONS LICENCE

In the following chapters I hope to apply some of the creative ethic that is an integral part of the works produced by our fellow military modellers. Irrespective of whether they produce dioramas, set pieces or single subjects, there is always an underlying feeling of 'tribute' to those who fought there or who drove or flew the original machines. That is not to say that they are in any way either pious or precious about their efforts. They simply set great store in their research and do their best to capture some of the atmosphere alongside the undoubted accuracy of their model-making. Without wishing to over-romanticize things – and I admit to being a fairly frequent military modeller myself – it's a bit like a handshake or a salute back in time. Perhaps it's a way of saying 'thank you' and keeping the memories alive.

In a short poem Sir Christopher Foxley-Norris described a Battle of Britain pilot as *'a common, unconsidered man, who, / For a moment of eternity, / Held the whole future of mankind / In his two sweating palms – / And did not let it go'*. I would like to think that bygone generations of enginemen and shed staff merit a similar outlook from railway modellers. They too were ordinary men whose lifetime's work it was to constantly maintain the nation's arteries, in all weathers and with machines that were at best primitive and at worst clapped-out. They deserve our respect and admiration and, if we can convey any of this on our layouts, the better modellers we will be.

RESEARCH

One of the great things about engine sheds is the plethora of potential research information. I accept that field research is a bit of a non-starter since most sites have long since been buried under bypasses, car parks or supermarkets. Those that do survive, like

Steam as I remember it: a pair of 'Caledonian' blue Kings pose alongside a newly built BR(W) Britannia. All three are long-term performers on the author's 'Wessex Lines'.

Didcot, Carnforth, Tysley or Swanage, are either very much changed and 'sanitized' or, as in the latter case, are generally inaccessible. Desk research, however, has never been easier. It can be roughly subdivided into three broad groups: technical, inspirational and anecdotal. The first category covers reference works that show the layout of the sheds, their key facilities and the site plans; they also often include the locomotive allocations at various times. Most of these are based on the individual BR regions and may include one or more photographs of the depot at some point in its history. The second category includes the innumerable 'on-shed' photo albums, which are also generally presented by region and are sometimes dedicated to just one establishment, usually a major motive power depot (MPD). It goes without saying that the shed buildings are often little more than the backgrounds to their resident or visiting engines. The final group comprises the many autobiographies from the footplatemen and sometimes from the Shedmasters. These are essential reading for anyone who wants their model shed to 'feel' like the real thing. The earlier chapters usually provide better reference points since enginemen, like everyone else, started at the bottom and their working lives then rarely took them much beyond the confines of the shed yard.

It is difficult to know how best to guide readers along the path of research. If we were discussing it within an academic environment it would be considerably easier, since one could reliably expect that all the students were at roughly the same point on the learning-curve. In this particular context, however, no two readers will share the same levels of experience, the same levels of skill or have layouts at the same level of development. In order to be fair and to offer something useful to the newer entrants to the hobby, any advice must begin at the beginning, even though that may risk being too simple for the more experienced modellers. The reverse is, of course, equally true. If everything is pitched at a level to match the aspirations of those who are already into the more advanced aspects of modelling, it inevitably means ignoring the needs of the newcomers.

It is indeed a dilemma, but with due apologies to the older hands, who can skip the more basic techniques, I'll start by setting out some of the initial guidelines regarding research. The first of these is that it should, above all, be a pleasurable experience and not a tiresome chore that keeps you away from modelling.

POSSIBLE SCENARIOS

Most modellers probably have at least a vague idea of the sort of layout they would like to build and it is equally likely that there is an engine shed somewhere within that idea. Another assumption is that the prospective layout will be largely hypothetical in location and probably quite loose in its time-frame. Now there's nothing wrong with returning from the nearest model shop with an armful of track, a few buildings and some engines and rolling stock, shoving it on a baseboard and 'playing trains'. The ultimate aim, after all, is to simply enjoy watching the trains running, no matter how sophisticated our layouts.

A few hours of research, however, can transform those rather haphazard beginnings into the start of a well thought-out model railway. It is immaterial whether our ambitions are constrained by a lack of funds, time or space, or whether we can confidently envisage building a major layout. The branch-line terminus or main-line junction will both be the better if they originate from some prototype research rather than just a convenient way of filling the available space.

I like to think of research as a sieve for ideas. We start with a very coarse screen, just browsing through all the available sources – print or internet – eliminating that which doesn't appeal or is not really relevant to our original idea. Anything that gets through the sieve should then help to give a better idea of some aspect of the following key elements:

Swindon's running-sheds on a Sunday morning in the early 1950s. *BEN BROOKSBANK AND LICENSED FOR REUSE UNDER THIS CREATIVE COMMONS LICENCE*

Geographic location: This might be Home Counties commuter belt, Midlands industrial, North Country mining, Welsh mountains, Wessex rural or something else.

Parent company/BR region: The choice of LMS, LNER, Great Western, Southern or BR (Scottish) will obviously be influenced by the chosen location.

Size of shed/operations: This is where reality impinges on the dream. What we can actually build will be governed by the space available, which in turn will govern the level of operations that we can envisage. This is where you must decide between a branch line or a main line.

Allocation: This is probably the most contentious issue facing most modellers: do we try to find a shed that can accommodate the engines that we want (or already own) or do we limit our choice of motive power to that which would be the most likely to be allocated? My head of course says the latter, but my layout proves the former!

This first trawl through the various sources should, when put together with your original ideas, enable you to come up with the vital foundations for a satisfying layout. It will, of course, need some refining but there is now sufficient information for a viable back story and perhaps for a few tentative track plans to see what you might be able to fit into the allotted space. I would advise you to get into the habit of writing things down. It need not be anything elaborate; just a simple ring-binder and an A4 refill pad will suffice. Use the back pages to jot down ideas and references, perhaps adding some photocopied images, and use the front of the folder for your back story and any essential elements. If you'd prefer, the same exercise can be done on your keyboard. Your back story will already have combined the answers to those previous questions: the probable location, the company or region, the size of the shed and the likely traffic needs, and finally the necessary engine types. Now you can start the more focused and finely filtered research.

It's best to discard any sources that are no longer relevant to the plot. Wherever possible concentrate your searches on those works that are specific to your chosen location/region or at least feature them to a significant extent. The two areas where you can justifiably stay broadly based are track plans and autobiographies. The former may give you a near-perfect track plan from Devon that ban easily be transferred to north Northumberland, while the experiences of an engineman in Leeds will be little different from those of a GWR man at Laira.

MODELLING THE SHED

At the risk of making yet another assumption, I would suggest that the vast majority of layouts rely upon kit-built sheds rather than on scratch-built examples of specific prototypes. We are fortunate that the current offerings from the trade are both many and varied; indeed, if one then adds the ease with which they can be extended and altered, it almost eliminates the need to even consider the scratch-built option.

In the following chapters we will be constructing many of the available kits from the very smallest up to those better suited to the larger MPDs. Some of these are based on actual prototypes, but the majority are what might be described in ecclesiastical terms as 'non-denominational', or more commonly as 'one size fits all'. Any of these can be quickly re-regionalized with the simple application of new paintwork in the appropriate livery. Most steam sheds, however, rarely saw a paintbrush once they were commissioned and several decades of smoke and soot rendered them in the same smut-covered colours from Penzance to Inverness.

Any 'shed' is going to be much more than just the building itself. The shed-yard and all the other essential facilities are key factors in creating a realistic and 'railway-like' model. They were as varied as the sheds in both size and presence: one would not expect to encounter mechanized coaling plants and locomotive hoists at the end of a rural branch line. Similarly, no large MPD would expect its coalmen to refill a score or so tenders working with just a shovel off a sleeper-built stage.

Sherborne shed on 'Wessex Lines' is the author's rather reduced interpretation of an MPD. It's a scratch-built exercise based on a single small image of the former LSWR shed at Salisbury.

Steam on shed in the twenty-first century. This ex-Db 2-6-2 awaits its turn of duty at this large and very popular steam centre in the Netherlands.

All of these facilities will be looked at in some detail and as appropriate to the type of shed and the scale of its activities. The emphasis will focus on the available kits, but the various dioramas will also include a degree of scratch-building and adaptation. It also goes without saying that no shed scene would be complete without its allocated locomotives, the enginemen who drove them and the small army of shed staff who kept them on the road. That thought brings us neatly back to where we began.

I suspect that there are very few of today's modellers who had access to a shed on a normal working day, apart from the elite group of former footplatemen or shed staff who are still active in the modelling world. Some of the older generation of spotters might possibly have enjoyed the occasional official weekend visit to a shed, but that is not the same. Lastly there is that very small minority of former enthusiasts who

may have worshipped in these 'cathedrals of steam' on a weekday (if the noble art of 'bunking' a shed without being caught can be described as a religious experience).

It was always the men who worked them, however, that gave them their true status and character. It is not enough to present them as shiny plastic drivers, acrobatic ever-shovelling firemen and labourers in neat overalls. They were ordinary men going about their daily routines and should be portrayed as such. Yet it was those same men who gave us 'linesiders' so many treasured memories and have since gone on to inspire generation after generation of modellers, many of whom were not even born when the last sheds were demolished.

Ensuring that your modelling is truly 'railway-like' will help to provide a fitting tribute to the fast-vanishing family of steam-era enginemen.

CHAPTER ONE

SMALL ENGINE SHEDS

THE ENGINE SHED IN THE STEAM ERA

Most modellers, even those who are still only just emerging from starting with train sets, like to include an engine shed on their layouts, even if it this may have little purpose beyond being somewhere to park any spare locos when they are not in use. This has always been the case, even in the days when the choice of sheds was limited to the single-road plastic kit from Airfix or the larger two-road card version from Bilteezi. Many layouts in the 1960s were graced by these models, often using two, three or even more kits combined into a larger structure. Today, however, there are far more choices on offer in both kit form and as ready-to-site models from Bachmann and Hornby.

If we wish to stick to the intention of achieving truly 'railway-like' and prototypical appearance and operations, which I outlined in my previous book on modelling goods trains, we must delve deeper into what the steam-era shed was all about. Fortunately, there is plenty of archive material available in books, magazines, on DVD and via the web. This can range from major titles featuring all the sheds within a specific BR region (with photos, track plans and even stock lists) to the autobiographies of enginemen or shed staff that deal with life at one particular depot. To these can be added the ever growing library of steam albums, some of which are specifically shed orientated and most of which include at least a handful of shed shots. Film archives, lovingly remastered onto DVDs, can be an endless source of information and inspiration. These are able to capture shed life almost minute-by-minute with

The small shed at Marlow, Buckinghamshire. The fireman is loading the bunker of his 14xx tank directly from the steel-open. This is an unusual practice but would be interesting to model. Note the familiar ash heap and that the coal is in the form of briquettes. The very prominent notice warns of the low headroom.

AUSTIN ATTEWELL

Much Wenlock shed, seen here in GWR days, is a typical Victorian structure sturdily built of local stone with considerable decorative work. Note the cramped interior, the massive doors and the water tank at the rear of the shed. The water tank could also be located over the entrance. COURTESY
STEAM MUSEUM OF THE GREAT WESTERN RAILWAY SWINDON

locos arriving, being serviced and going off-shed, all amid the atmospheric smoke and smother that epitomized the steam-era depot.

Irrespective of its size, the loco shed, like the goods shed and goods yards featured in my earlier book, shared many common features and common purposes throughout the land. Locomotives could be housed there under cover between duties. Resident or visiting engines could replenish their coal supply and take on water. In many cases engines could be turned on a turntable or make use of a convenient 'triangle junction'. Even the smallest branch-line shed had the facility to drop the fire, dispose of the ash and clinker, and carry out the vital oiling and some basic repairs. Larger sheds would provide a far wider range

of facilities, such as boiler wash-outs, wheel-drops, hoists, repair shops and mess-rooms. Something that most of them shared was that they were definitely only for the staff, with absolutely no official public access. They would often be some distance away from the end of the platform and any waiting trains-potters. Even those that were temptingly close, such as Bournemouth or Bristol Bath Road, remained tan-talizingly inaccessible to the enthusiast.

Sheds were universally, and unavoidably, dirty and potentially dangerous environments in which to work. Irrespective of the enthusiasm of even the most autocratic shed foreman, little could be done to keep it and its environs clear of the inevitable muck and clutter resulting from round-the-clock

Tetbury shed is more typically Great Western in appearance, being of brick construction and with far less detailing. The coaling stage has a shovelling platform in front of the storage area and is built back into the steep hillside. AUSTIN ATTEWELL

Tetbury again, but this time from Prototype Models and here representing the branch shed at Watlingford on the author's 'Wessex Lines'. The small coaling stage was built to fit from balsa strip to replicate the usual sleeper constructions.

operations. All of this can present a real challenge to even the most experienced of modellers. It stretches one's capabilities as a scenic expert to the limits. Thatched country cottages, trees, fields, ponds and fully detailed working farmyards are much easier to model than any attempt to capture accurately the appearance and atmosphere of a busy steam shed. In later sections we will show some of the ways that this can be overcome, but first it is worth examining the principal facilities and key features. Once again the simplicity of a list is the easiest way to approach the subject from the modeller's angle.

Regionality: This can be defined either as the originating company, a BR region and/or a particular geographic area. All of these factors will influence to some extent the design of the buildings and the materials likely to be used.

Size and role: These factors are interdependent and will be governed to a large extent by the back story to the layout and the available space. If you are modelling a typical branch-line terminus, a single-road shed housing one or two small locos will be adequate. If you have more grandiose ambitions and are assembling a secondary or main-line layout, then you can justify a multi-road shed with full facilities and a stud of twenty or so suitable locomotives. To do this, however, the available space will have grown from a square foot to at least a square yard.

Siting: Where to place your shed needs careful consideration. Bigger sheds indicate more intensive operations, for which you will require easy physical access. Ideally it should be away from your passenger platforms and, if possible, also quite separate from the goods yards.

Shed design: There is a wide range options here that can be summarized into three principal areas:

• Straight sheds, which may have either an end-wall or through tracks;
• Hipped roof or transverse north-light versions;

• Offices, messing, stores, workshops and so on, all of which may be built-in or separate structures.

All of these will be examined in later sections.

Basic facilities: Essential facilities include a coaling point, watering point, inspection pit, ash pit, work-bench, stores, and mess-room. (The last of these may be no more than a grounded van body or a small lean-to attached to the main building.)

Extended facilities: These will apply to larger sheds: a sand furnace, workshops, mechanized coaling, multiple watering points, an ash-shelter and coal stack (both immediate post-war only), offices, loco hoist, wheel-drop, cycle racks or sheds and a turntable. The bigger the shed, the more of them they will have.

Personnel: Even a small shed is likely to have two or three sets of footplate crew: three sets per loco is a safe bet for most depots. If there are two or three allocated engines, then the non-footplate

An excellent example of how the original builders dealt with the modeller's problem of lack of space. This is the shed at Kingsbridge, complete with inspection pit, coaling stage, ash heap and water tank, squeezed into the narrow gap between the platforms and the hillside.
AUSTIN ATTEWELL

staff might run to a shedman and perhaps a resident fitter. Larger sheds will see a larger number of crews either preparing or disposing of locomotives. Crews would book-on to allow at least an hour preparation before they were due off-shed. To these can be added cleaners (in teams of four) and the shed staff themselves. A reasonably large shed, such as Reading, with about ninety locomotives, would have had close to three hundred crews and more than fifty shed staff. Many of the latter would be working in civilian clothes rather than any official dress. In the 1950s a considerable amount of hard-wearing, ex-service clothing was in evidence. Loco men would generally be in well-washed and faded overalls. The GWR men wore jacket and trousers on the footplate, but these were not always regulation issue.

Surfaces: By the mid-1950s most sheds had been in daily use for more than a century. In the busiest areas the mixture of crushed ballast, cinders, ash and coal dust had built up to at least sleeper height, leaving only the chairs and rails remaining above ground level. These created the inevitable hazards for crews preparing locos within the wet, windy, stygian gloom of a winter's evening, illuminated only by the flickering flame of a flare lamp. In many instances even the sleepers in the four-foot had disappeared and the accumulation of general detritus had reached the top of the rails. The uneven ground meant that puddles were numerous, caused by the engines themselves as well as by the weather. In the winter months the whole shed yard would appear to be a blend of almost shiny greys and blacks, while in the summer the tones would be the softer, paler and with much dustier greys and oily browns. The areas around the coaling stage were coated in coal dust all year round, while the disposal roads and ash pits would be covered with a liberal coating of almost creamy-white ash and char.

Debris: More of this would be found later in the selected period as the railways struggled to find staff, especially among labouring grades. Typical junk would include piles of brake-blocks, boiler tubes, fire-bars and broken fittings around the workshops and the shed walls. Around the yard would be brooms, buckets and bent discarded fire-irons. Sheds needed several different grades of oil, so multi-coloured barrels, full and empty, could be seen piled up awaiting collection. In the earlier years of the chosen period morale and

Another of the author's models, this time inspired by the timber-built shed at Fairford. The actual carcass is the old Airfix (Dapol) plastic kit, but it has been completely covered with planking and re-roofed with tile-paper. The crew accommodation is an ancient 'Toad' brake van and the water tank is a Wills kit with coaling platform beneath. Some scrap plastic stonework helps to tie the scene together.

staff levels were that much higher: pride in the job and the sense of being 'company servants' generally led to a much tidier environment.

Track layouts: These are infinitely variable, from the ultimate in simplicity with just one siding serving a single-road shed at a branch terminus to the maze of tracks and point-work needed for a major MPD. Every track plan will be unique, but there are still some aspects you may wish to consider. Wherever possible you should endeavour to have separate access to the ash pit, coal stage and turntable, as distinct from the shed and storage roads. This enables visiting locos to be serviced without impacting on shed movements. Try also to have spare trackwork even when most of your allocation is at home. Shed yards rarely looked full of locos except overnight or at weekends, and even then some movements were still possible.

These general pointers may help to guide your eye as you study your various references and they should give you plenty of ideas for your project build. As always there is much to note and probably too much to remember. My own technique when researching is to have a notebook or scrap pad handy to jot down, or even quickly sketch, any items and ideas that could prove useful when building and detailing the sheds.

In the subsequent sections many of these features will be re-examined in more detail. In particular we will look at their relevance and suitability for the specific projects and how they might best be replicated in miniature.

SMALLER SHEDS

The most appropriate description of the first subject we will tackle is a small single-road engine shed, usually found at the end of a branch line or at sites with a specific role for no more than one or two engines, for example at the foot of a bank.

Most of this country's railways began life as pretty small affairs. They were promoted in the main by local merchants and industrialists seeking to get raw materials in and finished products out more cheaply,

quickly and reliably than by canal or turnpike. Even when the steam railway and locomotive haulage replaced horse power it still needed to be stabled, fed and watered in much the same way. The locomotive shed, or what might be described in Victorian terms as a 'commodious engine-house', would be the first structure to be built and brought into use.

Its purpose and the way in which it was worked would, unlike the locomotives it housed, remain largely unchanged from the mid-nineteenth century to its probable demise more than a hundred years later. The actual design of the sheds was very simple and their construction pretty basic. Structurally they were little more than three tall, solid walls with the fourth containing the entrance doorway. The roof was most likely a straightforward pitched version, although north light and hipped versions were not uncommon. As a rule the shed would feature large windows and a system of roof vents to allow smoke and steam to escape.

The general layout of the shed yard was infinitely varied depending on the immediate geography surrounding the site, which could range from wide, flat and open fields to the constraints of being squeezed against the face of a cliff. The sizes of the actual sheds themselves were equally variable. One of the main reference books on the subject, E.Lyons's *An Historical Survey of Great Western Engine Sheds*, 1947 (Oxford Publishing Co., 1974), notes that there were no fewer than eight different widths for single-road sheds, while they varied in length from a diminutive 40ft (12m) to more than 100ft (30m) for the largest structures. Out of the forty-six examples I examined in search of some common footprints, the best I could come up with was just five that measured 20 x 60ft (6 x 18m). Stretching the width slightly to 22ft (6.7m) yielded just two more examples. In modelling terms, those dimensions translate as 80 x 240mm, or nearly 10in long, which makes it a hefty item to squeeze into the often restricted available layout space. The two models selected to begin the projects will be of more modest dimensions.

Building materials would vary as much as would the actual designs. In most cases the choice would be locally sourced bricks, but if the builders had access

The Prototype kit of Sidmouth shed on the Southern Region. Here it is home to the resident banking engine, a kit-built 72xx 2-8-0 tank, on 'Wessex Lines'.

to cheaper dressed stone from a nearby quarry, then that might be the preferred option.

It is quite common to refer to some major sheds as 'cathedrals of steam'. The railway architects, like their colleagues in industrial and civic architecture, were strongly influenced by classical and ecclesiastical buildings. That being the case, the single-road engine shed could well be termed a 'chapel of steam'. Certainly their simple robust design closely resembled the growing number of rural and suburban chapels. On those few occasions where sheds were built of timber or corrugated iron, the resemblance to the once familiar 'tin chapel' could seem even more marked.

These simple structures alone, however, would not be enough. The locomotive could at least be securely locked away when not in use, but the iron horse was then, and is now, a greedy beast and requires regular and ample supplies of coal and water. It also needed to be repaired and maintained, so the shed immediately became a small self-supporting facility with adequate resources on hand to keep the locomotive in profitable daily work.

Internally there would be a workbench with vice and enough tools to keep the wheels turning. There would probably have been a small forge, anvil and water trough, cupboards for storage and a noticeboard. It would have somewhere secure for storing oils and lubricants, as well as a container for sand. Among the more readily available items would be the loco's oil lamps and undoubtedly some flare-lamps (like Aladdin's and still in common use in the 1950s). Externally three features would dominate, with first a stage or dump and perhaps a rudimentary hoist for loading the coal. Second there would be a water tower close enough to the track to fill the loco directly. This may also have had a pump housed either adjacent to it or located within the supporting walls. The final visible feature would be the dump for ash and clinker. Somewhere within that small yard area, probably outside the shed doorway, would be the loco pit, where ashes could be dropped or works carried out to the underside of the engine.

What of the staff? Obviously there would be a driver, although from the dawn of the railways to the demise of steam he was more properly known as

Access to the shed via a turntable was fairly unusual: it is also very difficult to reproduce in model form. These turntables were quite small and there seems to be nothing suitable in either ready-to-install or kit versions. This example is still in use on the Swanage Railway.

the 'engineman'. His colleague, then and now, is the fireman. They were responsible for the resident locomotive and at the smaller sheds they would probably have to carry out the preparation and disposal themselves. When a second and perhaps third locomotive was allocated, the company might recruit a couple of general 'shed men' to take over some of the less pleasant or technical tasks. They would be dropping the fire, emptying the ash pan and smokebox, ensuring that the bunker or tender was replenished and lighting up the engine before the shift.

Originally all these men would live in easy walking distance of the shed, as some of their shifts could be long and usually irregular. Once this initially simple shed became part of a proper station complex with goods and passenger facilities, the respective companies would often build railway cottages on an adjacent plot. This would almost certainly be the case if the shed was in a more rural location and often well beyond the outskirts of the town it served. As one might guess, such were the huge variety of locations, the different roles of the lines themselves,

and the differences in traffic and timetables, that any description of a typical working day is quite impossible. Nonetheless there are some common elements that can be put together to create that 'railway-like' atmosphere and 'prototypical' working.

TYPICAL DAILY ROUTINES

Branch lines rarely, if ever, operated at night. Traffic levels scarcely warranted it and the expense of even the most rudimentary safety measures for running after dark would be prohibitive. That said, the start and end of the working day in mid-December would undoubtedly be somewhat nocturnal activities. As an example, we will assume that the small shed is home to two tank engines and that they are safely locked up for the night. The first arrivals will be the two shed men, who will set about the task of lighting up the engines: to give them a head start, they may have left a few small coals smouldering overnight. Both engines will be prepared, the one in front for the early morning workmen's service to the junction, the second for the goods working that takes the full wagons and empties that had accumulated the previous afternoon.

When the crews arrive the respective firemen would join in by raising steam, gathering up the tools and doing some of the less accessible oiling up. The enginemen would come on duty at least an hour before they were due off-shed, checking the locomotives and completing the oiling, doubtless pausing for a chat over a pipe or a cigarette while they studied any traffic notices. Once steam had been raised they might well draw up to the water crane to ensure the tanks were full, with the fireman standing on the tank top to put the bag in while the engineman worked the valve. The shed men meanwhile may be topping up the bunkers from the coal dump. Eventually, and probably after a quick sluice at the shed tap and a well-earned cup of tea, the two locomotives would whistle to the signalman, if he was on duty, or set the road themselves, and then ease away to pick up their respective trains.

All that is left for the shed men to do is tidy up and complete their morning routines. To all intents and purposes the shed is now deserted: in winter there

would be little need to reopen the big doors until the locomotives return at the end of their shifts.

During the day the resident engines would return periodically to replenish coal and water, with the frequency depending on the timetable, the length of the branch, loads and gradients. This offers modellers plenty of scope for licence. Other movements might include a visit by a larger engine off some special working, and the shed itself would probably have had a daily 'full coal in and empty coal out' and maybe even a weekly 'empty in and full ash out' working.

At the end of the working day the two locos would return to the shed. Their arrivals would probably be juggled to ensure the appropriate 'first in/last out' stabling. The first tasks would be to replenish the coal and water. Next would come the fire-dropping, clearing out the ash pan, removing any clinker from the fire-bars and finally removing the soot and 'char' from the smokebox. If this were done properly, there would be just enough boiler pressure remaining to roll the engine gently back into the shed. Lock the doors and that's it. After a quick wash-down under the tap, the grubby over-

This outstanding model, based on the 100ft (30m) installation from Launceston, has graced the world-famous Dartmoor scene at Pendon Museum for many years. ANDY YORK, COURTESY PENDON MUSEUM

alls would be hung up and the crews and shed staff could cycle off to their allotments or nip across to the pub for a swift pint.

The ancillary facilities around the shed are highly variable. We have already discussed the need for a water tower, with or without a separate water crane. The coaling stage may be little more than a shovelling platform open to the elements or it may have some rudimentary tin (corrugated iron) shelter and a simple hoist or crane. Crew 'accommodation', a loose description if ever there was one, can be a purpose-built small annexe or a grounded ancient coach body. The latter is often modelled, but there are several known alternatives, such as a discarded horsebox or goods brake van, that would add interesting character to your layout.

Optional extras can include a tin-roofed shelter for drums of oil, grease and kindling wood for fire lighting. This might also be where the inevitable pedal cycles, or even the motorbikes of the younger firemen, can be stored. There may even be, if access permits, somewhere for an ancient car to be parked. Lastly toilet facilities might be little more than another tin shack round the back, or if the shed still exists in the 1960s, it might be graced by a Portaloo. External lighting would at best be sparse, but a couple of convenient posts carrying electric power or telephone cables, with lamp brackets attached, would not be out of order. That is all there might be to a single-road shed at the end of the branch line.

The other location, as a base for a banking engine, will look and work much the same. The key differences, if any, are that the locomotives would probably be larger and more powerful. Their daily comings and goings would be much more frequent and may well involve at least one crew change. The banker may also be on call around the clock, which could easily justify extra lighting and more frequent coal deliveries.

Both locations would be officially designated as sub-sheds of the nearest larger MPD. This provides the excuse for an engine change at least once a week so that the allocated loco or locos can return to the depot for boiler wash-outs and any fitting jobs that couldn't be accomplished on site.

It is to be hoped this relatively brief description will help point modellers to their own versions of these small steam outposts. They certainly provide a wealth of opportunities that can go towards the creation of a 'railway-like' atmosphere together with prototypical operations, and all in a relatively small space.

MODELLING THE SINGLE-ROAD ENGINE SHED

The biggest single factor in choosing which of the many offerings one should opt for will undoubtedly be the available space. Unless the layout is intended to replicate a prototype location, the chances are that it will be a question of 'how do I squeeze in the engine shed?' With that in mind, and in the knowledge that the structure can always be customized or regionalized to better suit the geography, I will survey some, if not all, of the kits in ascending order of footprint or, more simply, starting with the smallest and working my way up.

BUILDING THE ALPHAGRAPHIX SHED

They don't come any smaller than this: the main structure measures a mere 105 x 60mm. In scale terms that is 26ft long and 15ft wide (7.9 x 4.8m) and I am aware of only two of this size on the whole of the Western Region. Despite its low price of less than £5.00, it is a very complete and well thought-out kit. It includes a built-on office or storeroom, together with a water tower that can be added to the shed itself or constructed as a stand-alone item. The kit also includes two sets of double doors, enabling it to be built as a through shed, and the interior is reasonably detailed.

The package comprises just four sheets of printed A5 card. The main buildings are rather thin sheets with the stonework represented in a monochrome sepia/brown hue. These two sheets are commendably matt in finish. The two detail sheets are of a somewhat heavier gloss card and are almost full colour, being orangey-brown and black.

Alphagraphix has produced a small and inexpensive kit that is excellently designed, well printed and includes a comprehensive set of parts, but it takes some extra effort to get the best from it.

Despite its small size and low cost this is not a 'quickie' kit. This isn't because it is complicated, but rather because, in my opinion, it requires some improvements and customizing to get the best from it. This particular project will take the form of a sort of combined operation in which any additional tasks are integrated with the build itself.

Options and preparations

Using a new sharp blade in your scalpel or craft knife, cut out all the main walls for the shed, the office and the water tower. Score the various marked 'folds', carefully using the back of your blade rather than the empty biro suggested in the instructions: with small kits like this, clean sharp folds are essential for best results. Next bend everything into shape and offer it up to your layout or proposed site plan. I used an A3 piece of foamboard marked with a 3in square grid and with a length of straight track loosely positioned as a guide.

The kit can be assembled in various configurations and a test run will help you decide which version best suits the site and the intended operations. The main building can be modelled as a through shed with normal access from either end. In this case the office will need to be attached to the side of the structure, as in the illustration on the packaging. The water tower then becomes a stand-alone item or perhaps incorporated with a coaling stage that you will need to design and build from scratch or buy an off-the-shelf version

Alternatively, the office stays at the side and the tower is built on to one or other end of the shed, so making it a single-door version but modelled with access from the left or right to suit your plans. There is a fourth configuration that is slightly less straightforward and, needless to say, that's the one I selected. I opted to attach the office at the right-hand gable end, so the door faces outwards, and located the coaling stage and tower beside the left-hand entrance doors. This kept

The walls have only a nondescript finish and it is down to the modeller to paint them or cover them with an appropriate pre-printed sheet to suit the chosen location. To illustrate this, I used watercolours to do one section in red sandstone and the other in a pale grey Purbeck stone.

the whole complex within a 12 x 3in footprint, even with the extra depth needed for the coaling stage.

At this point, whichever configuration you choose, you have two major tasks ahead. I suspect you will have already spotted that the card supplied is very flimsy and a layer of reinforcement is essential. The second decision is one of finish. The printing is acceptable, but the dull brown on sepia card is neither visually attractive nor particularly prototypical. You could cover everything in a brick or stone pre-printed paper in the time-honoured manner or you could carefully use a planked finish or even corrugated iron. This would be an appropriate occasion, however, to introduce the scratch-building technique of painting stonework over the printed sheets.

Reinforcing the walls

This is a straightforward task but it does require a modicum of care and a good sharp blade. I chose to use the card backing from an A4 pad. This is thin enough to be easy to work yet still quite thick enough to provide the required structural strength. The process is simple; each wall is laid on the card and its outline together with any doors and windows are traced out with a sharp HB pencil. In cases like this I usually draw and cut the long sides to their full size and then reduce the width of the various gable ends by 1mm each side; this enables them to fit securely between the main walls. Ultimately, as is shown on the accompanying photo, you will end up with almost two kits. When it comes to laminating them together with PVA, I recommend you fit the glazing to the main sheet shed first and then fix the reinforcing panel. This keeps the final appearance more realistic. For the office, which features bent-back stone reveals for the door and the windows, fit the reinforcing strips first so that the stonework retains the required depth. Do not go any further with the assembly at this stage.

Quick mock-ups can be used to explore the various configurations that could be assembled. It's also a certain way to verify the need for additional reinforcing and bracing.

Painting

I chose to vary the painting of the stonework on the project example, completing one side and the end in a more reddish tone, not unlike that found around Penrith in Cumbria or on the West Somerset Railway. The other side I finished in the greyish/white stone common to many other areas in the UK. I left the office and water tower until later when I had determined the final finish.

As we have not previously discussed painting in any great detail it is worth having a look at the pros and cons. The major factor in its favour is that it gives the modeller total control over the end finish and delivers a unique appearance. The disadvantage is that it is not a quick process and takes time, practice and perseverance to get right. Personally I favour it and use it wherever possible, but that's writing with the experience of whole villages and fully detailed farmyards behind me.

For the project I used a simple No. 2 brush for the stones themselves and a long fine-pointed '0' for the shading strokes. Fortunately the kit includes a small section of printed card that is not needed for the assembly (the arched portion of the water tower base); this provided a sample on which to test the practicalities. One thing it did highlight was the un-prototypical size and brightness of the mortar courses, so the first step was to give all the walls a quick blackish wash that was little more than dirty water. Each stone was then painted individually with, on one side, a blend of reds straight from the palette, most of which were mixed with white to tone them down. The second set of sides were similarly treated, but with white slightly strengthened with some black and grey tones. The job is laborious and not made any easier by the deliberate lack of definition of the original print. For the record, each set of a side and gable end took about four hours. I like to replicate the three-dimensional effect of stonework by adding fine black shadow shading to the bottom right-hand corners of most stones. A steady hand and fine brush are prerequisites for a decent job.

The question remains, however, whether all this painting is worth the extra effort since it almost doubles the build time. My opinion is that it is more than justified as it is now very much your own work and unique to you, while also enhancing the prototypical appearance.

Assembly

Although no separate instruction sheet is provided with the kit, logic and the helpful guidance notes are more than adequate. All of the three obvious versions can now be assembled in the normal way and

The main kit components are seen here together with their reinforcing sections, cut from the back of an A4 pad.

the only extra work is to cut out the roof bases, which are not supplied, from scrap card to the dimensions given. You may also wish to add some judiciously placed corner strengtheners to maintain the necessary square and rigid structure.

If you are following the option I chose, you have an extra task involving the water tower. Cut off the whole of the pre-painted back wall and simply use the reinforcing panel at this point. It is not going to be visible on the final layout and you now have a better use for those stones. Cut out two strips 15mm deep and put them to one side. These will be the supporting walls for the coaling platform. Glue the office to the right-hand gable end of the main shed. Its width will be an exact fit and this will leave the upper part of the old access doorway exposed. Offer up your remaining piece of spare stonework from the back of the tower, mark it out on the gable end, cut it to fit and stick it in place.

Once everything is solidly together, attach the roof templates to the shed and office. There are no guidelines for the finish of the roofs but I would suggest that slate is the most realistic choice. I used my usual Superquick Grey and did not attempt anything fancy.

Finally add the provided details as supplied with the kit, together with any improvements such as guttering and downpipes, and a watering facility on the tower. Basic versions can now be weathered to choice, but my design first requires us to construct a simple coaling stage.

Modelling the coaling stage

One could almost say that there were as many different versions of the coaling stage as there were sheds. Each was simply the optimum size and shape needed to fit the site and fulfil its purpose. Construction methods and materials could, and often did, reflect the style as the shed itself, but it was just as likely that recycled sleepers and basic earthworks served the same purpose.

For the project I opted to face a timber-covered earthwork with an extension of the same stone used for the shed and water tower, giving this mini-complex a more attractive and unified appearance. This is also a case where 'size does matter'. This is

a functional and working environment that may well be used several times a day. The two critical aspects are that there must be sufficient room to store and access more than a single wagonload of coal, and sufficient space for that coal to be shovelled up into the bunker of the resident tank loco. There should also be room for the barrels of lubricating oil, fuel for the pumping engine in the water tower and a heap of kindling wood for lighting up. Together that would require a minimum platform width of 60mm (15ft) and a length of not less than 100mm (25ft). A quick mock-up using a standard 10-ton coal truck and the allocated engine should demonstrate that this will work.

Your back story can contribute to the plan in that the length and frequency of service on your branch line will determine the amount of coal you will need. The average small tank engine has a bunker capacity of between $2\frac{1}{2}$ and 3 tons; even if it manages to do a day's work on one full bunker, your coaling stage will still need at least two 10-tonners each week. Increase that consumption and it's easy to see how the shed will need a wagonload to be brought up on the morning goods every other day; and don't forget to dispose of the ash at least once a fortnight, if not more frequently. Sometimes the coal would simply be offloaded into a heap, but a sleeper-built retaining staithe will add to the overall appearance.

For the project the stage was knocked up out of scrap card, and the staithes were formed by balsa strips to represent sleepers and by plastic tubes, cut from cotton buds, to represent recycled boiler tubes. The rest of the surface was planked using sleepers made from coffee stirrers and the platform was faced with stone using the pre-painted offcuts from the back of the water tower. A simple water supply crane was made up from a scrap of cotton bud stem, some folded masking tape and a length of model chain to control the on/off valve.

Installation

Although this is not mentioned in the instructions, the shed is designed so its stone floor rests on top of the sleepers. That means we need to use play foam to build up the surrounding areas and then site the

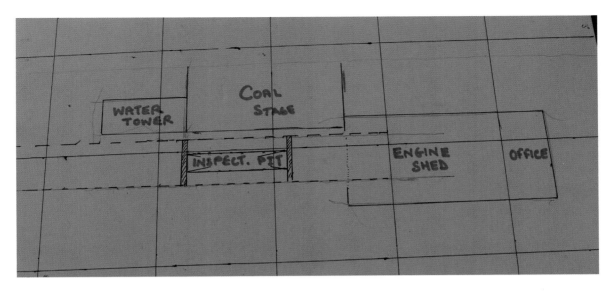

The final layout drawn full size onto the foamboard base. The 3in (7.5cm) grid provides a visual reminder of the space available.

structures on top of this. We also need to create an inspection pit somewhere in the complex. In most cases this would probably be within the shed itself, in which case it needs to be sorted before the various structures are sited. However, it is an interesting feature and all too rarely modelled, so it makes a good subject to install alongside the coal stage. In this instance the additional ash pit found at larger sheds is less necessary. With only one engine on shed, the fire would be dropped outside and the ash and clinker simply shovelled into a heap beside the track.

Adding an inspection pit

The inspection pit should between 15 and 20ft long (60–80mm or 8 to 10 sleepers). Select exactly where it is to be sited and mark it out on the trackbed/baseboard by simply 'dotting' between the appropriate sleepers with a ballpoint pen, and also 'dotting' the sleepers that need to be cut and removed.

If, as on the project, you are using a base of single or multiple foamboards then this part of the cutting process simply requires a scalpel. If you are using a single sheet, I would suggest adding one or more small sections beneath the board where the cuts will be made. This will ensure that your pit has the required depth. Seal the hole with a strip of card on the under-

side. If your baseboard is made from one of the wood options, then you will need to carry out some surgical carpentry. The usual method is to drill through the four corners with a large bit, perhaps adding a couple more along the sides. Connect the holes with a piercing saw and finally square them up with a heavy duty craft knife or Stanley knife and sand them smooth.

Cutting the inner sections of the sleepers requires a degree of care. It is important to maintain the integrity of the chairs and the supporting webs in order to ensure that the track gauge remains

A sharp and comparatively heavyweight blade is needed to cut the Peco 'streamline' sleepers. A curved blade proved the most satisfactory. It is not a quick task and requires considerable pressure in a downwards rocking motion. The track must always be on a firm surface and held steady.

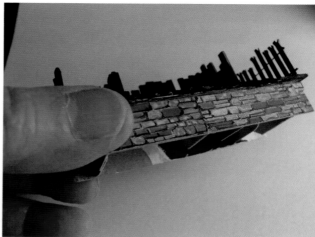

Cutting the play foam/foamboard base is much easier than cutting the sleepers. Keep the scalpel vertical and ensure the cut is properly square. A sharp blade is essential to hack through more than 10mm of fairly dense material. Don't worry if it looks ragged, as the ash pit will eventually be lined with brick paper.

It took just a couple of hours to make this coaling stage from scrap card, a recycled coal staithe from an earlier project and some cotton-bud 'boiler tube' fencing.

constant. The best method is to use a slitting disc in a suitable mini power tool, which makes for less stress on the track panel. If, however, you do not have this piece of equipment, then your craft knife or scalpel will be suitable. Keep the work well supported throughout and make cuts just inside the chairs working from the topside down.

Completing the scene

Laying the track, ballasting and scenic work is exactly the same as for the goods yard modules featured earlier. The main point to remember is that this whole area will be well-trodden by the feet of several generations of enginemen. There will be ample evidence of coal dust and oil stains everywhere and a few puddles near the water crane would be appropriate. You also need to feature piles of ash and clinker beside the track; a mound of ready-mix filler (or similar) with some coarse sawdust or ballast grains to add relief will do the job. Ash is usually a creamy grey colour and you can use the genuine article if you still have a coal fire at home.

Typical extras for the shed scene would be a couple of model cycles, a wheelbarrow or two, full and empty colour-coded oil drums, fire-irons and spare shovels on the coal heap. 'Huminiatures' can be justified even when the resident loco is off shed. A relief crew might be wandering up to book on or sitting around waiting for their turn. The shed's coalman might be tidying the heap, lounging on his shovel or perhaps talking to a fitter or one of the station staff. All these little features add interest and visual appeal and can be glimpsed in the accompanying photographs.

We will now take a look at building some of the other single-road sheds and see how well they fit into our little 'diorama'.

BUILDING THE KITMASTER/ DAPOL SINGLE-ROAD SHED

Dapol is to be congratulated for continuing to market what is undoubtedly a true 'steam era' shed. It was originally produced in the early 1960s by Kitmaster, whose once familiar logo again adorns the current packaging, and was later rebranded by Airfix. It has to be among the most popular railway accessory kits ever produced.

Just opening the packet is a trip back in time for older modellers. I am delighted to say that the kit has most certainly weathered the years in fine style and can

The completed models are checked against the grid to make sure that the initial plan is holding up. Everything appears to be in order, so they can now be fixed in place and the trackwork and scenic design can begin.

The Alphagraphix kit, built into a small but typical shed complex with the addition of the coaling stage, a van body for storage and the inspection pit. The latter is just visible and has not yet been lined.

The shed complex in position at the end of a rural branch line. Pannier tank 1368 from Weymouth Docks is on a running-in turn following a 'heavy-intermediate' at Swindon. Something is clearly adrift: while the inspector is waiting impatiently for the fitters to turn up, the crew are quite happy to enjoy an extended lunch break.

The Kitmaster/ Dapol shed, seen here positioned behind the Alphagraphix version, is almost half as big again.

stand comparison with most other plastic kit structures currently on the shelf. It is cleanly and crisply moulded with very little flash, and is comprehensive to the extent of including drainpipes, light fittings, a noticeboard and even a small wooden shed, the purpose of which is perhaps best left to the imagination. The design recognizes and encourages the modeller to combine kits into larger structures, either side by side or end to end, and it includes the extra fillers to facilitate this. The relief detailing of the brickwork and roof tiles is accurate and not overemphasized – a definite advantage when so many plastic kits boast mortar courses several scale inches deep. The instructions are simple and well supported by exploded diagrams, making it an easy option even for those completely new to the game. For the record, the footprint is roughly 140 x 75mm, which scales out to 35ft by just 20ft, more than adequate for most tank engines, even up to the larger 2-6-2s.

The first exercise is to remove any flash carefully with a scalpel and, in so doing, familiarize yourself with the various components, which are about thirty in total. The kit can be assembled using either tube or liquid polystyrene cement; I opted for the old-fashioned tube version. There are several conversion and customizing options open to the modeller, but the project will start with the straightforward assembly of the basic kit, before looking in more detail at methods of transforming it.

The actual assembly process is completely straightforward and the instructions tell you almost everything you need know, but there are a couple of tips that I am happy to pass on to fellow builders.

Window frames and glazing

This must be cut from the large sheets of acetate supplied. It is best done before the windows are fixed into the walls. Each piece must be an exact 'push fit' in the frames and secured with a small spot of poly in each corner, making sure that you avoid getting any adhesive or finger smears on the acetate. Before fixing, paint the outside of the frames first. You may still, however, be somewhat disappointed by the finished result. The window's glazing bars are simply far too chunky, scaling out at more than 3in square, which is far too big to represent the normal inch or so of the typical cast iron framework one would expect to find. This is not intended in any way to reflect unkindly on this otherwise excellent Kitmaster / Dapol product, but you should remember that it was first introduced more than a half century ago, when plastic kit technology was still in its infancy. The delicate tracery of the current offerings was still some way in the future. Remember, too, that this whole range of railway and lineside accessories were designed with the toy market in mind and were priced accordingly.

Two of the newly carved windows compared with those supplied. Note how the attempt to disguise one of the originals (left of the noticeboard) with darker paint fails to convince.

In an attempt to find a solution I looked through my selection of pre-printed acetates and my bits box for alternative mouldings, but nothing offered a speedy replacement. It would have been possible to go down the scratch build route, retaining the outer frames and then building up the glazing bars with plastic strip on the pre-fixed acetate. It can work, but it is far from easy. I finally settled for reducing the existing mouldings by carving away the excess with a sharp scalpel. The plastic is easy to work and a mixture of cutting and scraping delivered a more acceptable end result. It needs patience and you should allow twenty to thirty minutes for each window; a careful scraping of a light taper to each bar adds a final touch. Then paint and add the pre-cut acetate and insert the assembly into the wall as per the instructions. Note that if your shed or sheds will only be viewed from one side, you can omit this process from the windows on the back wall.

Smoke vents

These can be a bit tricky. Fix the ends of each set of louvres to the gable ends and allow the cement to cure. Then invert the model and, working from the inside, run a thin seam of cement along the join between louvre and the main roof sections. Carefully align them and hold them in place until set. Check each part. The walls, gable ends, roof sections and smoke vent are not identically fixed at both ends in order to facilitate the possible end-to-end combination of more than one kit. They simply won't work if you erroneously try them the wrong way round.

The average modeller should be able to complete the kit in two or three hours prior to the painting stage. During this first phase of the project I decided to work towards a slightly different result than the originally intended end-to-end combination of kits. Instead I would try for a 'back to back' and finish up with a through road shed, making it capable of being worked and accessed from either direction. This seemed to offer a more flexible option for most modellers; it also meant that I could combine the wooden lean-tos into a single structure sited on the long side of the main building. The rear of the single shed is therefore not fully painted since it is due to be discarded.

Painting

Like most routine operations there are almost as many methods as there are modellers. The painting of plastic brickwork is certainly no exception to this rule and every 'how-to-do-it' guide and magazine featured will probably come out with a different interpretation. Once again I will refrain from any rash statement about 'best practice', but simply describe my own technique and leave you to compare it with the numerous alternatives.

The engineer's blue brick decoration in watercolour shown in more detail and compared with the plain wall still being worked on. Note the very fine '0' brush being used.

Main walls: A painted finish is essential and somehow one needs to achieve a matt end product without obscuring too much of the relief brickwork. I chose to use two Humbrol enamels for the main walls: for the centre panels I mixed four parts of Humbrol Matt 63 to one part of Humbrol Matt 37, using the latter straight from the tin for the outer surrounds, gable ends and ridge tiles. It is essential to get the consistency right: too thick and it will obscure the detail, too thin and there's a danger of losing the required dead matt finish. Unfortunately I made that mistake with the centre panels to the extent that they dried 'shiny'. A rummage in the pastel box, however, found a near identical shade and this was generously applied. Luckily it worked without obscuring the mortar panels. You will also see from one of the accompanying illustrations that I treated the walls of the additional second kit at the same time, in order to ensure consistency when the two were combined.

While I was happy with the chosen colours, the end result still looked bland, unrealistic and un-railway like. I therefore abandoned the enamels

The purpose of the small curved upturns along the eaves was a bit of a puzzle. In the end I decided, rightly or wrongly, that they were intended to represent the guttering: the outer sides were therefore painted in house-green and the tops in matt black. Although the same moulding exists on the smoke vent roof and could become equally decorative, I felt this would be too much and so used the matt black.

in favour of the greater precision of watercolour and a '0' detailing brush. Using Winsor and Newton Indigo, I set about picking out some simulated engineer's blue decorative brickwork. It is a laborious task and requires the usual steady hand and concentration, but I find that it helps to completely transform an otherwise dull structure. If you intend to undertake a similar task, then the following tips may help. Always use watercolours since they are easier to apply, simple to touch up, have 'zero' consistency and can be quickly wiped off in the case of errors. Make sure your basic paintwork is dead matt or you will encounter problems applying watercolours. Allow enough time as there are a lot of bricks: somewhere in the region of five hours should suffice to detail the double shed assembly

Roofs: Attention needs to be given to the painting the roofs, including the smoke vents. I find that attempting to reproduce slate roofs realistically, whether with enamels on plastic or watercolours on paper, is one of the most difficult tasks to face the modeller. The colours of slate, perhaps 'tones' would be more accurate, are both elusive and constantly variable in changing light conditions. It is also true that in our chosen scale slates have almost no thickness, so the existing mouldings actually work against us. The roof is the most consistently visible part of our model buildings and it therefore demands as much care as we can lavish upon it.

It is best to start with fairly pale warm grey: enamel 64 from Humbrol is as good as any. If you are going to combine two or more kits, delay this task until the assembly is complete as uniformity is all-important. Apply the 64 across all the surfaces, ensuring that it is sufficiently thinned to cover without leaving brush-strokes and yet it must remain completely matt. Once it is dry you can pick out a few individual slates with lighter or darker tones. From here on I prefer to rely on pastels to enhance the underlying slate colour while also adding an element of weathering and soot fall. Keep things light. It will be better if you are able to access some colour photographs of similar roofs, as these will offer something to aim at. The location is obviously a sooty one, but that should not be used as an excuse to blacken every square inch. Judicious use of black pastel dust is acceptable, but uniform coatings of a dark-bluish grey are more visually appropriate.

Interior: After testing several trial positions and, more importantly, several viewing angles, I concluded that there was little point in doing any work on the interior. Apart from a very small area near the doorways the remainder is not visible. The most that is possible and practical is perhaps a board for the various traffic notices. As a general rule I am happy to leave the nearside untouched and treat the far side with a thin wash of matt black.

Details: There are very few to be considered, apart from windows, doors, lights, drainpipes and guttering. I wanted the building (single and combined) to have a vaguely 'Southern' feel, which meant Malachite green and buff enamels, with white for the glazing bars. I

also chose to add barge-boards to the gable ends and use the curved up turns on the eaves of the main roof to represent guttering.

Conclusions

Despite the age of this kit, it remains well worth considering among the many more modern offerings. Naturally it is more suited to those layouts already committed to plastic construction for its buildings. However, those who favour the card and brick-paper option should not discount it, since it is no more difficult to customize by re-covering it with pre-printed brick paper than any of its card counterparts. Those who want to make something different can always prepare their own pre-painted sheet, or paint *in situ*, a stone-built version.

EXTENDING THE KITMASTER/DAPOL SHED

There is an element of trial and error here since the instructions are not too helpful on the exact processes required. They certainly make no reference to combining the two kits into a through-road version. The project also involves adding the second kit to one that is already built and fully finished. There is a further complication in that we shall be constructing this one as a structure with only three walls and minus its rear gable end.

I elected to join both walls to the entrance gable end, constantly checking that they are absolutely square and horizontal. When they were solid, I next fitted the two main roof sections, once again checking carefully throughout. Departing from the original sequence, the two louvres or smoke vents were then offered in place, ensuring that they fitted precisely at the top of the gable. Once comfortable, the louvres were duly cemented to the roof.

Turning attention now to the first shed, we need to carefully remove the rear gable end and the small timber lean-to. This was not difficult since the cement had been fairly sparingly applied in the beginning. There were now two 'half kits' and some small 'extras' needed to help join them together. This is where a flat, ideally glass-covered modelling desk would come into its own.

The Dapol sheds are not designed to be combined back-to-back. Substantial bracing pieces are needed on both the walls and the roof sections. For the project I am combining the two sheds as a 'retro-fit' exercise with both structures already completed.

Carry out as many dry runs as you feel are necessary to get the optimum joining sequence and a near-seamless end product. When I first tried to 'dry join' the two sheds, I was surprised to be unable to find the purpose and locations for those extra bits. I eventually realized that they were designed only for the end-to-end combination, with the front of any subsequent shed joined onto the back gable of the first. In these cases the additional pieces coped with the overhanging roof at the front of the next shed. Taking my chosen route of a back-to-back through-shed meant relying on just a simple butt joint all around. That, however, is not the simplest of tasks: end-on joints always require considerable care and this is certainly the case where we have to deal with two full-height wall sections, the two main roof portions, the smoke vents and their roof – eight joins in all. It is essential that the front wall joint and the viewing side of the roof and the smoke vents are accurately aligned and not marred by excess cement. After some deliberation I opted to assist, and ultimately strengthen, the joints by first cementing a 2cm wide strip of (at least) 0.75mm plastic card to the inside of the first shed to produce a step on which to position the second original. The photo will clarify this.

Retrofitting

It is then best to get the front wall and roof fixed and ensure these are registered as accurately as you can. This may throw the near joints slightly out of true,

but this need not bother us too much since on this project they will ultimately be out of sight. As well as testing the feasibility of the back-to-back combination, I also wanted to check that this operation could be carried out as a retrofit, that is to say whether an existing fully modelled shed could be enhanced by adding a second unit. As you will have seen, the two structures were made more or less simultaneously, right through to basic painting. This experiment showed that it is possible. It is a bit of a struggle to maintain all those joints in perfect alignment, but the end result is quite acceptable. You'll need patience and persistence, but they're all part of modelling. In any case it's surely better to 'extend' than to 'scrap and build'. It's certainly cheaper and allows you to more easily capitalize on the potential for change.

Conclusions

If you are still be at the planning and design stage and are looking for a through shed option, the Kitmaster/Dapol will fit the bill. In terms of its footprint, two sheds combined are 80mm wide and 280mm long (20 x 70ft), while adding a third unit gives a scale length of just over 100ft. This is about the maximum for a shed of this type and would be likely to house several tank engines or some smaller mixed traffic 0-6-0 or 2-6-0 tender locos. Even the double-length shed would still be fairly generous for the average small branch line. Perhaps a more fitting location would be a larger branch serving a sizable town, a

The Kitmaster/Dapol shed in a rural setting. The addition of barge-boards and a vaguely 'Southern' paint job has helped to disguise its rather simple form. Note how a few figures, sensibly posed, add life and character to these mini-dioramas. One crew is reading the racing pages while the relief driver scans the notices and his fireman chats to the ever present Inspector. Their bikes are propped up against the grounded van bodies and the resident R1 0-6-0 tank waits for its next turn. Don't forget the coal deliveries and the regular visits of the ash wagon. The ash heap seen here is nothing more sophisticated than a blob of plasticine covered with cigarette ash! Cameos like this keep things interesting even when no locomotive is on shed.

There is sometimes a potential problem when 'retro-fitting' a second shed to an already completed model. The wall join is easy to disguise with a carefully positioned drainpipe, but the roof joins would need a careful application of plastic filler or disguising beneath tile-paper. Building the combined version from scratch would largely eliminate this. This double-length, through-shed version would be about 70ft (21m) long to scale; while by no means the largest of this type of facility, it's probably as big as the average layout could accommodate.

Sheds of this size would appear more at home with at least one extra stabling road to accommodate some extra locos. Here the R1 has been coaled while an ROD and Q await their turn. The large 2-8-0 gives some indication of the shed's covered accommodation. The shed roof and louvred vent have been covered with Superquick D5 grey slate to improve the overall appearance.

A typical, but rarely modelled, shed scene showing the accumulated ash and clinker being shovelled into the weekly wagon to return to the main depot with the outgoing coal empties.

holiday resort or an industrial station centred on several coalfields.

Despite having only a single road, a shed of this size could be justified at a busy mainline junction with a couple of branch lines and some local traffic junction or more important terminus. As such it could be home for the usual types of tank engines, but could also be home for a larger mixed traffic 4-6-0 to handle special workings. One example that springs to mind is Weston-super-Mare on the old GWR/BR (W). The shed was a single-road structure and only four feet longer than Stamford without the water tower. Throughout its life it invariably had as its resident locomotives a 4-6-0 Hall or Saint and pannier tank. A similar-sized shed at Winchester Cheesehill could keep both its 4-4-0 and 0-6-0 tender engines under cover.

BUILDING THE PROTOTYPE STAMFORD SHED

This is an updated version of a much admired range that was justifiably popular throughout the 1970s and 1980s. It is currently marketed by Freestone Models from Witney, who have carved out a niche specializing in card kits and accessories. It compares well with other more contemporary offerings and you get quite a lot for your money.

There are five pages of general guidance notes and detailed step by step instructions that are easy to follow, especially if you read them carefully while studying the pre-printed cards. There are actually

four A4 cards, plus a thicker sheet supplemented by its own A4 templates sheet, that yields the necessary reinforcing sections. The excellent printing is well detailed and perfectly matt. The kit, however, does require more modelling skills than those, for example, by Superquick or Metcalf: it is not pre-cut or fretted so you need to scalpel out carefully each of the hundred or so components. The cut lines, though, are clearly marked so the task is nowhere as daunting as one might think.

The Stamford engine shed kit from Prototype Models contains more than 200 separate components. The tools needed are very simple: glues of your choice, 12- and 6-in rulers, a scalpel and tweezers to position the pre-glued smaller components. The palette knife will be used to spread the PVA adhesive evenly when laminating the various larger sections. You will also need watercolours and pastels to paint the exposed card edges and for general weathering.

Early considerations

It is down to you whether you cut only what you need when following the instructions or attempt, as many of us do, to cut out the whole lot in one go. If you take the latter course, make sure you transfer any necessary part numbers to the back of each component. It is also a sensible step to place all of the related items into separate envelopes as you go along.

Although the guidance notes recommend UHU as the main adhesive of choice, I have found that any of the other all-purpose, clear impact glues will do just as well and some are slightly less prone to stringing. When it can be found, my preference is for a Scotch quick-dry adhesive that resembles an enhanced PVA and is clean, quick and easy to use.

Another adhesive that I find essential is ordinary craft PVA. While the previously mentioned types are sound choices for joints and the final assembly, they are perhaps overkill when it comes to laminating sections and adding the smaller detailing components. Indeed any form of glue in tubes usually releases far more than is necessary for things like windowsills and is difficult to spread evenly when sticking overlays together. I simply squirt a large blob of PVA onto a tin lid and then pick up the precise amounts needed with the point of a palette knife. For laminating overlays it is simple to use the same tool and spread the PVA evenly over the whole surface or surfaces. For the smallest components, lay aside the palette knife and use the point of a cocktail stick or a simple matchstick cut to a chisel point.

The kit is designed to offer some variations in the final assembly, allowing the modeller the choice of where to site the water tank and the small restroom or office building. This enables one to juggle the eventual footprint to best suit the space available on the layout. For the purposes of the project I have assembled the shed to match the illustration.

Take your time

Before embarking on building the kit it is worth discussing its complexities as well as its virtues, which are essentially two sides of the same coin. On the 'tails' side, this Prototype kit is not a particularly good starting point for a first-time builder. Allowing

Cutting out the thin card is easy, but you should always use a cutting mat and a steel ruler. Where possible use the full length of the blade's cutting edge so that most cuts can be achieved cleanly in a single pass. For the numerous semicircular cuts around the arches, however, you will need to use the tip of the blade. Keep the scalpel as vertical as possible, hold the workpiece steady and then rotate it to make the cut easier and more accurate.

for the number of components that are replicated, there are about two hundred items that must be cut carefully and cleanly from the printed card. Many areas require multiple laminations, with at least one piece stuck on top or behind another. As well as the need for precision in both cutting and gluing, patience and thoroughness are needed. There are many similar components that are often differentiated by less than half a millimetre of printed brickwork, so mistakes are easily made.

On the other hand, the advantages of this well thought-out, well-printed and very accurate Prototype kit together add up to an intriguing and absorbing challenge to the modeller. This is not something you can put together on one night for instant gratification. I would suggest that even an experienced builder, putting in several hours of work each evening, will still find themselves with work to do after three or four weeks. It is not a rush job.

However, a trainee modeller who really wants to test and develop their skills would be hard put to find a more suitable test piece. The finished structure,

Prototype kits rely heavily on multiple laminates of relatively thin card to add strength and detail to finished buildings. The best way of ensuring that these items are securely and evenly bonded is to use a palette knife to spread a thin coating of PVA across the whole surface. This is difficult, if not impossible, with any tube-glue.

in any of its various forms, would grace any layout and, indeed, would not look out of place even on an authentic 'P4' system.

The project build

The illustrations show the shed in its real-life form with the main entrance from beneath the built-on water tower. In this role it can be operated as a through shed with access at both ends. If space is limited, however, either set of doors can be modelled firmly shut and the shed worked from one end only.

The instruction sheet enables the water tower to be constructed as a separate assembly sited apart from the shed itself. To capitalize on this option I assembled both structures as stand-alone models. Research revealed a number of instances where the space within the base of the water tower was put to good use as a covered coaling stage. This, of course, yielded two benefits: it made for a more interesting visual feature and provided a useful space-saving device by eliminating the need for a separate structure.

The doors and any other smaller components like plinths and buttresses can be treated in exactly the same way. It is useful to have a selection of palette knives in various shapes and sizes, as they can serve as very useful multi-purpose tools.

Adding a coaling stage

The additional work is relatively modest, although I went one step further to provide a brick lining to the interior. This was formed from a spare sheet of thick brick paper glued beneath the arched entrances. The space beneath was filled with a platform base, modelled in the same way as the previous examples and with its parts cut from the surplus reinforcing card. Rather than making the actual surface timber covered, I chose some spare paving slabs and covered the supporting walls in the nearest suitable brick paper. Add the coal heap itself and glue the sub-assembly in place. If the stage is to be worked from one side only, it is necessary to insert a brick or timber wall across the far arch. I decided that this depot could be fairly busy, so I laid a coal siding at the rear to permit offloading without interrupting the other movements.

Strong and square

When assembling the four sides of the main shed and the four sides of the tank base, you may find it somewhat flimsy and inclined to warp out of true. This will not be improved if the various brick overlays on

Some small irregularities are almost inevitable no matter how carefully you cut and stick these laminated sections. Inspect each batch of sub-assemblies very carefully and tidy them up before they get to the final build sequence.

which the tank base sits, three strips deep, are not properly meshed. These problems are quite common on many card kits and are more likely to occur with thinner card. Prototype's card is barely 0.3mm thick, so there is not much to stick.

One solution that works for me is to leave off the overlays and concentrate on getting the plain walls well stuck and properly square. Make full use of any card formers, reinforcing triangles and square-section balsa wood to keep the structure as square and robust as possible. Then add the overlays, ensuring that each strip butts neatly against the very small 3mm overhang of its predecessor. Work your way around the building, then repeat on the tank as necessary where these multiple layers are concerned. This principle would, I think, pay dividends on the water tower base, which also has minimal internal reinforcing, as well as the very large doorway voids on two of the walls. This operation should also eliminate any need to trim the overlays after assembly.

If you opt for this route then it is better to glue the corner reinforcing to the two 'inner' walls first, ensuring that they are absolutely flush to the edge and properly set before adding the overlapping second pair.

Finishing off the workshops and office. With the subassembly inverted it is easier to identify and rectify any requirements for extra bracing or reinforcing.

ABOVE LEFT AND RIGHT: *Offering up the Stamford shed model to the existing A3 site shows the size of its footprint. To squeeze it into the previous space would require some shifting of the track and removal or repositioning of much of the ballasted shed yard. Further adjustments would be necessary when the water tower was re-sited as a separate entity.*

It is not satisfactory having just a spur serving the back of the coaling stage behind the tower. Even that would require a specially designed buffer stop or rail-mounted stop blocks. If the layout space permits, and if viewing is possible, I would extend the platform and move the coal road further out, thus clearing the pump house chimney and extending the line's capacity. It could even become a loop, with two more storage roads fitted between it and the shed wall.

A bird's-eye view of the site, with the water tower in its new site and doubling as a coaling stage, shows that it is still a tight fit. It might just be possible to fit a turntable offstage to the right at the far end of a second A3 board, but access to the shed from the left would need yet another board. The shed yard would then require a total space of 48 x 10in (1,200 x 250mm).

The supreme test is always the eye-level view as it's important that the buildings and all the other elements hang together to make an attractive, but still properly 'railway-like', scene. A photograph taken from these low angles should look as close as possible to the real thing.

Improving the water

The kit includes a sheet of clear acetate to represent the surface of the water tank. In the real world this would be exposed to both the natural elements and man-made debris, and as such one would expect it to look pretty scummy. The acetate supplied is far too shiny and toy-like and it tends to detract from the otherwise realistic appearance of the buildings. One solution is to pour on a layer of PVA and spread it evenly across the surface with your palette knife. This gives a better impression of stagnant water, especially if you have first remembered to paint the interior with a random mix of greens and black.

Conclusions

This Prototype model is probably close to the zenith of the card-kit offerings. The amount of work involved brings it very close to the demands of scratch-building but without the preliminary work of drawing, measurement and finish. Even the task of touching in the exposed edges will take several hours. Here's one last tip in respect of that particular exercise. It is almost impossible to get an exact match of watercolour compared with the printed surfaces of absorbent card. One way of disguising these joins is to touch in a few of the adjacent bricks with the chosen watercolour and to paint a few black bricks across the corner edge.

CHAPTER TWO

SCRATCH-BUILDING A SINGLE-ROAD ENGINE SHED

CHOOSING A PROTOTYPE AND DISPELLING A MYTH

Even though scratch-building has always been an integral part of railway modelling, in recent years it has been elevated to the status of a mysterious black art. I've no idea when this began or even why it began. Like so many fads and attitudes, it seems to have crept up on us and simply acquired its degree of credence through repetition. The very mention of the fact that something has been scratch-built seems to award it some kind of higher accolade that all too often is ill-deserved.

In fairness, I have the greatest admiration, tinged with a significant portion of downright envy, for the immensely talented modellers who produce locomotives and rolling stock from sheets of brass and pieces of nickel-silver. They are not just modellers or scratch-builders, but are truly 'engineers' in every sense of the word. I also have enormous respect for those at the top end of our own premier league, who contribute to museums like Pendon or who earn their living making world-class model townscapes to order.

For those of us who still model for pleasure, however, and who enjoy a challenge, scratch-building is almost part of the day-to-day routine. After all, any building, from a crofter's cottage to a city's cathedral, is still just a box with a lid. Some boxes are indeed much more complicated than others, but the principles behind their construction remain largely the same. Any modeller who can make a halfway decent job of assembling a kit can easily make the transition to scratch-builder. The additional skills that are needed are quickly mastered, since they are little more than the ability to calculate or measure dimensions and then to draw them as a series of horizontal and vertical straight lines.

In no way is it either a black art or rocket science. If you elect to work with card, it becomes even easier and is almost ridiculously inexpensive: an accurately scaled farmyard can be built for less money than just one ready-to-site farmhouse. So don't be put off. Scratch-building is not the sole preserve of a few talented individuals. It is there for everyone who wants a layout that is uniquely theirs and not merely yet another example of an out-of-the-box train-set.

CHOOSING A PROTOTYPE

Since the scratch-build exercise in my previous book was the goods shed at Corfe Castle, on the preserved Swanage Railway, it is logical that we should now consider as our prototype the line's only engine shed. This is conveniently located just down the road at the approach to the terminus. This example not only has every necessary quality in respect of size, operating characteristics, build appeal and visual interest, it would also make the perfect counterpart for the goods shed since they use the same materials and are built in the same 'house style'. There is a further benefit, too, in that the shed is generally inaccessible and there will be no opportunity for measure it on-site. That means we will have to rely heavily on calculations to obtain all the relevant dimensions. This may be a new technique to master, but it is one frequently needed by the steam-era scratch- builder.

The last half-century has seen dramatic changes across the entire landscape and especially across our railways. Nothing remains as it was in the 1950s. Desk research and historic photographs are our only sources of information. In this case, however, this need not be too much of deterrent as the shed still exists in almost daily use, and is thus easy to photograph from several angles. The advantage of this, if not

Swanage in 2015, showing the general appearance and clutter typical of any preservation shed. This is as close as one can get to a square-on shot; the presence of 80104 in the doorway and the stores van on the turntable may help when calculating the dimensions.

An earlier summer view from the same spot. This time it's the height of the worker near the entrance that may help when judging the relative dimensions.

immediately apparent, was that both site visits could take place in the same few hours, thus ensuring that lighting conditions would be virtually identical and would produce equally identical colour values on the photographs.

DESK RESEARCH

Despite the fact that our choice is more or less predetermined, the usual preliminaries shouldn't be neglected and some initial desk research will be beneficial. There is no shortage of photographic and documentary information about this attractive feature on such a popular railway. There are literally scores of images of Swanage from its earliest days in the late 1800s, through the many decades of steam working and into its rebirth as a major heritage line. The shed itself did not change significantly over the years (apart from a successful attempt by a runaway M7 to remodel the entrance in the late 1950s), so many of the photographs will still prove to be very useful. At least half a dozen images, all taken from slightly different angles, at different times and under different lighting conditions, are to be found in Andrew P. M. Wright's *The Swanage Branch in Colour: The Ultimate Archive* (Waterfront Publications, 2013). Similar albums also show the quite significant alterations to the various facilities and the immediate surroundings. Many of these views were taken from angles that are no longer easily accessible. Track diagrams and descriptions of shed workings will also contribute to our knowledge and subsequent planning.

Several important points will have emerged from even the most cursory glance at the research material. The shed site is narrow but quite lengthy in proportion and the shed itself is only accessible via a small turntable. The facilities are modest and the site is cramped. In the steam era the shed had a small water tower and coaling platform. The site is located immediately under a tall stone wall retaining the higher ground of the parish churchyard and on the right it is bounded by a graceful stone bridge spanning all the roads. Behind the shed, and continuing to the left, there is a tall row of ancient chestnuts and other trees. The very delineation of the site's limits —the high stone wall, the stone

Despite the strong shadows, the iron-framed windows show the variations in height and shape caused by the arch. When calculating the verticals, always use the centre upright glazing bar as your datum. This close-up also demonstrates the random nature of the stonework in which no two pieces are the same size or shape. The general style could best be described as 'laid-to-fit'.

This slightly more square-on image shows further details of the stonework. The gas cylinders are also useful to gauge the dimensions: in model form mine measure 20mm (5ft).

overbridge and the background trees – is a positive advantage. Only the approach, or the left-hand end, is lacking any clear definition, but this would be of little consequence since on any model it would simply represent 'the rest of the world', just as, in reality, it leads to the rest of the branch.

The real headache will be the turntable as it is too small to be successfully replicated by any of the commercially produced types. Unfortunately these are all far too big to fit the site and it will have to be omitted from any plan and replaced by a simple access road. All the other elements can be constructed, including the disused arched doorway that betrays how the original intention had been for it to be a 'through' shed. If this entrance could be brought into use on the model it would certainly improve its operating potential, as well as helping to relieve the access problem following the omission of the turntable.

Armed with all this information, and perhaps with a few additional ideas sketched out, it is now time to visit the site.

FIELD RESEARCH

As already mentioned, this will be largely a photographic survey. Unlike any earlier trips to the goods shed, there will be very little that might be achieved with a tape measure or measuring-stick. In situations like this where full access is denied to an existing building to be modelled, it is sensible to jot down the key elements that need to be noted and photographed. There is nothing more frustrating in the middle of a model-making exercise than to realize that the one image or sketch that could have made all the difference was never taken.

Returning to the actual Swanage trip, but with the proviso that the advice holds good anywhere, the obvious starting point is determining exactly those places to which you have access and those you don't. In this case the likely areas are the picnic and viewing-point immediately facing the shed, a convenient gap between some vehicles further along and the road bridge a few yards from, and overlooking, the entrance. From these three positions it is possible to see nearly everything one needs to construct a pretty realistic model.

A closer shot of the entrance detail reveals just how little of the interior can be glimpsed. In its original state with the arched doorway, almost nothing would have been visible.

This slightly different angle on the entrance may enable us to make better use of 80104. Try using a model of one these 4m-high tanks to get the actual height to the top of the bunker from ground level and then plot it on the image to calculate the heights to the valence and ridge.

The checklist should include:

Square-on shots of the side elevation
Square-on shots of the side elevation
Square-on shots of the front elevation
Square-on shots of the front elevation
General shots to show background
Detail shots with wide-angle or telephoto

Full-frame
Wide-angle to show background
Full-frame/telephoto lens
Wide-angle to show surroundings
trees, church, bridge etc.
windows, buttresses, entrances, stonework, roof detail, smoke
vents, stores, coal platform, retaining wall, general detritus, any
interesting features that might be worth modelling and are not
date-sensitive

This close-up shows just how shallow are the mortar courses. They are very variable and the actual shapes of the stones have more relief than the mortar separating them. Such small details are almost impossible to model in our scale.

The plinth is not very pronounced: the 4in measured on the Corfe goods shed would also seem correct for here. The use of an extra layer of picnic-plate polystyrene appears to give a fairly realistic interpretation.

Take any notes that might prove useful in fixing dimensions or may help to put the clock back to the steam era. Sketch any possible revised track layouts to realistically replace the turntable or facilitate the through-shed option.

Armed with this, you can now confidently embark on the survey in the knowledge that you will have gained not only the necessary facts but have also soaked up some of the actual atmosphere. You should not, however, expect everything to be as easy as turning up and following your brief. Only rarely will you get exactly the angles that you want and remember to record that vital bit of detail. It might not seem to be a problem until you came to model it. Many of the images accompanying this section will surely prove the point.

Another shot of the interior proves that there is little point in spending time on the windows on the back wall. They admit no light and could easily be represented by a photocopy or simply omitted.

PREPARATION

ASSEMBLING THE INFORMATION

The first real task will be to draw the shed's elevations on the chosen construction material, but there are some essential preparatory jobs before committing pencil to card. Start by checking your recent photographs and get them into a useable format. These days it is most likely that they will have been taken on a digital camera and this should be an easy task for those with their own computers and printers. Provided their quality is satisfactory they can simply be printed off. The elevations are vital and these should be printed as individual items as large as possible on the usual A4 sheet. The remaining shots can be printed as you want, but a good rule to follow is the larger the better, and this is best done now to save time later. Those who lack the technology at home or who still rely on 35mm cameras will

All scratch-build projects should start by assembling all the relevant detail from the desk or field research. It is also advisable to enlarge any decent photographs to at least A4 size. This makes the eventual measurement easier and more accurate.

have to do this initial work through their local photo printing or copy shop: either way, those A4 subjects remain essential.

Your own data file can then be augmented with the best and most appropriate images from the desk research. Once again these can be produced as monochrome photocopies, even though the originals might have been in colour: your own photographs will provide all the colour references that are needed.

TOOLS AND MATERIALS

The next item on the agenda is to assemble the necessary tools and materials. In this particular instance, where card or mounting board is the main medium, the usual basic tools are more than adequate. As a quick reminder, they should include pencils and erasers, a scrap pad, a pair of compasses and dividers or a Vernier scale, a set square, steel rulers, needle tool and, of course, one or more scalpels with plenty of spare blades. At this stage we need not concern ourselves with any additional items needed for the various assembly jobs.

TRANSPOSING THE INFORMATION

You can now get down to the business of extrapolating the information from the A4 elevations to create accurately dimensioned artwork for the eventual mounting board 'kit of parts'. This is best done in easy stages on the scrap pad rather than jumping straight to the finished artwork.

The first thing is to decide on the principal dimensions. Normally this a tricky task since stone-built structures deny us the usual method of counting the brick-courses and making the necessary calculations, but in this case you may have the substantial bonus of the accurate dimensions you may already have measured on the goods shed. The ones we need are the window sizes as they, fortunately, appear almost identical in width (4ft) to those on the engine shed, although the panes on the latter seem to be somewhat deeper. Make a note of their calculated width and height as transposed into 4mm scale as on the finished building. For the record these are simple: each window is 4ft wide and made up of sixteen panes that measure 12 x

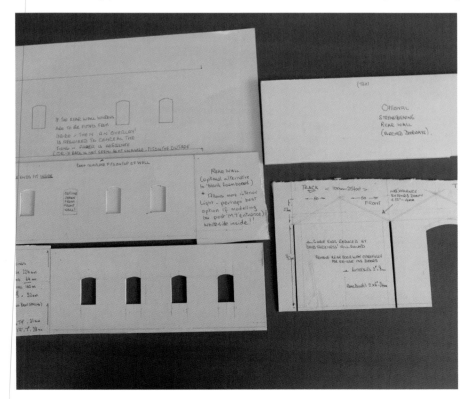

The kit of parts for the two main walls and the gable ends. The front wall is lower left and the north gable end, with its original arched doorway, is on the extreme right. The various notes on pieces serve as reminders during the build sequence, much like the instruction sheet provided for commercial kits.

21in at the centre of the arch and slightly less at the sides.

The dimensions that we will need are the width (4ft) and the maximum height (7ft). Using the dividers or the Vernier scale on the A4 elevations, set them to the precise corners of the windows, starting with the width, and then 'walk' them along the facing wall to calculate its length in 'windows', converting them to feet and inches in the usual way. Next do exactly the same to get the height. Use that width setting in the same way on the A4 front elevation to get the dimensions across the entrance. You can now start creating the working drawing on the scrap pad as you have established the length, width, wall height and footprint. That probably sounds a bit simplistic, and some more detailed calculations will also be needed, but this is the basis of establishing the vital end results included in the accompanying illustrations and captions.

Reset the dividers to the equivalent of precisely one foot as on the A4 images. You will probably need to make a few trial runs to get this spot-on. Once correct you can now measure all the other features on the structure, transpose them to 4mm scale and add them to your main drawing. It may prove helpful to produce some separate scale drawings of individual items. This avoids making the main drawing too complicated too soon. It will also give you an early insight into how the eventual kit of parts might best be created. Above all, don't lose sight of the fact that you are not attempting to model to the nearest inch but are only after a well-executed, accurately proportioned and instantly recognizable creation.

CHOOSING THE WALL FINISHES

It is fortunate that the Swanage shed is a relatively simple structure and that what complexities there are lie mainly in the roof details, which we will get to in due course. There are, however, some things that must be attended to even at this early stage. One decision that should be taken, since it may well affect some other aspects, is how you intend to finish the building. The carcass will definitely be made from mounting board, but you can then choose from the following:

Picnic-plate polystyrene, used to clad the walls, is cheap, easy to cut, simple to work and gives a highly satisfactory result. The centre sections of two plates are needed for the front wall. These are first given a priming coat of thick white emulsion paint.

- Draw and paint our own stonework straight on to the card.
- Cover the card with suitable plastic stone-sheet or pre-printed stone paper.
- Coat the building with a thin plaster/PVA mix and scribe the stones before treating them with water-colour.
- Clad the carcass with polystyrene cut from picnic plates, prime it with a quick coat of emulsion and then pencil on the stonework.

The actual stonework is not in any particularly recognizable style, but it is distinctive, attractive and matches that found throughout the line. This sadly rules out any shop-bought solution and leaves us with just three choices: painting directly on to the card or a scribed plaster skim, or having another go with the picnic plate idea, which seemed to work well on the Corfe goods shed project. If the last of these is chosen, you can still try the plaster version on the rear wall, despite the additional work involved. Having taken that decision, there are some additional and useful tasks that can now be undertaken.

As usual, the windows will be as important as they are undoubtedly tricky. The metal glazing bars have almost no thickness and the widows as a whole are set well forward in their recesses. They are best sourced from one of the commercially available pre-printed sheets, but you may well have to fall back on the hand-drawn approach. This was the only solution to the previous problem at Corfe and could well apply again in this case, but it's worth digging around in the spares box. Draw at least one on the elevation on the scrap pad and use this as a 'master' against which any examples can be tested.

The walls will be quite a time-consuming exercise and the more you can practise now, the better will be the final result. Place the elevation photos and any useful close-ups in front of you and then, with a soft HB pencil, attempt to draw as much detail of the stonework as you can manage onto your scale artwork. This is going to be a laborious task at the best of times, but it's one that can't be rushed, let alone skipped. There is no need for absolute accuracy, though, as the eventual building will be a working model and not a museum piece. Any small differences against the real thing will be undetectable and unimportant. You should, however, practise getting the various rows to run horizontally and picking out the more interesting or obvious details.

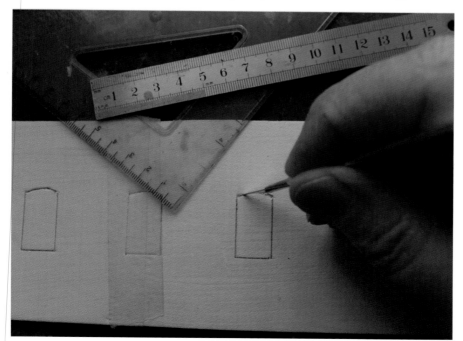

The two pieces of polystyrene have been taped tightly together and the windows drawn on. Use the wall as a template and keep the pencil very firmly pressed against the card. The material is very easy to cut, but you must take special care around the arches as these curves are notoriously difficult to cut with any accuracy.

You may find it helpful to rule the whole piece with guidelines roughly 1mm apart, in the same way as one does for brickwork. Look for missing or broken stones, any with a markedly different colour, and pay special attention to the arrangements around the windows, the corner buttresses and the entrance. All of these are likely to be focal points when the model is *in situ*. The reason for this rather concentrated exercise is simply that, when you are doing it in the build phase, it will be achieved by scribing on the chosen finish and mistakes can't be rubbed out. It may seem a bit excessive to go into so much detail in this scrap pad phase, and if you are already an experienced builder the you might be forgiven for going straight to the finished artwork.

ROOFS

The final element of the preparation concerns the roof. Using the same techniques of drawing, measurement and calculation, prepare some templates for the two half-roofs, the smoke vents and louvres. Check your stock of pre-printed slates as I certainly do not recommend trying to produce these for yourself. You may have to settle for a near-match, but even that is more likely to convince the eye than a hand-painted version. This rooftop detail is probably the most difficult part of the whole project, as these 'mini-structures' are what give the shed much of its unique character and they are also its most visible features when on the layout. Although it is not essential, you may find it worthwhile to carry out a few quick test-assemblies using any spare scraps of thin card or thickish paper you have to hand. These trial runs should prove which material, card or paper, is better suited to each component and sub-assembly. They may also help you discover the easy way to put each piece together and so save valuable time and stress in the actual building phase.

ALTERNATIVE MATERIAL

One thing that all model engine sheds have in common is their inherent instability. Unlike most other buildings, they have neither a floor nor a ceiling to help keep the structure square and robust. This problem has already shown itself in previous projects

and it is more than likely that it will be encountered again with Swanage. The answer is to fall back on the principle of the false ceiling, discreetly hidden behind the tops of the walls. The most effective material for this task is thick foamboard, the 7mm version being ideal: this has the twin advantages of being warp-free and it also offers four times the depth of a comparable piece of card.

On the later MPD project (*see* Chapter 4) this same foamboard will also be put to good use as extra-strength back walls. This could be easily repeated on the Swanage shed as the far wall is completely hidden from view against the equally unseen portion of the churchyard retaining wall. What little of the interior that might be glimpsed through the shed entrance is easily disguised and foamboard is, in any case, not that much different from the usual card.

These suggested revisions have no significant impact on this preparation phase, but they would need to be taken into account at the final artwork stage.

DRAWING THE KIT

The procedures for the engine shed are no different from any other scratch-building exercise where card is the material of choice. This is a task that requires patience and sometimes even a few practise runs would not come amiss. A good, sharp pencil is a must and on balance I would always opt for an HB, which produces a clean line while still being soft enough to make it easy to erase any errors.

The first step is to cut the large A2 sheet of mounting board into more manageable sizes. Two pieces about six inches deep and cut across the width of the board should be more than enough. The piece with the machine-cut edge will be used for the artwork that forms the walls; the other piece will be for the roof, and anything else, and can be put aside at this point.

WALLS

It is better to draw the walls with some extra depth, or foundations, that will enable the finished building to sit in the terrain rather than to stand on it. The optimum depth is about 2in (50mm), but even if you are working on a solid table-top baseboard I would still advise allowing an extra two or three millimetres at the base. This will help you to get a neater finish to your painting, it helps to avoid the risk of damage during any cutting and it is easy to disguise with ballast and weeds. For the purposes of the project however, it will be simpler to go for a table-top type or zero foundations, so the starting point will be the bottom of the artwork. The alternative would be to draw a horizontal line 3mm above the machined edge and across the full length of the workpiece, which would then become the ground level.

The next bit requires a moment's decision making, which is usual on all scratch-building ventures. You need to determine whether the assembly will be a complete wraparound of all four walls or whether it will use butt-jointed corners. The easiest method is to use butt joints and these will, in any case, be conveniently hidden by the buttresses. It will also allow for substitution by a foamboard 'blind' back wall at a later stage. This will further allow us to test what is the usual alternative to the score-and-bend method used with great success by many modellers.

Starting at the left-hand edge of the piece, plot the exact width of the left gable end and draw a full-height vertical. Follow this consecutively with the verticals for the front side, the right gable end and the rear wall. All these measurements would normally come from your own efforts on the scrap pad, but are shown on the accompanying illustration and repeated in the Appendices. Take the exact height of the walls up to the eaves and draw a precise horizontal across the whole piece. You may wish to follow me and draw the four walls as separate pieces of artwork. It makes a degree of sense as we eventually intend to assemble the kit by butt joining.

For either of the options you now need to complete your artwork by drawing in the gable ends, the four window apertures and the two entrances, Where the last of these is concerned you need to decide which period you are modelling. The present 'M7 modified' front entrance is suitable from about 1958 to the current preservation era, but if you are recreating the Southern or early BR periods you

must feature an arched doorway identical to that at the other end. If this is your intention, do note that these entrances and the through track are slightly offset towards the front wall and the running lines. This completes the artwork for the main parts of the shed. The four walls, the windows and the chosen entrances can all be cut out.

Buttresses

The four corner buttresses and the low plinth can now be drawn, but I should warn you that the former are relatively shallow features and you may prefer to model them as a wraparound construction to hide the corner joints. This tends to rule out the use of mounting board since it would make them too bulky and is, in any case, very difficult to score and bend in such small sections. Since the whole building is due to receive polystyrene cladding, these elements can be realistically made from the same material. If we were working with the plaster finish, I would suggest using the 200 gsm paper that was used on some of the previous projects. In either case, take the dimensions from your scrap pad, draw them up and cut them out.

Vital adjustments

There is one more job that can be carried out before these parts are set aside and a start made on the roof. The intention is to assemble the four walls with butt-joined corners, but this cannot be done when all of them are to the exact size. One pair must fit inside the other. You need to decide which option to choose, but there is no one preferred choice. Probably the best and easiest is to fit the gable ends inside the two long walls. In order to keep the dimensions correct, and to allow the use of mounting board for the roof templates, the gable ends must be reduced by the thickness of the card all round. When the walls and roof templates are fitted it all gets back to normal. This method also offers additional strength to the structure as the templates are now able to sit squarely along the full length of the two main walls and can eventually be glued in place more securely.

Even when this essential adjustment has been made there will still be a need for a further similar exercise when we come to the assembly stage. This will enable us to deal with the extra thickness of the cladding and the buttresses. It is best left until then in order to ensure the requisite accuracy, which can only be achieved by dealing with the 'as built' actual models.

ROOFS

There is now more than enough information to hand to enable you to draw and cut the various components that will form the main roof and those rather challenging smoke vents. The roof itself is very simple and requires no more than just the two half-roof templates from the mounting board. These match the dimensions of the walls, but with a couple of minor changes. The length of each half should be increased by 4mm to allow for an overhang at the gable ends and the front half should be made deeper by the exact thickness of the board. This then neatly overlaps the rear half to give a clean ridge-line. When planning and fixing these roof templates it is best to work 'white-side up' as the dark underside eliminates the need to paint beneath the eaves. The roof will eventually be clad with the chosen slate-paper and this will need to overhang the eaves and soffits by a few inches.

Pre-printed slates

These papers are notoriously thin and this is an opportune time to deal with the problem. Rather than leaving the job until later, fix the slates now. There is nothing complicated involved, simply glue (spray mount or paper-glue) sheets of copy paper to each half-roof, making sure there are no creases or air bubbles and allowing some overhang all round. Using the same approach, apply the slate-paper and then place the work beneath some hefty books to ensure it dries properly flat. When this is done, trim the now thickened slates precisely to the edges of the gable ends, but allowing a 2mm overhang along the eaves. To complete the task, carefully paint the exposed edges and the underside of the overhang with the usual watercolours. These little jobs take only a few minutes and they are far less difficult and more controllable than if left until the roof is in place.

An alternative approach is to delay fixing the slates until later, but to prepare them now ready for installation. Instead of gluing them to copy paper, I chose to use a good quality thin card (0.2mm) or roughly 150gsm. The card was cut to size by offering it up to the roof templates and then adding the small margin for the overhang; the slate sheets were then trimmed to fit.

Smoke vents and chimneys

The louvred vents and smoke chimneys, which are such a characteristic and attractive feature of the shed, are quite complicated affairs. They must be an absolutely correct fit to the roof from every angle and are therefore best treated as part of the final detailing when the main structure is complete.

FINISHING THE WALLS

This is one area in the whole field of scratch-building where practice really does make perfect, or at least near perfect enough to convince most viewers. The picnic-plate cladding is applied in exactly the same way as one would fix plasticard or brick paper. The four walls were liberally brushed with craft PVA and the thin polystyrene sheets pressed into place. Two pieces were needed for the long front wall and these should be pushed together quite firmly to disguise the join. Once dry, the new surfaces are duly scribed, or perhaps just drawn on as very little pressure is required, with a hard pencil. The job will need the centres of at least six plates to complete and it is best if these are given a quick coat of matchpot emulsion before the wall areas are cut out. This helps to stabilize the surface and makes it easier to work. When fixing the cladding, make sure that all the edges and openings are firmly secured. It is a good idea to stipple on a further thick coat of emulsion to hide any brush marks and give an optimum surface for your detailed pencilwork.

The pre-agreed test piece of the rear wall can now be covered in its thin plaster skim. (I know it isn't really plaster, but it's used like it and it's convenient to call it that.) The actual area to be treated is quite small and the entire surface barely adds up to a few square inches. If you consider it worthwhile, you can always include any visible portion of the inside of the rear wall. Now is probably the opportune time to decide whether to keep the rear wall as mounting board or to replace it with the more robust 7mm foamboard. It isn't the last chance – that only comes with the assembly phase – but if you want to include extra plaster detail you should make up your mind now.

There is one other thing to do before we discuss the plaster and its application. If the whole building is being done then the four corner buttresses need to be folded into their sharp, right-angled forms; unless this is done, it's pretty certain that the plaster finish will crack and probably flake off when you try to bend these items. The 200gsm paper is strong stuff and the backs will need some vertical scoring to help form that all-important angle. The long low plinths can also be glued into position; remember to fix them above the 'ground level' if your version has foundations.

Plastering

Turning our attention to the plaster mix, this is where the practice begins. The base is an ordinary DIY tub of ready-mix filler, ideally one the lightweight interior versions. (I find that the Wilko own brand 600ml tubs are easy to use and have a long shelf life.) To improve its adhesion properties it needs to be blended with a small quantity of PVA. No two makes of PVA or filler have the same characteristics, so it is quite impossible to offer a recommended mix of these two constituents. If you have tackled this process before then you will have reached your own conclusions. If you haven't, I would advise that you mix a small quantity of filler on a saucer (or similar) until it becomes a smooth paste and then add a few dribbles of PVA, blending it completely with the filler. Some care is needed with the choice and use of the PVA. The large containers available cheaply from most arts and crafts shops are always a good buy, but

The rear wall was used to test the viability of using a plaster skim as an alternative cladding. The constituents are ready-mix lightweight filler, white emulsion paint (as a thinning agent) and PVA (to aid adhesion).

they have a habit of becoming congealed as the container is emptied. These 'blobs' remain quite useable for several tasks but are certainly not suitable for mixing the paste. Always select a more runny version.

With a palette knife, spread thin layers on several pieces of scrap card and leave them to harden. Once it is really hard try tapping it, flexing it and test-scribing it. If it withstands this brutal treatment then the mix is certainly correct; if it fails, mix another sample with some more PVA added and continue until there is proven satisfactory result. Don't discard those pieces as they will serve for the next exercise.

Something else you can do that may enhance the finished stonework is texturing. Although the plaster has a more realistic feel than the ultra-smooth appearance of card, it is still someway short of the roughness of hewn rock. When the paste or plaster is almost dry, gently stipple the surface by dabbing it with the bristles of a toothbrush or nailbrush. Don't overdo it and don't be too surprised if your efforts appear to go unrewarded, as the results may not be really discernible until you apply the final light dusting with pastels.

The test piece was prepared in such a way as to illustrate any difficulties rather than show a nicely finished result. While I would in no way wish to discourage modellers from having a go with this method, it is time consuming and needs considerable practice to get the best results.

Scribing

You can now practise the art of scribing. Select your tool with care as an instrument that is too 'needle-like' will produce grooves that are narrow and deep; screwdrivers err the other way and leave over-wide grooves. The better answer is an actual pointed scriber or blunt map-pin. In any case, do not press too hard. This is the moment when your initial pencil efforts to draw the stonework will begin to pay dividends. This is not an easy practice-piece since the original builders did not stick to one particular style or pattern when laying the stones, but seemed to vary their approach according to what they had to hand at the time. Some parts of the walls appear regular with dressed stones of a similar size being laid in almost brick-like courses. Other parts are far more random in style to the extent that they almost resemble the rough stonework more usually found on the boundary walls. This is not a task to be tackled freehand nor by immediate scribing, unless you have some previous experience.

The first thing is to find the best pencil for drawing on plaster. This will almost certainly be an HB, but which one? Test all of them as they will be slightly different: the best choice will be that which can be sharpened to a really good point and leaves a fine but clear line for the scriber to follow. The other important tool is a set square; the simple plastic school type is ideal. Do a few trial runs on the scrap test pieces to build your confidence and get yourself familiar with the relative sizes of each course and of the stones themselves. To put it bluntly, the ease and accuracy of your scribing are entirely dependent upon your initial drawing. Always remember that you can't erase a scribed line. When all the pencil-work is complete, you are at last free to start scribing.

The completed picnic-plate front wall is there for comparison while the plaster test piece is being scribed. The pencil horizontal guidelines, which may just be visible, are vital on a job like this where the small and irregular stones make it easy to run 'off square'.

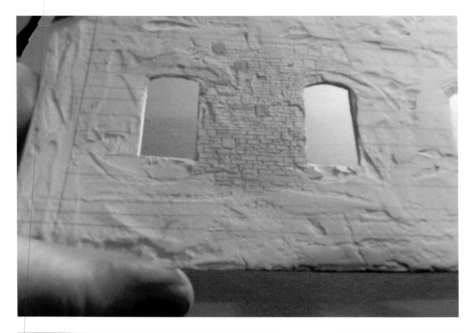

The scribing of any form of plaster cladding takes time, effort and concentration. This small sample took well over an hour to complete – almost as long as it took to do the whole picnic-plate wall. On balance, I could see no benefit from the extra mess and the additional hours needed.

A closer view of the completed front wall demonstrates how well this material captures the feel of the Purbeck stone. As a modeller I really appreciate the lack of fuss associated with its use. The only tools needed are an H pencil, not too sharp, a square to draw the horizontal guidelines, a steady hand and a modicum of patience and concentration. This method might yet come to replace my usual watercolours on card.

Don't forget that the mortar courses are almost flush with the surface and not much more than a half-inch deep. Indeed, if you re-examine the photos taken square-on in bright sunlight, they are barely discernible and it is only when viewed from an angle, or when the wall is lit from the side, that their shadows and staining become apparent. Keep the scribe vertical and do not press too hard. One thing you will probably discover is that each stone will require several small 'scribings' to get right, unlike our chosen material, which requires just the one simple pencil mark.

That, however, all comes under the heading of 'useful information', since the one wall done this way is really only a test piece and picnic-plate polystyrene is a much less hazardous option.

WINDOWS

There now remains only one fairly straightforward task to complete the walls prior to their actual assembly. This is the selection and fitting of the four windows to the main, front-facing, long wall. The three alternatives that can be examined are the same no matter what building you are working on. The first and most ideal choice would be a pre-printed version from one of the accessory suppliers, but of course they must exactly replicate the actual windows in design and size. Sadly the chances of finding that exact match are pretty remote. The second option is to look through the sheets of industrial windows to get a close match for style then cut them to the correct size and stick them in place. This is a somewhat laborious exercise but , if successful, guarantees good-looking Victorian iron-framed windows, The final option, and probably the least satisfactory, is to resort to a DIY approach by choosing a reasonable thickness of plastic glaze, carefully drawing on the glazing bars and repeating the task four times.

If possible I would avoid the last of these at all cost. Sixteen-pane iron-frame windows are very difficult to reproduce with any accuracy, the glazing bars themselves are very fine and the glass is set within them. To attempt this with the usual mapping pen and drawing ink, while not impossible, requires an ultra-fine nib, a very steady hand and a phenomenal amount of concentration and patience. If I'm forced down this route, my preferred method is to draw a 100 per cent accurate version in the centre of a reasonably sized piece of mounting board. This then becomes the 'master' and the plastic glaze securely taped down on top of it. Then it is a question of very carefully aligning the ruler over the drawn bars and frame and tracing them with the pen. I have tried the professional pens by firms like Edding and Rotring that come in white ink versions and they can give excellent results, but they aren't always happy on shiny plastic nor are they exactly cheap.

The twin purposes of the stippling exercise are to mask any brush marks left in the emulsion priming coats and to impart a little surface texture. The second of these is of little importance and the whole process can be ignored if masonry paint is used as a primer.

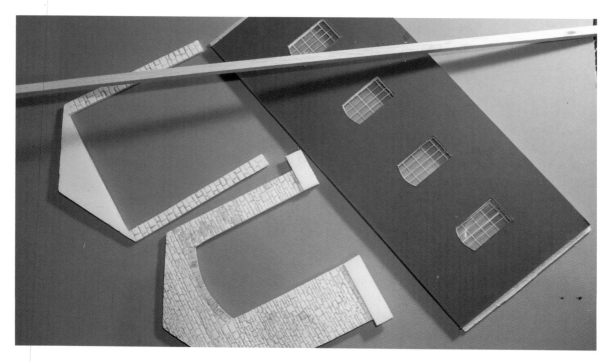

Seen here are the inside of the front wall and the outsides of the two gable ends. The small plinths are shown with the extra length that will be trimmed back to form a neat chamfered joint with their neighbours. The corners will be braced with ¼in balsa strip.

Installation

Whichever method you are able to use, once you have the four windows they are glued behind the apertures in exactly the same way as on all the previous projects. There is also an option to create a glimpse of the window on the back wall nearest the entrance. This actually admits so little light that it could be represented by a correctly sited photocopy or a hand-drawn version without any need to create a proper aperture. Don't forget that, since we are using a cladding that is almost the same thickness as the inner walls, the glazing should be inserted between the two layers. A word of warning here, don't make the mistake of trying to glue your windows behind the polystyrene cladding in the same way you would with a card wall. This is not the time to use UHU or other universal type tube. Polystyrene and these glues do not mix —even the smallest smear will have your carefully prepared cladding melting before your eyes (as the accompanying photograph demonstrates).

Never fix windows to polystyrene walls with UHU or other clear glues, as the wall will quite literally melt before your eyes.

DOORS

The only doors and doorways to be considered are those at the back entrance to the shed. The solution is obvious. When you cut out the arched doorway, put the removed card to one side and subsequently use it to create the actual doors. Incidentally, if you are modelling the arched front entrance of the earlier years, I can find no images that show any trace of the doors. I would guess that they were dispensed with some time ago, but if you wish to have them still in place, simply repeat the above procedure.

ASSEMBLING THE WALLS

I prefer to carry out this job as soon as all the components are ready. This serves two purposes: it gives an early 'heads-up' on any possible errors or problems and gives a genuine sense that real progress has been made. If your workbench is as cluttered as mine, it also prevents those precious components being lost or damaged during the remaining jobs. Assembly is the same sequence as for any other kit, but a polystyrene-clad project requires some extra scalpel work. Offer up the gable ends to the inside of the front wall so that the outer edge is exactly square with outer edge of the corner buttresses. Mark the cut lines and then very carefully remove

the thin strip of card wall and cladding. Take your time over this and do not damage the outer buttresses. Offer up again and your gable ends should now sit neatly behind the said buttresses. You can now take one final step towards near perfection, but it is not without an element of risk. To remove the visible edge of the buttresses very carefully, shave away the inner polystyrene with a scalpel until you are left with little more than the paint-covered outer skin. This will now give a corner so precise as to make the stones appear solid from all angles.

Glue the two gable ends to the front wall, ensuring that they are absolutely square and vertical. Add strengthening fillets or bracing for added security. When you're happy with that, fit the rear wall and reinforce it if necessary.

If you have decided to use a plaster finish, this would be the point to fix the four pre-shaped buttresses into place at the corners and to make sure they are in their correct positions by comparing the stonework with the photographs. Finally double-check that they blend well with the plinth.

False ceiling

When everything is firmly fixed it is now possible to plot the dimensions of the false ceiling accurately. The

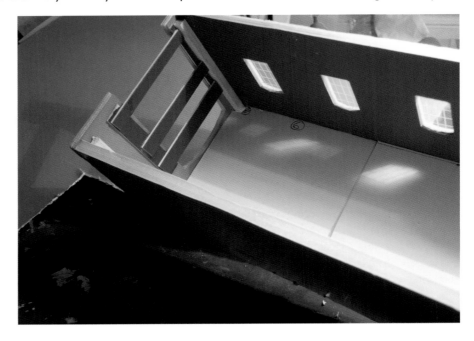

The model has been inverted to show the balsa corner braces and newly fitted false ceiling. The additional strength and support of 7mm foamboard for the rear wall is very apparent. The card strips will allow the large double doors to sit firmly within the arched doorway.

simplest way is to place the structure on the chosen piece of foamboard and prick the four corners with a needle-point tool. Then join the dots with a scalpel and steel rule, making sure that the cuts are absolutely vertical. Examine the piece very carefully and, if there is any doubt about its quality, make a better one. Test fit it just below the eaves, but don't glue it in place at this stage as you will need to access the underside when securing the roof.

SMOKE VENTS

Even though this is a small shed and is likely to be a home for only the resident tank engine, it boasts a more than generous provision for smoke extraction. There are louvred vents at each end and two rather attractive smoke chimneys. These four subassemblies may well prove to be the trickiest parts of the whole kit. It is important that each pair looks identical when in place and this suggests that batch assembly is the best answer. All the components for each pair are drawn and cut in one exercise to ensure they are identical in every respect. In order to get this right, you first need to do some design work on the scrap pad and determine the best materials for the job. These mini-structures need to combine an element of strength but with the appearance of relatively lightweight construction. There are several ways of achieving this, but the easiest is to use mounting board and something like a better quality postcard or record card.

This design work requires more than just the accurate drawings of the finished structures. They must also be broken down into manageable components while maintaining a clear idea of their eventual assembly sequence. This then establishes the numbers of each item that need to be precisely drawn and cut. It is a good idea to have some blow-ups of each item, taken from your best photos or desk research, and use them as a constant source of reference.

Louvres

These are complicated structures and could be described as a series of holes joined together with strips of wood. In some cases, though not this one, the end formers that straddle the ridge are of solid appearance and this makes the model much easier to design and build. At Swanage the ends, as well as the sides, are slatted and this creates the problem. The most realistic result will come from doing the whole thing as one single piece of accurately drawn artwork on good quality card. If you can find it, something about 0.2mm thick would be ideal. The key to success is to get the 'vee' at each end to exactly match the slope of the roof and to be dead-centre on the ridge-line. The sketch and dimensions should be sufficient for you to have a go at it.

If you are prepared to sacrifice the accuracy in return for a quicker and easier option, however, then a 'slab' construction of rectangles of mounting board will just about pass muster. Some thin strips of card detailing will help disguise its solidity and this approach will at least guarantee an accurate fit to the roof. Once again the sketch plan should be easy to follow. Each vent requires six pieces cut to 42 x16mm and four pieces of 35 x 10mm, all from the mounting board, together with two roof halves of thin card made slightly larger at 46 x 18mm. While you have the thin card to hand, cut several lengths approximately $1/16$in wide (just over 1.5mm) to be used for the final detailing. Assembling these 'layer-cake' louvres is best done in their correct positions on the tiled roof. This way everything must conform to the actual roof profile and is therefore almost error-free.

Both options are roofed the same way, using card templates covered with slate-paper and with a quite generous overhang at the eaves. In fact they are simply smaller versions of the main roof.

Smoke Chimneys

These are going to demonstrate the problem I mentioned earlier where a missed opportunity to photograph some details can create unforeseen difficulties at a later stage. I really thought that the chimneys were going to be simple to draw, plan and build. When it came to building them, however, it became apparent that they had not been identical throughout their long lives and I could not fathom how they were put together. Fortunately the present versions appear to be identical and

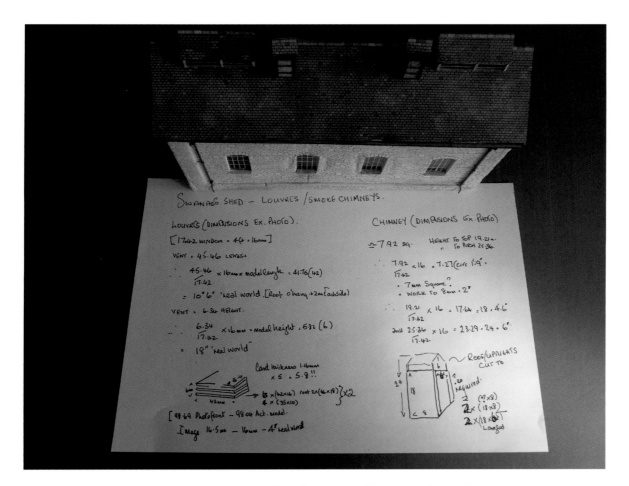

Calculations and sketch plans to determine how best to tackle the roof details.

they have been rebuilt in their most attractive form, so these will be our prototypes.

When I studied all the images the only positive facts to emerge were that the chimneys are positioned on the near side of the roof to cover the offset track beneath, the main corner uprights and cross-braces were all timber, and the insides appeared to be clad with asbestos. The other piece of information concerned the small pitched roofs, which disappeared during the late 1950s but were reinstated in the preservation era. What I had not been able to determine, however, and despite innumerable sketches and exploded diagrams, is how those wooden frames were designed and assembled. Swanage is within an hour's easy drive from home, so a return trip

would have been possible, but I decided it would be better to work with what was available since most modellers in the same situation would not always be able to make another visit.

The chimneys are hollow structures and could therefore be built in either of the methods discussed above in respect of the louvres. The single sheet of folded card, with slightly thicker card strips added later to represent the wooden framework, would be the preferred option, but this could be rather flimsy when it comes to fixing the little roofs. A more robust solution is to again fall back on mounting board to form the inner core. This would provide a more secure foundation to the card strips and hence a firmer support for the roofs, which are the same lightweight card and paper as elsewhere.

CLOCKWISE FROM TOP LEFT: *A pigeon's-eye view of the more recently refurbished roof detail, showing complicated carpentry that will not be easy to reproduce with thin card at a scale of 1:76. Note the essential lead flashing and the extra-thick modern ridge-tiles. These are the shots I should have taken on my first visit.*

After laboriously calculating the dimensions, I settled on 2ft square chimneys standing some 4ft 6in tall at the front and reaching 6ft at the top of the ridge. This seemed too narrow on the scale drawings and presented further problems with the corner posts. Trial and error finally produced a workable compromise: I would keep to the scale 2ft (8mm) mounting board core but would then make the corner posts from $^1/_{16}$in balsa strip. This made the finished chimneys 3ft square and provided just enough strength to carry the neat little pitched roofs. The balsa was glued to the innermost edges of the four board walls, leaving a small amount showing on the outsides that conveniently allowed some more $^1/_{16}$in thin card strips to slot in and represent the cross-members.

The accompanying illustrations should clarify these points. On balance I would not recommend the alternative method as too fragile and too fiddly. The chimneys are built on the workbench and continually offered up to get the correct dimensions and profiles. They are best painted at this stage, but do not fix them until the very last bit of detailing on the shed has been completed.

FINAL ASSEMBLY CHECKS

Putting everything together has been very little different from assembling any other kit, but in case you have worked to a slightly different sequence, here is a general reminder of what needs to be done.

Fit the two roof half-sections to the pre-assembled walls, the rear one going on first. Make sure it is properly square and securely glued to the gable ends and along the eaves. Invert the model and run a further seam of glue to the undersides. Repeat the process with the front half-roof and double-check that the ridge-line is correctly formed.

With the model still inverted, run a bead of glue just below the eaves around all four walls. Carefully ease the tight-fitting false ceiling into place and fix it with the glue. A further seam can again be added to the underside for extra strength.

Using the photographs and plans as references, glue the louvres and smoke chimneys in their respective positions. Remember that the chimneys should be offset and located above the loco-road beneath. A line from the centre of the arched rear doorway will provide a datum.

The completed model is influenced as much by archive steam-era images as by the recent photographs. It seems to have captured the essence of the shed and would not look out of place within a diorama of the whole scene.

Another view of the complicated stonework. Anyone seeking to model the shed in its current state will struggle to locate all the essential clutter that inevitably accompanies a busy working environment.

A timeless view of the north gable end. The hinges are cut from thin card and the large double doors are simply the portion removed when the arched doorway has been cut out. Before the late 1950s this would have been replicated at the south gable entrance.

The roof detail as modelled has here been covered with Superquick grey-slate pre-print. Comparing this with the close-ups in the earlier photographs will demonstrate that it is wrong to model slate roofs with overlapping strips, just as is the relief shown on moulded plastic versions. Real slates are, to all intents and purposes, flat.

RIGHT AND OVERLEAF: *The shed frontage, showing a glimpse of what might have existed inside during the steam era. This, though, is only an artistic guess. If this were a model shed of the arched doorway period almost nothing would be in view.*

It is impossible to over-estimate the importance of the period details.

The final stage is to add the details, including the barge-boards, the soffit, drainpipes, ridge tiles and doors. When fixing the last of these you need to take account of how the model will be worked. If it is as the original, then the rear doors should kept closed. If you intend it to become a through shed, however, then they need to be permanently open. This would also be the case with the front doors if the shed is set prior to the damage caused by the M7 and assuming you have modelled them.

The building is now ready for painting with water-colours and 'house style' enamels for the woodwork. Attend to any last-minute weathering and it can then be sited on the layout. It's a reasonably large building, but one with plenty of character that could quite easily be finished in different materials and colour schemes for installation other than in the Purbecks.

If you have sufficient space and the idea fits in with your overall plan, you could do a lot worse than place the shed in its proper setting. The immediate scene at Swanage is surely one of the most attractive on the entire system, and particularly so in the actual steam era. The published images provide a good starting point and the desk research will be more than enough for you recreate the picture exactly as it was in the 1950s. Study them carefully and you'll see that even the omission of the turntable still fails to spoil the delightful character of this unique little depot. The coaling platform is pretty basic and the water tower in the Wills range looks very similar.

THIS PAGE AND THE TWO FOLLOWING PAGES: *These views of the current scene at Swanage should help in making an accurate miniature of this attractive, though cluttered, little depot. The distinctive stone water tower could just about be worked up from a model in the Wills range. It is worth noting that in the steam era the large trees, mostly lime and horse chestnut, extended well beyond the far end of the shed. They also provided a backdrop to the coal stage and water tower, as shown in the black and white image overleaf.* STEAM MUSEUM OF THE GREAT WESTERN RAILWAY SWINDON

SCRATCH-BUILDING CONCLUSIONS

I began by saying that you should immediately dismiss any of the implied mystique and status that is often attributed to 'scratch-building'. I stand squarely behind that statement. This project and the additional comments will, I hope, have convinced most modellers that it is worth a go. The tools, materials and techniques are all very basic and are well within the grasp of even the most recent entrants to the hobby. Above all it is surely the only guaranteed way of achieving a railway that is truly your own and that is wholly down to your own skills and perseverance. I accept that today's ready-to-site buildings are attractive and that their ranges cover almost every imaginable need. However, they can never be anything more than 'cheque-book modelling' and do little or nothing to distinguish your layout from the next man's. Indeed, the only skills involved are in opening the boxes and amassing enough funds to be able to afford them.

As a scratch-builder, no matter how inadequate your first efforts might seem, you have taken that all-important step towards being a real modeller and not just a purchaser of models. It's more fun, it's less expensive, it's more rewarding and it's far more memorable. Should you need any further excuses, remember that it always places you in total control. If you need to adjust the actual scale measurements so that a building is a better fit on its chosen site, and this can be done safely without altering its essential character, then go ahead as no one will be likely to spot the difference.

Before ending this chapter I should make a confession. Nagged by the uncertainties surrounding the smoke chimneys, I returned to Swanage to obtain a few extra images to assist any modellers intending to construct their own version. Close-ups of the chimneys show that the current structures are actually wood-planked and not asbestos, and their small roofs are not slated but covered with nailed-down tar felt. I remain happy with my interpretation, but the photos will allow other modellers to construct a more accurate version of the shed in the twenty-first century.

CHAPTER THREE

LARGER TWO-ROAD SHEDS IN THE STEAM ERA

WORKING THE LARGER SHED

Much of what goes on at this size of shed is no more complicated than the routines at its smaller brethren: there is just more of it and it happens more frequently. Every steam locomotive coming on-shed or going off-shed requires the same routines, whether at Swanage or Nine Elms, Keswick or Camden. For the sake of this brief discussion we will place our two-road shed at a mainline junction serving perhaps two branch lines. The shed's allocation will be somewhere between ten and twenty locomotives, depending upon their relative size. (It also depends upon the real space available on the layout and the very real limitations on the modelling budget.)

The majority of the stock will be smaller tank or tender engines for the branches, a few larger tanks or smaller mixed-traffic locos for any mainline duties, and perhaps one express loco for specific fast vans, parcels or passenger runs to London. All of this, as in every instance, will reflect your back story. The more comprehensively you have thought this out, and preferably written it up, then the more realistic will be your eventual allocation.

If you haven't yet attempted this exercise then the hypothetical 'extract' on the opposite page may help guide your thoughts. My apologies to any non-Great Western enthusiasts, but I'm sure you'll be able to translate it into your own region or location.

The shed is located in mid-Somerset on the main Bristol–Exeter line. The station serves two fairly long branch lines, one (A) to cover the seaside resort, the other (B) northeast to the coalfield. (See also the sketch map in the Appendices.)

Now I'm not suggesting that this is a real-shed/real-world example. It is no more than an indication of an entirely hypothetical set of rosters. However, I

hope it may inspire others to produce similar detail within their back story. This can apply irrespective of whether the shed is a stand-alone project simply feeding a sector plate or cassettes, or one that is incorporated within a larger layout.

It provides some ideas on the sort of locos that should be allocated (and that also means purchased) and the probable level of activity that could be shown as cameos around the yard. The concept can be extended still further if your back story includes other potential traffic sources via the branches or mainline. Typical of these might be a slaughterhouse or cold store (for which vacuum braked-fitted locos are essential), a Ministry of Defence ordnance depot (perhaps tank engines with spark arrestors) or a quarry or cement works (headed by a 0-6-2T for sharp curves and heavy loads). The list is endless but the more realistic and convincing the back story then the more enjoyable and fulfilling will be your shed operations.

BUILDING THE SUPERQUICK SHED

The Superquick engine shed kit has been around for more years than most of us care to remember. It was one of the earlier entrants into their range and has, I think, remained largely unaltered since the 1960s. Indeed the only version with a longer shelf life has been the 'flat' sheet from Bilteezi. Needless to say the Superquick model does show signs of its age. It is, after all, a near-contemporary of the steam age that it represents.

As with the other items in the range, the brickwork and colour scheme is designed to fit in with their own unique ambience. The station buildings, platforms, signal box and sheds all feature the same

Typical Duties

SSX = except Saturdays and Sundays

Branch A

SSX	Hourly 'all stations' from 08:00 until 19:00 (trip time 1½ hours)	Requires 3 locos
SSX	09:30 pick-up goods all stations, return 18:30	Tank or tender loco
Weds only	Livestock ex-yard and pick up en route, return empties	
SSX	Daily through-goods to terminus (trip time 1 hour), return with empties	Mogul or large tank
	Service incoming branch, loco off semi-fasts ex-terminus, turn	
Sats only	12:00 holiday down special	Hall or Grange

Branch B

SSX	07:00 workman's train (return with coal, leave stock)	Tank as available
SSX	07:30 coal-empties ex-yard, return full-coal	
SSX	09:30 coal-empties ex-yard, return full-coal	
	14:00 coal-empties ex-yard, return full-coal	2-8-0 or 0-6-2(T)
	09:30 pick-up goods all stations	
	Hourly 'all stations' from 08:15 until 19:15 (trip time 1½ hours)	Tank or tender loco
	15:15 pilot to 'all stations', return workman's train depart 18:00	

Mainline

SSX	09:05 semi-fast Bristol, return down-semi via Exeter	Hall or Grange
	06:30 yard pilots light engine, return 14:30	Small tanks (2)
	10:30 yard light engine for up-vans to Bristol	2-6-0
	10:35 yard light engine for up-coal to Bristol, return empties	2-8-0
	14:00 yard pilots (shift change) light engine	Small tanks (2)
SSX	14:30 semi-fast to Bristol, return down-semi via Exeter	Hall or Grange
	18:00 yard light engine for up-coal to Bristol, return empties	2-8-0

characteristics, enabling the modeller to create a correctly uniform setting. While this is an advantage on the one hand, however, it is a problem on the other. Superquick's choice of yellow glazing bars, almost yellow woodwork and green doors render it inappropriate to any prototype region or company. The model also suffers from the print colour being rather shiny. This is a great shame since the actual 'brown brick' finish is well executed and, if matt printed, would not be out of place in any 'midlands' or urban setting.

The actual construction of the model appears quite an easy task, since the building itself is very simple and has but few additional features. There are a couple of construction sheets and some quite useful tips on how to achieve the best results. While their recommended adhesive is no doubt quite adequate, I prefer to use my own mix of craft PVA, clear or universal glue, and the enhanced quick-dry type from Scotch. I positively disagree with the instructions, however, where they recommend fixing the

The Superquick two-road shed, which has been on the market for several decades, is still reasonably priced and is relatively easy to build. The artwork is crisp but is somewhat weakened by being in the familiar 'house-colours' of the original range. It is also rather shiny, but you can help to gain a bit of texture by placing a medium-grade sandpaper over the print and pressing firmly down with a decorator's roller.

glazing acetates with Sellotape or similar sticky tape. It is a fact that the card used in the kit is pretty absorbent and that sticky tape also loses its 'grip' over a period of time. The acetates, as stated, are to be held in the 'sandwich' of the outer and inner walls but I am far from confident that this offers a truly permanent solution. So, despite the fact that the individual acetates have very little overlap for fixing, I still suggest clear universal glues are the better bet.

One further word of advice is that the separation of the frets is not always as easy as it might be. Many of the allegedly simple 'push outs' need the judicious use of a scalpel to free them from their surrounds. All that aside, the model goes together pretty well and most of the various fits and joins can be aligned without too much difficulty. However, the sheer length of the unsupported side walls, coupled with the rather unusual 'groove fit', can cause problems. It certainly remains well within the scope of even the most inexperienced of modellers, which no doubt helps to explain its constant presence on the stockist's shelves. In an uninterrupted session the kit could just about be completed in a single evening; spread over two sessions, however, it makes for a leisurely and enjoyable project.

During the build I used the sandpaper/roller technique in order to go some way towards reducing the shine and providing a better surface for the eventual pastels. On balance the gain is not that discernible, but then the extra effort is any case pretty minimal. I also scribed the vertical planking on the two small interior offices and added one or two braces, cut from the window push-outs, to reinforce the corner joins.

CUSTOMIZING THE SHED

The finished shed would be adequate for the majority of smaller junctions and, at 300mm long (75ft to scale) long, it will house four reasonably sized tank engines with maybe there is just enough room for an 0-6-0 tender locomotive and a shorter tank on one of the roads. However, there are examples of quite small sheds having an extra solitary 4-6-0 mixed-traffic engine allocated to them for specific workings: a Hall, Black 5, V2 or Arthur could easily be accommodated. The finished model is attractive but it is pretty basic. The modeller who is seeking something that is more prototypical needs to put in plenty of thought and some scratch-building to enhance its appearance: given the shed's likely multi-engine allocation, the

The assembled kit makes a handsome structure, albeit with a few weaknesses and omissions in its basic design. The very small wooden offices inside the entrance, for example, are too small to serve any real purpose. The kit also lacks any proper workshop, stores, sand furnace or messing facilities.

existing kit certainly lacks a number of essential features. It should surely have had sufficient office space for a shed foreman and probably a clerk; half a dozen engines would need facilities for possibly eighteen loco crews; there would be the fire-lighters and cleaners; and there would be a couple of fitters with a small workshop; and finally there would be stores with the necessary supplies of oils, tools and basic spare parts.

The kit has an exterior office scaled at 20 x 8ft and two interior 'cubicles' measuring just 7 x 3ft, scarcely sufficient to even open the door. The only short-term solution I could come up with was the addition of more accommodation as separate structures representing later improvements to the building. In order to have a reasonably realistic back story, the existing office was given to the foreman/clerk and the small inner office on that side adapted into a signing-on point. I then added a tin-sheeted block at the other end of the wall to act as both stores and crew room. Finally, another tin structure was tacked onto the back as the fitters' workshop. I acknowledge that this is really moving basic customizing into the realms

of scratch-building, but there is no alternative if the shed is to be seen as a proper working installation.

If the tin additions are not to one's taste, it may be possible to find matching brick and tile sheets in Superquick's accessory range, although this cannot be guaranteed. If this can be done, the extra buildings shown can still be replicated, but they will now have the same finish and give the appearance of having been built at the same time as the main shed. One final point is to cover the printed drainpipes with modelled versions, either made up from the bits box or from one of the available accessory packs. Once that is done, the building should be weathered and then placed in its chosen location. Superquick has provided some sections of paving slabs in the kit, although they will definitely need substantial weathering to produce the required oil-stained and grimy effects. Steam sheds were, and still are, filthy. On the project I considered using the slabs inside the shed to provide walkways along both walls. This, however, can only be done after the building is *in situ* and everything, including the tracks, is in place.

The small external office could be sited almost anywhere around the walls. The archives certainly show that there was no favoured position for this feature.

Scratch-built additions

These are very straightforward lean-tos and require no great skills to reproduce. If you are thinking about adding one, however, it may be worth looking back to the end of the previous chapter where we looked at scratch-building, since the basic principles are the same.

Although a lean-to has only three visible sides, it is best modelled with all four in place. When two small-ish structures are concerned, as here, then I prefer to work on both simultaneously.

Select a workpiece of mounting card large enough to yield all the parts needed for the two 'kits', The crew room needs side walls 10ft wide (40mm) and the front and back walls are 30ft (120mm). The height to the rear (to match the existing shed) is 12ft 6in (50mm) and at the eaves 8ft 6in (34mm). The fitter's workshop to the rear of the building can have the same dimensions but a shorter frontage of 16ft (64mm). The roof sections (to sit on top of the walls) should be 12ft (48mm) wide with lengths of 124mm and 68mm respectively. The two floors that sit inside

the walls will be 116 x 40mm and 60 x 40mm. The workpiece should therefore be roughly a quarter of the original A1 sheet.

Draw the twelve sides, roofs and floors accurately to the dimensions shown above. Then draw on the windows and doorways. I have used the dimensions of various bits of spare glazing and doorways from the bits box. The apertures could still remain the same, but with the frames and glazing bars drawn on plastiglaze and thin card used to fabricate the doors.

With a sharp scalpel, cleanly remove the above apertures and then cut out the twelve main individual sections. Separate the two 'kits' and mark them with pencil so you do not get them muddled.

The next step only applies if you are going to use brick paper. Glue the appropriate brick paper to the various walls with paper glue, allowing about a 2mm overlap at both ends of the front and back walls. Give it time to dry and then pierce, fold back and glue the surplus inside the window and door openings.

Using clear or universal glue, fix the plain glazing acetates or pre-printed acetates behind the windows.

The only solution to the lack of facilities included in the kit is to resort to scratch-building your own additions. These need not be complicated: the illustration shows the kit of parts for two simple structures drawn out on a section of mounting board.

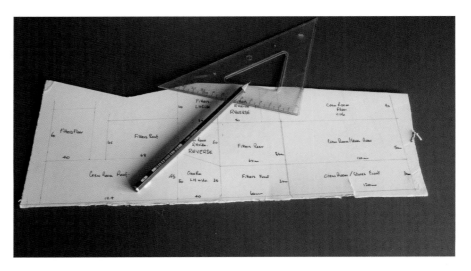

As usual, the only tools required to separate the various components are a steel rule and a sharp scalpel or craft knife. The eventual windows and doors can come from the bits box and their apertures cut accordingly.

All the components have now been separated. Note that each piece is identified and has its dimensions marked. This is always advisable when planning a complicated structure or when engaged in batch-building, and is particularly important when several components may be similar in appearance.

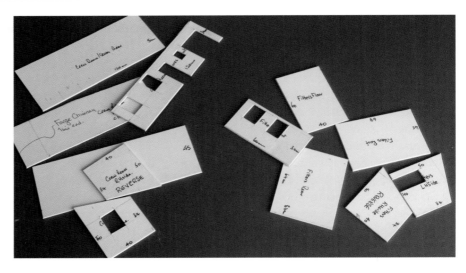

Assembly is quite straightforward as they are really no more than little boxes with lids. They are designed to look like typical tin sheds built on the usual brick plinths. Tin, or more correctly corrugated iron, is difficult to find in our scale, so I prefer to make my own.

From the bits box (or the pre-drawn or painted versions) fix the doors in position. To add animation, glue one open to pose a figure entering or leaving at some later stage.

Use thinner card or very thick drawing paper to make up the three chimney stacks, all of which could then be covered with brick paper that is the closest match. Do not forget to add some additional strips to represent the proper capping. Set them to one side to dry and settle down.

Take the two floor sections and glue each of the sides in place. Next, glue the front and back walls in place so they exactly fit across the ends of the side walls. Check that they are square and upright. If the model is paper covered, carefully bend the small overlaps and glue down the exposed edges of the front and back walls. If this proves difficult, trim off the overlap and disguise the edges with watercolour paint.

Glue the chimney stacks in place. Offer up the roof 'lids', mark out the positions of the stacks and cut these out. Glue the roof in place.

When making the brick-paper version, the next stage is to cover the roof with the chosen tile paper. Add thin paper lead flashing around the chimney stack, then add the barge-boards, gutters and drainpipes to finish. Chimney pots can be from accessory packs or made from paper rolled into small cylinders. Glue to a solid section on top of each stack or set them into a plasticine base.

The alternative, when making a tin-roofed structure, is to cut out the smooth bases from foil baking cases or similar. With a ruler and HB pencil – not too

The very simple procedure starts with a supply of tin-foil baking cases. Remove the flat bases with scissors and then smooth them out using a round pencil as a rolling pin. Using a small steel rule and a not too sharp pencil, press the corrugations at roughly 1mm spacings. This is best done with the foil supported on a pad of kitchen-towels. Using a scalpel, slice the completed discs to give rectangular sheets equivalent to about 6 x 3ft (24 x 12mm). Lightly roll them again to remove any distortion and you have tin sheets in less time than it takes to describe.

sharp – score vertical lines across them all at roughly 1mm vertical intervals. Cut them into small sections roughly 6 x 3ft (24 x 12mm) and you have sheets of corrugated iron. This is a long job as you will need enough sheets to clad all the walls and the roofs. Tin structures were invariably built up from a brick plinth and I duly cut relief sections of six courses deep from scrap card. These were fixed and paper covered on the made-up buildings.

Stick on the first row of tin sheets, working from the top of the plinth and, when ready, from the front of the two roofs. This can be done with decent PVA or quick-dry Scotch glue, but the best option is carefully applied clear or universal glue. Each new sheet should overlap its predecessor by one corrugation. Repeat this for all subsequent layers, overlapping vertically by about 1mm. Do not worry if the rows are irregular: provided the corrugations are vertical, any irregularities will simply highlight the efforts you have put in. Avoid pressing the pieces down too firmly and apply just as much pressure as is necessary by running a pencil point down the grooves. The sheets are best cut with fine scissors. Measure and cut the ones around doors, windows and corners before fixing to avoid damage.

When all the walls and roofs have been covered, give the whole an overall coat of matt black, making sure that the paint is not too sticky or thick. Two thin coats are better than one that is too thick. While it is still drying you can usefully streak it with an almost drybrush technique of various rust hues. Augment the finished job with pastel weathering, adding any drainpipes, bargeboards and other details.

LEFT AND BELOW LEFT: *The two completed small buildings before adding any final weathering. They are certainly not architectural gems, but they will serve their purpose. The block on the left represents the fitter's workshop and the larger one contains the mess-room and, to the right, the stores.*

Touching in

One last point regards touching in the exposed card edges and any other areas needing attention. This is quite a lengthy job with a building of this size and is not made any easier by the long sections of capping stones that top all the walls. Be prepared to spend an hour or two on this task and do not be surprised if you have to revisit some sections. As stated earlier, the exposed card is very absorbent and it seems to leach out the carefully applied watercolours. Pay particular attention to the two sets of louvred ventilators. These can remain quite stubbornly shiny despite the application of several coats of black watercolour. A quicker and more satisfying solution might be to use Humbrol matt-black enamel.

ABOVE AND BELOW: *As with the offices provided in the original kit, the two additional tin shacks can be sited anywhere around the base of the main shed. They can also be positioned as free-standing items, perhaps serving different functions, and they will be shown this way later in the project.*

BUILDING THE PROTOTYPE NORTH LIGHT SHED

The Prototype two-road north light engine shed is a comparatively recent addition to Freestone Models' range of welcome reintroductions. I'm given to understand that this particular model was never fully marketed and that the Freestone version is still in its testing phase. There is some evidence of this in the kit kindly supplied for the project, most obviously in that the new printers used the glossy side of the card and not the requested matt side. The kit shown here is, quite literally, a prototype of the new Prototype.

The kit, however, is everything that one would expect from the Freestone/Prototype range. The artwork and print accuracy are excellent as always and the whole thing is well thought out. As with the single-road shed (see Chapter 1), there is a lot to be done with a scalpel. I once again followed my usual practice of cutting out and carefully numbering all the various components in one operation. These were then placed in clearly marked envelopes, noting their eventual functions and their places in the assembly process.

There are no particularly difficult aspects to this kit and no likely snags to look out for. It goes without saying that Prototype kits have never been intended to be 'quickies', but the extra time and effort needed to do them justice is well rewarded with a robust and well-detailed addition to one's layout. Indeed, the dozen or so original kits on 'Wessex Lines' were installed nearly thirty years ago and still show no signs of aging, even given their often inhospitable loft environment.

There is little purpose in giving the usual step-by-step construction procedures as they are well covered within the instructions, but a broad overview of the kit as a whole may be of help. A north light shed is an attractive proposition as these were found on almost every region within British Railways. This particular one earns well-deserved bonus points as the designers have thoughtfully included, at the rear of the building, a stores block that, quite properly, is only accessible from inside the shed. It has two chimneys, the smaller of which could well be the flue from the office stove or perhaps from a forge. The

The Prototype Models north light shed is designed and assembled using the same tools and techniques encountered with the single-road shed in Chapter 1. The joins between the bays are easy to disguise by adding drainpipes from an accessory pack or, as here, from green-coated florist's wire. The mounting brackets are small strips from an address label, shown oversized and unpainted for the photograph.

larger one is clearly that emanating from the sand furnace, which is an essential feature of any decent-sized shed. This welcome feature, however, reduces the length of covered roads available to the engines, limiting the capacity to four or five smaller tank locos or, at a pinch, a pair of 4-6-0s. In practical use this may not be a drawback, however, as I much prefer to have my engines on view in the yard rather than shunted into the shed at the end of their shifts. They are far too expensive to remain hidden away.

INTERIOR AND EXTERIOR DETAILING

The shed has four north light bays and the builder is offered the choice of whether to have windows in all of them. I opted to go for all four windows on one side and just two on the other. There is not much to be seen on the inside as no interior detailing is supplied with the artwork. However, if you want to site the shed so that you can obtain views through the large entrance, it is not that

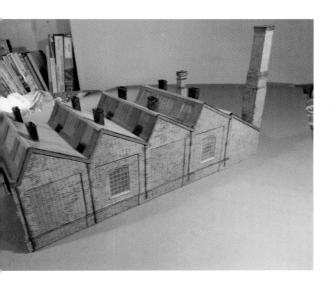

Compare this image showing the windows appearing on alternate bays only with the 'all bays showing' version on the opposite page. There is quite a difference between the two.

The finished structure would make a handsome addition to any layout. Like all north light buildings it has more character and individuality than a straight roof version. I particularly like the smoke chimneys and the provision of a workshop and sand furnace at the back.

difficult to create your own artwork. This need be little more taxing than using watercolours to paint a continuation of the back-wall colour scheme on a piece of copy paper. This can then be cut to size and fixed to the wall or walls with a glue stick. Some thin card noticeboards and paper notices would add a bit of appropriate detail.

There is not much to be done to the outside of the shed except to add drainpipes and some guttering to the extension at the rear. The kit includes some steel wire for this, but I chose to use my thickest green-coated florist's wire (1.15mm) to give the typical 4in downpipes with thin strips from address labels to represent the brackets.

It is not unusual to find that thinner card models require some extra bracing and general reinforcement. This is particularly true in the case of engine sheds, which naturally lack the strength given by the floors, ceilings and internal walls. The Prototype kit acknowledges this from the outset and provides some sections of ¼in square balsa strip to be strategically sited within the carcass. I chose to add some more to provide extra strength and rigidity. In hindsight, the addition of a further strip of mounting board along the base of each inside wall, rather like a

Engine sheds have a notorious weakness, with their main wall literally hanging from the roof. Extra bracing is needed on this model, over and above the ¼in balsa supplied with the kit.

Another underneath shot of the prototype roof, in which the extra bracing is just about visible. Perhaps it might have been better to use mounting board, with the dark side down, to reinforce each of the slate roof sections?

Many of the larger two-road are prone to a potential problem by which the walls tend to develop 'toe-in' at the base, as this photograph of the entrance clearly shows. The presence of central supporting pillars simply makes matters worse. If the shed can be permanently sited, then glue it down firmly with the walls and pillar set suitably vertical. If the shed needs to be moved for track cleaning, insert nails about 2in long into the corners and the pillar and seat them into pre-drilled holes in the baseboard.

plinth, would help to prevent any bowing or warping during the life of the model.

CONCLUSIONS

I have always enjoyed the challenge of attempting to get the best from these kits and this new-generation example was no exception. At first sight it may appear tricky for an absolute beginner. Indeed it has some of the complexities that are now associated with the more contemporary downloads. The instructions, however, are clear and comprehensive. Any possible problems can be quickly overcome with a few test fits and rereading the instructions. The usual strictures about touching in the exposed areas and some judicious pastel weathering still apply, but the end result should look at home even on a smaller layout.

BUILDING THE METCALF SHED

This model is an entirely appropriate companion for the Metcalf goods shed, which was extensively featured in the author's previous book dealing with goods operations. It has the same architectural style and the brick finish ties it in to perfection. Needless to say it uses the same construction methods and is

The Metcalf two-road shed is a genuine pleasure to build. It needs little, if any, additional work and the instructions are both clear and helpful. The kit design is such that the overlapping layers of thick card lock together to produce a robust and 'square' structure. In order to follow 'real-world' practice, I added lids to the smoke chimneys, although I should have checked all the corner supports with a spirit level before gluing them in place.

accompanied by one of the well-detailed instruction sheets that are the key to the success of this extensive range. The print quality is excellent, verging on outstanding, and the pre-punched frets are almost entirely accurate (only a handful required intervention with a scalpel). As is common with the Metcalf approach, the kit includes the numerous reinforcing cards that help to make these models consistently sturdy and robust.

The large sheets of components might appear a bit daunting to a beginner who is tackling a card kit for the first time. Provided you heed the manufacturer's advice, however, and spend a little time studying the frets and reading the instructions, it should soon become clear. It may appear a contradiction in terms, but while the kit is complex it remains simple to construct. It therefore needs very little additional step-by-step advice as all the necessary guidance is already well presented.

ADVANTAGES AND OMISSIONS

Among the many features in the kit's favour, I particularly like the inclusion of chimney-style smoke vents in addition to the more usual louvred vent along the ridge-line. More properly referred to as 'smoke chimneys', these were such a common sight on engine sheds as to appear almost universal. The kit also includes a small outbuilding identified as the workshop. It is an attractive addition, but I can find nothing comparable in my archive on sheds. Where such workshops existed, they were usually built as an integral part of the main structure to avoid having to lug heavy lumps of steel halfway across a rain-swept yard to a fitter's bench.

I cannot, however, help lamenting the absence of the shed doors and the lack of any accommodation for the crews and the shed staff. A facility of this size would probably have been allocated between six and twelve locomotives; that would imply perhaps

ALL IMAGES: *The cavernous interior of the Metcalf shed reveals that it also boasts pre-printed inner walls. This is definitely better than most of the other offerings, as I certainly find it irritating to have to decide how to treat the insides of these quite large structures. In this case I simply added some notices, a couple of pin-up photos and the obligatory duty or roster-board, all from the Sankey Scenics sheet. I also found a second use for the small tin lean-to additions from the earlier Dapol kits, though I'll leave their precise purpose to your imagination.*

twenty or more sets of enginemen, fire-droppers, coalmen, cleaners, fitters and storemen, in addition to the shed foremen and their staff. It could also see round-the-clock activity, which would require offices, stores and messing facilities that were far more 'prototypical' than a separate workshop.

We encountered similar problems with the previous Superquick shed and the same solution is needed here – scratch-built additions. In the case of this Metcalf kit, however, the task would be much easier as spare sheets of matching brickwork have been included. It should be a fairly straightforward exercise to design and build a small, single-storey annexe, either as a stand-alone feature or, perhaps a bit more tricky, incorporated into the shed itself.

The kit is well suited to some extra detailing, notably by fabricating some shed doors and adding realistic drainpipes. You could also fully customize it by re-cladding the whole building with alternative brick or stone papers. You would then be able to resite it and regionalize it to better suit your layout's geography and corporate ownership. If you embark on this rather drastic, but worthwhile endeavour, don't forget that all the paintwork will also need to be changed to the appropriate region or company colour scheme. The usual comments about touching in the exposed edges apply here as elsewhere, and it would be sensible to add barge-boards to the workshop and some lead flashing to its chimney stack.

ROOF DETAILS

While we are on the subject of chimneys, a little work can be done to improve the very prominent smoke chimneys on the shed roof. A further trawl through the archive revealed that nearly every such installation was capped with some form of protection, ranging from a simple flat lid to an elegant little pitched roof. (A similar situation was discussed in Chapter 2 in relation to scratch-building the actual shed at Swanage.) The caps on the chimneys are intended to let the smoke and steam out without letting in gallons of dirty rainwater. For the project we will keep things simple and stick with the flat-lid version.

The required number of lids are cut from mounting board to the exact dimensions of the chimney tops.

Each lid sits on top of four small uprights projecting upwards from inside the corners of the mouths of the chimney. These can be small lengths of balsa or hardwood, or even 2mm plastic 'L' girders, fixed securely to the inside of the chimney with about 2 or 3mm showing. Allow them to dry properly and then simply glue the lids in place so that they sit squarely over the mouths of the chimneys. Give everything a coat of matt black and liberally dust it with sooty pastel. Your shed will now be ready to receive its allocation of engines.

CONCLUSIONS

The Metcalf shed is a worthy addition to any layout. It is competitively priced and a pleasure to build and to detail. Its architecture is pretty universal, so it should be relatively simple to customize it to suit a location on any BR region.

ADDING A COALING STAGE

It may be more accurate to refer to knocking up a coal stage, rather than constructing one, as I can trace no references to any sort of common style, size or building materials. Each one was clearly developed over the life of the shed as generations of coalmen complained to successive shed foremen, who in turn badgered the Divisional Engineering Officers for such luxuries as a hoist and a rudimentary shelter. Invariably the end result, however much an improvement on what was there before, was little better than a flimsy eyesore. It is hardly a construction project requiring scores of modelling hours.

As is usual in this sort of situation, I would start by looking through the albums to get some idea of the general sizes and appearance. At best you will find only a few shots in which these installations may be seen somewhere in the background. However, with the track formation already loosely in place and with its eventual operations in mind, there may be enough information to make a few quick sketches or plans to decide upon the size, style and construction methods. For ease, speed and the use of materials to hand, I opted for a solid, brick-faced, concrete-topped platform with wooden supports to a tin roof.

CONSTRUCTION

A quick template was traced *in situ* in the optimum operating position. This was transferred to the usual mounting board card and duly cut out. Platform 'walls' were from the same material to 15mm in depth to give roughly the correct height for unloading wagons. The height of the roof eaves, designed to overhang the wagons and locomotives, was gauged from the top of the tallest tender (GWR 4000 gallon) with room for the fireman to level the load. This was fixed at 60mm above ground level and the uprights were cut from small square balsa strip. There was nothing scientific about it, simply selecting something thick enough to look capable of doing the job. This is, rather obviously, a task for balsa cement. It sets quickly and that is essential with uprights and end-on joints. Prior to gluing on this basic timberwork, cover the platform walls in your choice of brick or stone, and use small reinforcing squares of thicker paper or card to help maintain the key joints of the timbers.

Next you should measure the under- roof and roof templates. You will need two half-sections meeting along the ridge beam. On my version these will be 140 × 80mm on the loco side and 140 × 50mm on the wagon side. Fix these in place with balsa cement. You will then be able to design, cut and fit the extra strip wood to represent the trusses. A quick sketch and some offering up will reveal what looks like best. As these will be permanently on view, you should take your time. Once this is completed, paint all the woodwork with watercolour black or matt black enamel, including the underside of the roof template. Cover the platform surface with paving stone paper or paint it to give a worn concrete effect, as was done earlier on the pathways.

ROOF

In nearly every case the actual roof was provided by tin or asbestos sheets, which may be represented using a pre-printed or plastic sheet, either of which will provide the simple solution. On my example I decided to use the same technique as on the extra buildings and fabricate my own individual sheets with tin foil. It is a lengthy process but it does ensure the essential air of cohesion and consistency. Once the sheets are laid and firmly secured, the whole roof is then given a coat of matt black.

FURTHER DETAILING

At this stage we can turn our attention to the inside of the structure and see if any other small embellishments will help to add character. I chose to add

Creating a coaling stage in miniature is very easy in that there are no prototypes to reproduce and you can make anything you wish. The problem is that by their very nature they are flimsy and thrown together, and this is difficult to capture in model form. At this point we have the basic platform and the timberwork, using $^1/_{16}$in balsa strip, that will support the roof.

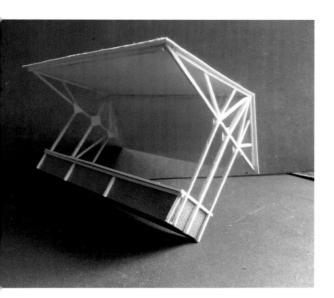

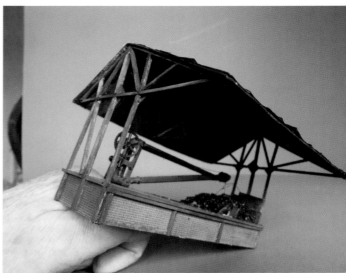

With the card roof-template in place it easier to see how, while the platform must fit between the tracks, the roof is designed to cover them. This is not helped by the fact that the site will only accommodate a roughly triangular shape. If that were not enough, one then has to take the pitch of the roof into consideration. I did try to produce a working drawing but finally settled for a 'cut-to-fit' approach. The roof trusses were made up in the same way.

This, together with the later illustrations showing the finished coaling stage, should provide enough information for anyone wanting to build something similar for their own shed. A facility like this is essential if your depot houses a dozen or so engines. On this model I chose to use my own handmade tin sheets, but a viable alternative would be the download version used on the ash shelter in Chapter 6.

some reinforcing braces to the uprights and to the platform face, implying an inherent weakness in the brickwork.

The hoist is a Wills yard crane, ignoring the instructions for a semi-working model. The scoop or bucket is made from plastic scrap and duly rigged with black-painted cotton 'rope'. I would advise that this is best modelled with the scoop on the platform fixed down and loaded or being loaded ready for its next move. For safety reasons, it would be better to fix the hoist at the wide end of the platform. A set of access steps, together with tools and other bits, will add character. The coal heap is a blob of plasticine with fine, crushed real coal. To add a human touch, select a couple of suitable figures in realistic poses, such as filling the scoop, unloading a wagon or tidying the heap. In all probability this small but essential cameo facility will take less time to execute than it has taken to photograph and write it up.

THE COAL DUMP

This is possibly the least interesting item you might be called upon to model. In their day, however, coal dumps were just as important as they were large. They were introduced after the industrial crises in the 1920s and '30s, which made the railway companies aware that they were vulnerable to disputes at the pithead. It was therefore prudent to create stockpiles of coal at most, if not all, key depots. I haven't been able to trace any evidence regarding the sizes or how many days of reserves were held, but autobiographies frequently describe these coal mountains as containing many thousands of tons. Given that a depot might well have sixty engines, all demanding to be fed with three or four tons every day, a thousand tons wouldn't last a week.

The stockpiles were maintained throughout the Second World War and many proved to be invaluable

During the Second World War, and in some cases even earlier, MPDs and larger sheds began to build up huge stockpiles of loco coal to prevent undue shortages in the event of disruption to supplies by enemy action or adverse weather. No doubt the threat of industrial action was also considered. These vast dumps, often many thousands of tons, were still around in the early 1950s, although some had been significantly depleted in the savage winter of 1947. The model version is no more than an upturned foil pie dish coated with plasticine and with real coal pressed into the surface. It's worth noting that the lumps could well be the size of tombstones and that the army wasn't the only organization to paint things white. Not surprisingly a family of 1:76 rats would not be out of place.

during the traffic interruptions in the bitter winter of 1947. Many depots still retained them even into the early years of British Railways and the nationalization of the mines, although it's fair to assume that most had disappeared by the late 1950s.

CONSTRUCTION

This is certainly not going to be a complex task. It will obviously be governed by the amount of space that you want it to fill and, of course, its shape. Ideally it should be long and narrow so that it can be accessed from a parallel siding for loading and removal. A site outside of a back road would be the most appropriate, but not essential.

All you need is a suitable container – a cardboard box or foil dish will do – invert it and coat it with well-worked plasticine. Smash a lump of coal into scale-sized pieces and then press them into the surface, placing larger pieces round the base to give some semblance of a sound structure. Continue this until everything is covered and then give it a liberal dose of the PVA mix used to fix ballast. As finishing touch, paint the lower portion white, which management would say was a safety measure during the black-out and still needed due to the inadequate yard

lighting. Cynics would say it was needed to limit pilfering by off-duty enginemen.

MODELLING THE ENGINE SHED YARD

In the real world two-road engine sheds appear to have been in the minority. In terms of quantity, they seem to be a small group sandwiched between the vast numbers of single-road structures and the host of much larger and complex units with three, four and indeed many more roads. Careful research reveals even fewer two-road through sheds. Although several boast an elevated coaling stage and a turntable.

Most of the examples sourced were located at sites such as junctions rather than at terminal stations. This is fairly logical since a branch terminus would rarely need to house more than two or three locos, while larger urban termini would doubtless be served from an adjacent major motive power depot (MPD). For the purposes of this introduction, at least, we can perhaps define the two-road shed as simply one that has a greater capacity to handle its own allocation together with an increased opportunity to service visiting engines.

Among the expanded facilities one could include a larger and definitely mechanized coaling stage, a larger water tower and strategically placed water cranes, perhaps a rarely modelled coal dump and increased numbers of office and stores buildings. One can also justify one or more engine sidings, together with adequate access to the shed facilities for visiting locos to be serviced without impeding the normal activities. Even though they existed, however, we will leave the elevated coal road, large water tower and the turntable to our next and final shed project, the fully fledged MPD (see Chapter 4).

PLANNING AND COMPROMISES

Earlier we deliberately set out to minimize the footprint of the shed itself and its immediate environs. While, as always in modelling, space still remains an issue, we need to acquire considerably more layout real estate and, where possible, introduce additional trackwork for both access and shed movements. That does not mean, however, that a space-strapped modeller cannot simply plan for a two-road shed to come straight off a single point from the running line or lines: there is a prototype example for almost any kind of track plan that you may wish to devise.

The critical factor here is the actual size of the shed building. Looking at the available kits this would seem to range from 115 x 245mm to 140 x 320mm; no doubt there are or will be other kits outside of these basic parameters. In order to appear properly railway-like, you must also make provision for a sensible amount of straight track in the shed yard. Sharp curves into the shed doorway are not an option.

The single-road sheds modelled so far have all been on a basic A3 sheet. We will now move up to the much larger A1 board, which should enable you to plot a variety of track plans and include some impression of a junction-type location. Once again the starting point for any plan is the marking out of a suitable 3in or 6in grid. Once this is done, and assuming your layout already exists, plot in your existing running lines and loops or at least those portions scheduled to include the point or points for shed access or that perhaps form fixed limits to your available space. (For further guidance see the sketches in the Appendices.)

You now need to plan how best to create the proper feel of a small but busy shed-complex. An A3 board was used for the single-road branch-line project, but this one will need an A1 version. The starting point is the 6in grid, shown here with the quick card footprints of the three completed sheds. The hypothetical running lines have also been sketched on. The Metcalf model seems to offer the best solution for size and visual impact.

For those still only at the initial planning stage, the some hints and tips may be of use. When you have drawn your grid, mark the outline of any external limits that you wish to apply. The next step is to take pieces of scrap card and cut out the exact floor-plan or footprint of the shed itself and of any other additional facilities, such as the coaling stage, stores or offices.

If you have already jumped the gun and constructed these items, then you will have them to hand. This applies equally to those remodelling their existing layout, although a word of warning might not come amiss.

If space is tight, and it invariably is, I would advise that you delay your purchases until you have checked the dimensions and shapes of all the available kits. We are tempted to cram in the largest, most impressive structures possible, but too often this leads to a situation that neither looks railway-like nor operates like one.

The key feature to consider when planning is the shed's access road or roads to and from the rest of the railway. This may be directly off one of the running lines, from a loop or perhaps off a line leading to a goods yard or carriage sidings. Whichever the case, it is likely to be a fixed location with a turnout

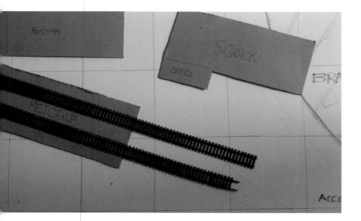

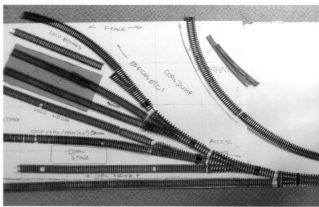

In order to obtain a clearer idea of the relative positioning and angle for the shed, some short lengths of Peco track have been added to the emerging mock-up.

(point) that will have an equally predetermined angle of access. You can vary this angle by the choice of point radius: trial plotting with your existing points, or the invaluable Peco templates, should help you reach the optimum decision. These steps should be more apparent from studying the later illustrations and captions.

Once the two critical factors have been plotted – the angle of approach and the outer limits – it is now possible to juggle the various components to determine the best track plan for both appearance and operational flexibility. One may be lucky, or simply constrained, and arrive at the ultimate plot from the outset, but more often than not various workable alternatives will present themselves. At this juncture it's useful to have to hand at least some of the actual allocated locos and any likely visitors, and to place them physically on the plan.

The moment you enter this three-dimensional world your layout, which previously seemed spacious, will visibly shrink, often uncomfortably so. It is indeed a rare thing to encounter a modeller who actually has less stock than his layout can accommodate; the reverse is definitely the norm.

Don't be too disappointed if you are forced to compromise on the track plan, the structures or the allocation. Compromose is very much the essence of modelling.

The plan is being developed in situ, which is probably how most of us work on our layouts. An extra sheet of scrap A2 has been added to test how well the shed yard could be incorporated into the 'V' of a junction on a larger scheme. Some of the key facilities have also been sketched in.

REMEMBER THE WORKINGS

It is useful to have some real railway images in view at this stage. While you may not be recreating an exact prototype, it is more than likely that your finished result will be either inspired by, or will feature, various aspects drawn from these originals. As you start to refine your plans it is also worthwhile remembering the basics of shed workings.

The two vital routines are 'disposal' (dealing with the locomotive at the end of its shift) and 'preparation' (getting it ready for its next spell of work). This is not quite as simple as it might sound, though, since some essential parts of the disposal process are actually the first steps towards preparation. On a smallish shed like ours many of the duties will fall to the footplate crew, while at larger MPDs they might well be undertaken by other staff.

The fireman on our loco will have already allowed his fire to run down while still retaining just enough boiler pressure to complete his necessary shed movements. The first task will be to 'coal up', replenishing the tender or bunker for the next day. Next they will top up with water and then run over the ash pit (or 'ash pile'), drop the remaining fire, clear any clinker and clean out the smoke box 'char'. Finally

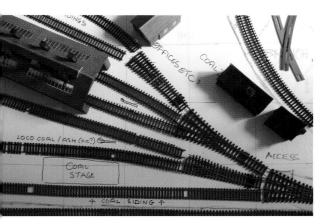

The next step is yet another mock-up, this time with some of the structures in their most probable positions. When planning by trial and error, as here, you may make plenty of errors before reaching the final version.

On any layout, from the smallest diorama to the loft-filling main line, the eye-level views are all important, as it is from just that angle that we see the real world. Aerial or high-level views are still essential for planning and for correcting the track geometry, but this is the aspect of choice where the finished product is concerned.

they should clean up the footplate, remove the tools and, with just a breath of steam left, the locomotive will be parked inside the shed or outside on a siding; where possible it will be in the correct sequence for its work in the morning.

Preparation will start with the fire-raiser lighting up and maintaining the fire to bring the boiler pressure round ready for the crew. When the enginemen arrive for their shift they will have a pre-set time to prepare their rostered locomotive. The time allowed will vary according to its size and type. The fireman will collect the necessary tools, lamps, sand and oil, and check that his fire is building nicely and that the boiler pressure is coming round. A quick sluice of the footplate with the prep-pipe and then he will probably start to assist his driver by beginning to oil round, first easing up as necessary to be over the pit. Doubtless he will have ensured she is in middle gear (neutral) and the tender handbrake firmly screwed on. He may even place a 'Not to be Moved' sign on the buffer beam. The driver having checked the notices, will then take over the oiling, although many an older or more corpulent driver would be happy to let someone younger and more supple attend to the inside motion.

Once the loco is ready it is probably time for a run to the water crane for a quick top-up. Then it's a quick wash, a brew of tea and the inevitable pipe or roll-up

before running to the shed access line and either whistling to the signalman or phoning for the road.

This prototypical detail is here to make our operations more realistic and, more importantly, to make sure that the planned positions for the various facilities are correctly and conveniently sited. I readily acknowledge that our locomotives operate at the press of a button, the turn of a knob or the flick of a switch, but it makes for much greater interest and involvement if we as 'enginemen' can reproduce these various routines in miniature with suitable real-time pauses in between.

HOW MANY ENGINES?

In terms of allocations, two-road sheds would seem to range from ten to twenty locomotives, mostly smaller tank engines 0-6-0T; and 2-6-2Ts and the smallest tender-locos for longer trips almost invariably mean some 0-6-0s. Some sheds, however, did run to Moguls and larger tank engines, but bigger engines meant that fewer could be accommodated. A quick glance back at the likely duties for our hypothetical shed will show that we've made provision for some heavier goods workings that will require the services of a 2-8-0 or 0-6-2T.

The A1 foamboard has now been covered with 2mm play foam. Once glued and stapled it is ready for track laying. For ease and speed, I have used some set-track curves in addition to the rest of the Code 100 flexible track. This final design remains very simple but still allows for the maximum amount of loco storage combined with considerable operating potential. Note that the ash pit has been excavated, while the main inspection pits are, at least hypothetically, out of sight inside the shed.

The addition of a single layer of white play foam covers those areas where the surface must be raised to sleeper height. The extra layers, marked '2', bring the surface up to rail height. Note that this is continuous immediately in front of the shed and will eventually make the rails appear set into the concrete finish.

That brings us to manning levels and to the facilities that the staff would need. For a start you can reckon on two sets of enginemen per locomotive. Shed staff would probably include a shed foreman, two coalmen, two fire-lighters, half-a-dozen cleaners, a fitter or two, a boilerman and a couple of shed-labourers. You will need a mess-room, toilets, stores, cycle-racks and maybe parking for the odd car and the inevitable motorcycles. This gives plenty of excuses to create the illusion of 'activity' even when perhaps no more than a couple of engines are still on shed.

The eventual track plan, compromises and all, will just about accommodate our engine allocation. Two water cranes have been provided, one adjacent to the coaling road, which would benefit visiting locomotives, while the second is between the shed roads for top-ups.

For the purposes of the project we have been planning around the Metcalf shed in the knowledge that, if it fits, then so will the others. Our hypothetical location is a junction station with the shed sited in the 'vee' between the mainline and a branch or secondary line. We will provide a 'modeller's allocation' that will

inevitably include some larger tender engines, but we'll stop short of the bigger 7P or 8P Kings and Pacifics. That said, Southern enthusiasts could certainly consider their versatile Bulleid Light Pacifics of the West Country and Battle of Britain classes.

DON'T FORGET THE ESSENTIALS

One important aspect that is all too often forgotten concerns coal supply. This has been discussed above, but it now becomes much more relevant. Given that our allocation is a mixture of ten engines, with tender and bunker capacities of three to four tons, they will create a probable daily demand of more than 30 tons. That is three 10-tonners or a couple of the longer 20-ton loco-coal wagons to be dealt with every day. This in turn means a lengthy reception siding ideally capable of holding up to six wagons at either side of the coaling point. Delivery and collection of the empties would be every third day; the empties being drawn out and parked on an empty loco road before shunting the six 'fulls' into place with the leading wagon on the stage. A depot of this size would also warrant ash removal and a stores van (oil and spares) at least once a week. Sheds are not just about locomotives.

With regard to the layout of the yard, given some extra length rather than width it would be advisable to extend the shed access road to at least 18in (45cm). As it exists it is too 'tight' to move around without encroaching on the running lines.

The ancillary buildings now include a fitters' workshop and stores (both part of the Metcalf kit) and two tin-built mess-rooms/offices. Both of the latter are scratch-built and could be used with any of the kits to make a change from the usual grounded coach-body.

So far we have rather mingled the 'prototype' with the actual model making. It is now time to concentrate solely on the construction project. As in the previous section, and already mentioned, the chosen medium for the baseboard is two A1 sheets of foamboard laminated together with PVA and then topped with play foam.

BASIC GROUNDWORK

A shed of this size and operating characteristics must have a ground surface that clearly demonstrates its level of traffic. It might possibly reflect the beginning of the decline in maintenance standards and the increasingly visible wear and tear. There are perhaps three different surfaces to consider. The first, and probably the easiest, comprises the stone or concrete paved areas inside and outside the main shed and the main pathways to and from any ancillary buildings. The second is the ballast between the sleepers and in those areas less walked-over. The last, and largest area, is the working part of the yard, which, as in the previous scene, is usually a well-trodden mix of ballast, ash and cinder worn almost smooth by scores of hobnail boots.

Paved and concrete surfaces

These can often be found as part of the pre-printed material in kits, but there is rarely enough for our purposes and it will not be wholly tailored to our needs. There are two alternatives: you can either use the commercially available pre-printed sheets in card or plastic or you can make up your own painted sheets. For the project we will use the second option since it involves more actual modelling and can be finished and fitted to precisely meet your require-

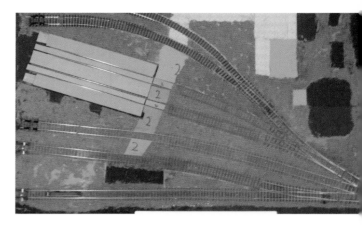

The basic preparation has been completed and any last-minute issues resolved. The pale inverted 'L' shape at the top is a cobbled area, around the staff entrance, where the offices, stores, workshops and other key facilities will be located. The dark patches to the right will be the sites for grounded van bodies and the large coal dump. Ballasting is now underway and the inset tracks extended into the main shed.

At this point the ballasting, painting and weathering is almost finished. The recycled and sieved ballast has been given a liberal coating of cigarette ash and a mix of grey and rust-coloured pastel dust. There is still some detailing work to be done but we are almost there.

ments. The first decision you need to make is the choice of material. In this instance I would favour the heaviest grade of paper, possibly that described as 'watercolour paper', which also benefits from a visible surface texture.

Next you need to decide whether to model it as paving slabs or as concrete. For the former you need to draw on the paving stones, which should be approximately 10 x 15mm. Take a sheet of scrap paper and trace the exact areas you wish to cover. Use this to mark the outlines on the workpiece and then cut it from the sheet with a scalpel. Start from the shed, mark the 10mm verticals that represent each row of slabs and continue these verticals all the way across your irregular workpiece. Next, rule each row in 15mm divisions to represent the slabs, make the alternate rows with the same ruled line, and then mark the remaining rows with the appropriate half-length overlap. A sharp pencil is best for this since it will remain visible through a watercolour paint finish and will also produce a very small indentation along the ruled lines.

You could then paint it as necessary, but this is a task best left until the end, making it easier to blend it in with the other surfaces. The palette is down to you but it is likely to include white, grey and sap green, with perhaps an appropriate pastel dusting to finish. Individual slabs can be picked out in slightly darker or lighter tones, but don't overdo this or your pavements will start to look like an outdoor chessboard, rather than big blocks of well-worn stone from just one supplier.

Concrete is a much easier and quicker option and is probably more realistic for the post-war period. Prepare the workpiece as above to produce the cut-out fret that can be positioned on the layout. Once again leave the painting until last to ensure a good blend of tones, but your palette will be the same as for the paving slabs. Concrete is a difficult colour to capture since no two mixes seem to deliver exactly the same tones. It is also subject to weathering to varying degrees, but there's no shortage of the stuff in real life so accurate references are readily available.

Ballasted track

Initially there is no difference here, in principle, to any other ballasting exercise. As with the previous project, however, the ballast is likely to be 'spent' and certainly very dirty, especially around the more heavily walked areas. The main ingredient will be the same ballast that you have used, or intend to use, on the rest of the layout. You can start the weath-

The finished scene. The tin-roofed coaling stage is prominent in the foreground, with the ash pit and heap to its left. At the top right are the offices and stores (the additions to the Superquick kit), the sand furnace, the Metcalf workshop and part of the coal dump with a small lamp hut in front. Note also the Wills cycle rack and the mix of sleeper and boiler-tube fencing.

The coaling stage, with more real coal, seems to blend well with the rest of the yard and would function correctly if the project was 'live'. The track in front is the disposal road, with engines going to the far end to drop their fires, then drawing back to take on coal before going on-shed. The track at the rear is the coal road with full wagons coming in from the right and pushing the empties out to the end of the siding on the left.

ABOVE LEFT AND RIGHT: *These eye-level views of the yard show that the scene fits well together. Given its relatively small size, it would adapt quite easily to fit most layouts. It could also provide a viable and interesting alternative to the over-modelled branch terminus.*

ering and dirtying while doing the layering. Either add some black powder paint to the ballast itself or introduce some black poster colour to the PVA or 'polish' adhesive. This is worth practising before you commit and the parts of the tracks hidden in the shed itself are handy for this. An alternative, and a probably more convenient and controllable method, is to leave this toning process until last to ensure that the whole scene takes on a uniform appearance.

The actual ballasting in a shed yard can be pretty crude and variations of depth between the sleepers would be commonplace. The shed's environs will be far removed from the gangers' 'prize length' on the mainline. (For information on adding inspection and ash pits, see Chapter 1.)

Other areas

As with the single-road shed discussed in Chapters 1 and 2, this is where you need to take the differences in levels into account. In some places the ground surface will have been packed up to about sleeper height. There will also be some areas, notably immediately in front of the shed, around the coaling stage and surrounding the ash pit or heap, where it is almost level with the rail-head. The answer to this problem is play foam: one extra layer will bring the surface up to sleeper height and a second will take it up to the rail-head. It is necessary to disguise

the visible 'steps' between the layers and using a mix of techniques is probably the best way to mask the joins. With a sharp scalpel or curved blade scissors, cut an irregular chamfer along where the visible join will be before you stick down the extra piece or pieces.

Lay the sections in place and then smear on small quantities of ready-mix filler with a palette knife until you have an almost imperceptible change in levels. A coat of matt black emulsion or acrylic will help blend the white filler with the black play foam. Beyond these raised surfaces, the rest of the yard requires only a thin layer of ballast, mixed with finely sieved sand or soil, and with selected areas given the benefit of some additional Woodland Scenics 'cinders' or genuine coal dust.

FINAL FINISH

This is where we stop being civil engineers and become landscape artists. First ensure that all the buildings and any ancillary structures are correctly positioned, either permanently stuck down or, as in the case of the shed itself, made removable for internal track maintenance. Begin by painting and weathering the track, following the practice described earlier. It is purely personal but I like to use a darker colour in shed areas than elsewhere on the layout. In places I also add some matt black to the chosen track colour to darken it still further. It is best to avoid the more orange-toned paints that represent the more recently rusted colours, since these are rarely seen anywhere except on very newly re-laid lines.

With this laborious task accomplished you can turn your attention to the yard as a whole. There is a temptation to do the whole job in sooty black. A shed might well look a bit like that on a dull and damp midwinter's day, but most modellers seem to prefer summer layouts upon which the sun never sets. This immediately lightens all the tones to give an overall greyish-brown or brownish-grey appearance. A good way of achieving this is to look for a DIY matchpot of suitably toned matt emulsion paint. If you can find a masonry paint version then so much the better. If it isn't exactly to your taste, you can improve it by adding, and thoroughly mixing, small quantities of the appropriate watercolour until you get what you want. If you are using watercolour in tube form, be careful not to overdo it as it is very strong and the smallest dab can have a profound and unwanted effect. Watercolours in pan form can easily be made up into a strong wash, enabling you to blend several colours before adding it to the matchpot.

The areas around the access line and associated point-work should receive only the weakest mix of the prepared paint, and then gradually strengthening it until you arrive at the 'smooth' area and the concrete paving. Again the mix around the buildings and on the outer reaches of the sidings and the yard can be weakened. When you have completed everything, leave it to dry and then return to it with a fresh eye. If it still looks 'right', the only glaringly pristine surfaces will be the paved or concreted areas. Get to work on these with watercolours, starting with a fairly weak wash and building up the strength until you achieve the desired result and a good match.

We are now moving into what can be the make-or-break exercise: weathering and finish. Colour prints or photos of sheds in action will prove invaluable. Prints or greetings cards by artists such as Don Breckon, Philip Hawkins and David Weston can be most enlightening. A signed print of *Nine Elms: The Last Hours* by David Shepherd hangs on the wall a few feet away as a constant reminder of just how much

The interior of the Metcalf shed with its noticeboards illuminated by a shaft of spring sunlight. There would be just enough room to pose a few enginemen studying the roster-board and traffic notices, and still allow locos to access the shed.

The small sand furnace has been borrowed from Sherborne shed on the author's 'Wessex Lines'. It was scratch-built from a drawing in E. Lyons, An Historical Survey of Great Western Engine Sheds, 1947 (Oxford Publishing Co., 1974). The tall chimney is a relic from a long-forgotten Faller factory.

There are ten engines in view and there is probably sufficient room inside the shed for another three. The hypothetical running line in the foreground is not ballasted and is only there for reference.

colour there is to be seen by the trained eye. All these artists have enjoyed first-hand experience of these scenes and have captured them in two dimensions in much the same way as we are seeking to do in three.

For your own efforts, however, you must now resort to pastels, maybe some talcum powder, certainly watercolours, a few wisely chosen enamels and, in my case, a carefully gathered store of cigarette ash. You will also need some scatter materials and sources of vegetation, but these will be used only sparingly. The final essential material is real coal dust, for which there is no viable substitute.

Detailing the shed yard

The following list of potential detailing is by no means comprehensive, but it does show some of the more common features:

- Coal dust all around the coal stage and several feet beyond.
- Oil stains around the inspection pits, near the oil tanks, if these are located outside, and also inside

and outside the tracks where locos will have been standing.
- Water and puddles are common around the water cranes and also worth including in spots where locos have been standing.
- Loose sand near the furnace, if modelled, or the store. It should also appear in small quantities where locos have had their sand boxes filled and tested.
- Footfall is noticeable as dark oily stains down the centre of the pathways and around the pits.
- Ash, widely dispersed around the ash pit or heap, is usually a creamy-white hue.
- Vegetation is limited across the site as a whole but grass, dandelions and taller thistles are likely to be found around the buildings, in areas where no one goes, and along the base of the boundary wall or fence.

At this point each modeller will doubtless choose how much, or indeed how little, of the above should be included. It is simply a question of experimenting, using as little as possible to start with and then adding tones and density until you have achieved a finish that is both 'prototypical' and pleasing to the eye. One tip in respect of oil-stained areas is that where these are most pronounced try satin-black enamel or even black 'metal-cote', but don't overdo it as it will draw the eye.

SCRATCH-BUILT AND KIT-BUILT STRUCTURES

As you can see from photos, the shed on its own would look pretty isolated, although the stores/ workshop and mess-rooms help to fill the gap. There are other features that might be introduced:

Cycle stands: These may come from Wills kits.
Coaling stage: A substantial platform capable of holding several tons of coal together with a hoist. The latter is a Wills kit with a scoop replacing the hook. The shelter is true to type in that there was no set design or construction method. The supports can be either timber or metal girders and the covering is most likely to be corrugated iron sheets. The roof

This kit-built N15x Remembrance has arrived off a special working and is in preservation order, hence its pre-war Maunsell colour scheme. The author has fond memories of the whole class when, in mid-1950s lined BR black livery, they spent their last days on Basingstoke shed.

could be half curved or with any variation of pitch. I chose balsa strip and homemade tin beneath an irregularly shaped pitched version.

Ash heap: This is simply plasticine covered with ash (*see* Chapter 1).

Coal heap: Coal was stockpiled shortly before the Second World War and the piles were maintained in the Austerity period as reserves against extreme weather or transport disruption. The base is a plastic pie dish covered with plasticine and the coal is real coal dust. Note the whitewashed edges.

Oil-stands: Smelly barrels of oil were never stored indoors. Outside trestles were far more convenient for the firemen or other staff.

Detritus: This term covers all the bits and pieces of broken and discarded equipment and materials, as well as items still in use, including fire-irons, empty oil drums, boxes, tools, buckets, broken lamps, barrows and shovels. It is probable that there might be heaps of worn out parts behind the shed or around the fitting shop, most commonly brake blocks and attendant fittings. All of the above are available in accessory packs or as loco detailing extras.

Fencing: The modeller has a wide choice when it comes to fencing a shed. You should remember, however, that this would only be necessary where the boundary was bordered by non-railway property. The project shed is in the 'vee' of a junction, so the only fence needed is at the back of the shed behind the buffer stops. In an urban area it would probably be a full brick wall with a staff doorway. In a rural area it might be a wall of sleepers, a fence of 6ft high boiler tubes or even a modern length of concrete-post security fencing. The easiest to model is the sleeper-built version, which requires lengths of 3 × 1mm balsa about 30mm long, planted upright and close together. They are braced or connected by two rows of 1mm square strip. Painted with watercolours these look very effective.

Huminiatures: There is plenty of scope for action or relaxed human cameos illustrating the coming and going of twenty sets of men, plus the dozen or so shed staff. It is down to each modeller to choose the scenes they wish to reproduce. Some are shown in the illustrations, including the following choices together with their suggested sources and finish.

The coalmen are sweeping their platform clear ready for their next customer having just replenished the visiting N15x. The full wagon on the far side is waiting to be unloaded and one of the cleaners might be assigned to help out.

The cleaners, under the watchful eye of the chargehand, are doing a grand job on the shed's Hall, which will shortly take the late-afternoon express-parcels to the capital and return with an evening semi-fast.

Remember that enginemen and firemen rarely wore neat, complete uniforms and the shed staff would be in a mix of regulation overalls and downgraded civilian clothes.

- Crews should be in the cabs of any locomotive going on or off shed. Other crews might be arriving or booking off, perhaps chatting as they hand over an engine. Others might be spare men awaiting a call.
- Coalmen are likely to be involved on the stage all the time. They were paid an incentive according to the tonnages shifted: even when not replenishing a loco, they would be busy emptying the next full wagon or using pinch bars to move away an empty one.
- Labourers might be seen sweeping out the shed, chatting to the foreman, fetching and carrying or shovelling ash from the pit or into a waiting wagon.

- Fitters could be working on a failed loco or perhaps at lunch on an outside bench.
- Firemen might be carrying lamps or tools to or from a loco, drawing oil or oiling round, or standing on the tank or tender of a loco taking water.
- Enginemen could be reading the notices, oiling round or chatting with the foreman or an inspector.
- Cleaners could be shown at work or generally skiving, perhaps playing football.

If your loco stud enables you to have engines consistently spare, or some of them are non-runners, a cameo can be made permanent or semi-permanent. In other cases Blu-tack or similar on the boots of your figures will enable you to ring the changes. Don't be afraid to be adventurous with any unpainted plastic figures. Careful selection, and equally careful use of the scalpel, will enable you to alter poses or combine anatomies.

CHAPTER FOUR

THE MPD THROUGH THE YEARS

THE BACKGROUND TO THE PROJECT

By this stage you should now be ready to embark on what will be the final project. Not surprisingly it is both large and complicated, combining the products of several manufacturers, ranging from among the oldest to one of the newest. We will try to discover how easy, or otherwise, it is to mix these different items and still achieve a visually coherent result. It will also give you the opportunity to reassess the varied techniques required and perhaps reach some conclusions about which kits you might prefer to use in your future modelling.

That could well be considered as quite enough for one project, but we are going to take it a lot further and illustrate what can be achieved by choosing different periods in the life of a single site. To keep it as realistic as possible there will be just one major build, which will initially feature our version of the motive power depot (MPD) in the heyday of the steam era. We will then attempt to show how it might have looked in the earliest days of the preservation movement. This will mean introducing a fair amount of natural and man-made dereliction. Some of our buildings may just be abandoned to the elements, while others may have already been wholly or partly demolished. Our final transformation will be to resurrect the site fully as a 'Steam Centre' and give it the appearance of an up-to-date, museum-type tourist attraction.

I'm not suggesting that other modellers might wish to go through this tortuous time-shift process, but it would make a challenging concept for a modeller with limited space and perhaps an innate desire for some long-term planning. It would certainly be a very cost-effective alternative to the more usual course of scrapping and rebuilding every couple of years. It also makes it very worthwhile to put in some extra effort on the truly permanent parts of the layout.

The sprawling MPDs were invariably shrouded in steam and drifting smoke on weekdays. It was unusual for public visitors to gain access when the sheds were busy, but this group at Norwood have plenty to look at. *BEN BROOKSBANK AND LICENSED FOR REUSE UNDER THIS CREATIVE COMMONS LICENCE*

One of the regular Sunday openings at Swindon. In contrast to the previous image, the engines are stationary and in light steam.
BEN BROOKSBANK AND LICENSED FOR REUSE UNDER THIS CREATIVE COMMONS LICENCE

An everyday scene typical of sheds across the country. This is Croes Newydd, a roundhouse with two main access roads. The numerous hazards that can be seen are great for modellers, but they could be deathtraps for railwaymen. BEN BROOKSBANK AND LICENSED FOR REUSE UNDER THIS CREATIVE COMMONS LICENCE

RESEARCH AND PLANNING

With that in mind a little longer than usual will be spent on the research and planning stage. It is obviously necessary to get the back story fixed in your mind and, preferably, on paper as well. Planning should be organized so that it is possible to progress through these three distinct phases easily and efficiently. A variety of kits will be used, the more complex of which will be for those structures that will be constant through all three phases. Cheaper kits and scraps from the bits box or recycled from earlier projects can then make up the rest of the changing scene in the next two phases. It will be the same with the track, and most of what is laid for the steam-era period will remain largely unchanged. New track may be installed for the final 'Steam Centre' version and, if necessary, provision could be made for any extra point-work by inserting small removable sections of track at the outset.

The concept will, I hope, provide some inspiration for creative scenic modelling. I hesitate to call it landscaping, since this is a long way from the gentle countryside of a rural branch or the heather-clad

All is peaceful and orderly in Llanelly's roundhouse, which is home to eight different classes of tank engine. BEN BROOKSBANK AND LICENSED FOR REUSE UNDER THIS CREATIVE COMMONS LICENCE

hills of a northern mainline. Nonetheless, nature will be making its presence felt in Phase Two and it will be much more in evidence in Phase Three, assisted by the Steam Centre's 'Garden Team'.

MULTIPLE CHOICES

Even if you simply wish to select just one of the phases and concentrate on that, this will still create a mini-layout that is far from common among one's fellow modellers. All three periods offer the perfect excuse to amass a whole range of locomotives and the opportunity to operate them, albeit within a rather limited space. The final 'Steam Centre' concept offers prototype scenarios in which *Tornado*, *Scotsman*, *Clan Line* and *KGV* can be seen cheek by jowl with the resident regional stud. Indeed, those with an interest in diesels could justifiably stage a visit by a Western or Deltic alongside your SECR-liveried 'C' Class and the T9 in the olive green Maunsell livery. It is a glorious excuse to buy whatever you fancy, or can afford, and no one can argue with your decisions.

This same freedom of choice also applies to the rolling stock. These can be posed in their pristine straight-from-the-box glory and representing newly

Bournemouth, with the shed directly opposite the end of the lengthy down platform, was a trainspotter's dream. It always seemed a rather ramshackle establishment in which to house its fleet of Nelsons, Arthurs and West Countrys.

PLANNING CONSIDERATIONS

The back story of any MPD is important since it will largely govern the make or type of the shed and the attendant facilities to be modelled. It will also direct some of the locomotive purchases. Part of the decision will be influenced by the space at your disposal, which for this project should comprise two A1 foamboards, totalling 66 x 23in (1678 x 585mm). That means avoiding sheds that serve cities or major rail centres and doesn't leave room for a stud of Pacifics. Even so, most regions will have at least one shed whose general appearance and 'feel' we can attempt to reproduce.

Basingstoke, which was also quite close to its busy station, was the only shed I ever 'bunked'. Note the typical flat lids on the smoke chimneys.

restored vehicles. Equally they can be pretty decrepit and awaiting attention or displaying an earlier overhaul that has seen some on-site service. There could be a place for almost any wagon or van you happen to like. Passenger carriages, too, can be in use on the later demonstration lines or presented as static exhibits. Older types can be in any of the many liveries they would have worn during their long lifetimes.

I hope these few introductory paragraphs have inspired you to have a go. For what it's worth, I found it to be one of the most fascinating ventures I have attempted in the course of fifty years of wielding scalpels, pinning track and painting.

Back Story Elements

Region/locality	Select your chosen 'Big Four' or BR region
Size of shed	2 roads, 4 roads or more? Size of the model footprint?
Type of shed/roof	Dead end or through? Straight, hipped or north light? Half round?
Features	Coaling stage or coaling plant? Turntable? Lifting shop or hoist? Sand furnace?
Track plan	Can it be tweaked to fit the available space?
Buildings	Which kits can be built or customized to suit?
Loco stud	Engine types and quantities? Visitors?
Models	Do they exist in r-t-r format and can you afford an appropriate allocation?

The answers to the above questions should give a pretty good idea of which sheds might be modelled or might at least provide some inspiration. Once you have looked around your model shop and scrutinized advertisements in the press and online, you should know which kits and materials are needed for the initial part of the project, not forgetting any new or additional features that may be needed for the present-day Steam Centre that will be the third phase of the project. Armed with any available photographs or other references you can now get on with yur plan.

Designing the track plan

I like to start with a few scribbles on a scrap pad, attempting to combine the prototype's plan as much as possible with the eventual track plan for the Steam Centre. These are then elaborated, still in very crude form, to incorporate the known footprints of the various structures, especially the shed itself, and the major impact that will be made by the coaling stage and ramp. A final sketch then attempts to envisage how the preservationists might run the site, particularly in respect of any running lines.

The massive pitched roof of this through-shed dwarfs even the bulk of the LMS 0-8-0 goods engine. The rather hazy view of the brickwork shows that it bears a close resemblance to that modelled in the Metcalf buildings.
BEN BROOKSBANK AND LICENSED FOR REUSE UNDER THIS CREATIVE COMMONS LICENCE

The first real test involves plotting this 'final' version on graph paper. This should be done on the largest sheets that you can handle, with point-work and radii plotted as accurately as you can. Problems are far easier to correct if you can spot them now rather than encountering them during track laying. Once you are happy with this smaller version, it is then time to transfer it to your baseboards. For this project that simply involves pinning the Peco point templates to the foamboard and drawing in the various tracks and features full size. Those working within an existing layout or on newly built baseboards are best advised to make up the appropriate dimensions from taped-together sheets of drawing paper. This will require the templates to be lightly stuck down with a dab or two of glue stick.

You are almost certain to discover a few new problems, especially regarding clearances around buildings and where the tracks run together at point-work. Some may require rethinking the plan and others may need no more than a note on the plan. You will see from the illustrations that it is a useful idea to mark the various tracks and features clearly. Colour coding and guidance notes for the phase changes are also helpful aids. This is particularly true if there are likely to be delays between this planning exercise and laying the actual track.

Cambridge was a fairly typical north light shed, apart from its rather unusual smoke-vents, which seem to extend between the bays. The watercranes are in the usual position. Note how the build-up of muck is covering the sleepers.
BEN BROOKSBANK AND LICENSED FOR REUSE UNDER THIS CREATIVE COMMONS LICENCE

The north light shed at Ashford has a rather quirky appearance as the cowl-roofs to the smoke chimneys face in different directions on the alternate rows. BEN BROOKSBANK AND LICENSED FOR REUSE UNDER THIS CREATIVE COMMONS LICENCE

Operating

If you intend to introduce live running you will need to include offstage sector plates or cassettes at the end of the active lines. These can be simple hiding places for the locos coming and going, giving footplate rides or being used for the brake van trips and weekend 'diners'. These extensions do not interface with any other lines and there will be no need to turn the stock: they can be viewed as little more than detachable storage roads. There is a similar need at the shed approach end, but here it needs to be a slightly more complex arrangement. This is the 'rest of the system' on which visiting locomotives can arrive and depart and the shed's own stock can all appear to use offstage point-work to change roads. Once these are in place, the modeller is then free to run back and forth using whichever available engine takes their fancy. This, however, implies the use of suitable-length cassettes or a sector-plate that can serve more than one entry road.

THE MPD IN THE STEAM ERA

WHAT MAKES AN MPD?

Having examined and built examples of both small and larger sheds, we can now turn our attention to the MPD proper. Every shed is in essence a 'Motive Power Depot', and every MPD is a shed but we will

here define it as 'a large shed capable of undertaking most repairs and servicing short of sending the locomotive back to the nearest works for full overhaul'. It can therefore be said to include the scores of sheds from every region that had allocations from about thirty engines up to the giants with close on two hundred on their books. One generalization that may be useful, however, is to accept the original British Railways decision that defined anything with a shed-code as an MPD.

A few companies favoured the hipped style of roof, such as this impressive example at Sunderland. They seem to occur more frequently in Scotland and northern England. BEN BROOKSBANK AND LICENSED FOR REUSE UNDER THIS CREATIVE COMMONS LICENCE

Bricklayers Arms in Bermondsey was one of the Southern Region's biggest freight MPDs. The original north light shed on the right was expanded with the addition of a more modern pitched-roof shed. Flat 'table-top' vents were quite common on this region. BEN BROOKSBANK AND LICENSED FOR REUSE UNDER THIS CREATIVE COMMONS LICENCE

There is little point, however, in dreaming about a Nine Elms, Camden, Old Oak or 'Top Shed', as they are simply too complex to consider and much too large to model. Instead we will approach the subject from back to front and create an MPD, at least in part, which has most of the key features present, but one that will fit into a module made up of two A1 foamboards. We can begin by restating that the basic shed operations will revolve around the locomotives and these will be no different from those that we have already examined. These, and the environment in which they are carried out, are simply that much more of the same. It is the enhanced scale and atmosphere that we want to capture, along with the other additional features that might be replicated. The MPD in our chosen period would be likely to have provision for most of the features listed below. We may not be able to show them all within our limited resources of time, cost and space available, but the constraints of the project need in no way impede your own modelling aspirations.

KEY FEATURES

Coaling plant: This would at the very least include a ramped approach to a raised coaling platform. At larger MPDs this would be sufficiently extensive to coal at least two engines at the same time and accommodate about a dozen wagons. Many depots had the 'cenotaph' type of concrete fully mechanized coaling tower. They were not installed on the GWR/BR (W), however, as its coal was especially soft and no fireman relished a tender full of dust.

Water: Plenty of water was needed and huge tanks were often sited on top of the coaling stage or as separate structures. These provided constant pres-

Watford MPD is another illustration of growth and expansion. This time it's a hipped roof that has been joined by a newer and cheaper pitched version. BEN BROOKSBANK AND LICENSED FOR REUSE UNDER THIS CREATIVE COMMONS LICENCE

sure to the whole site and ensured limited supplies in an emergency. The bigger the MPD then the bigger the tanks would be, often holding 100,000 gallons or more.

Sand furnace: Another essential.

Stationary boiler(s): These were vital for the weekly wash-outs of loco boilers, for pressure-cleaning before servicing or repair and for the site's domestic hot water. They might be just boilers and fire boxes salvaged from scrapped ancient engines. In some cases almost complete withdrawn engines were pressed into service.

Ash pits, ash roads and ash shelters: Engines produce a lot of ash, so the pits would be extensive

A compact arrangement of shed, sand furnace and water tower, even though the smoke-vents appear in need of attention. BEN BROOKSBANK AND LICENSED FOR REUSE UNDER THIS CREATIVE COMMONS LICENCE

and there would be a separate loop or dead-end siding adjacent for emptying. Ash shelters were erected in the 1940s to conceal the glare of fire-dropping from enemy bombers. They were simple constructions running the length of the pit and were no more than an open shed built of asbestos or tin-cladding on a steel frame. Many survived the war and some lasted as long as the depots themselves, albeit in a battered state.

Loco hoists: These were often installed under-cover as part of the workshops. The building could well be specially constructed for the purpose and would be taller than the original sheds. In other examples they were in the open at the entrance to the workshop which, in such cases, might also be part of the original shed.

Wheel drops: These were frequently installed but rarely visible, being an integral part of the workshop building.

Turntable: This now becomes another essential feature. MPDs would be required to send engines to work in both 'up' and 'down' directions, so turning was essential. This was usually done when they came off shift for disposal. It was also necessary to turn visiting locos coming on-shed for coal and water before working back to their home depots.

Workshops: These would be proportionally larger than those at smaller sheds. They would be able to deal with most repairs to their allocated engines as well as to those from their outlying sub-sheds. As a general rule they would have a go at everything short of the regular Intermediate, Heavy Intermediate or Full Overhauls carried out at the appropriate works.

Shed Buildings: Everything will be bigger and more complex than we have encountered so far. Sheds would be multi-road — anything from four to twenty — and lengthy enough to house several large engines buffer to buffer on each road. Many of these larger MPDs were 'round houses' with large turntables under cover serving a score or more storage roads. There is little scope there for the Modeller, though, since all that is seen is a large square building with one or two entrance roads. Many MPDs would have more than one shed, sometimes as newly built-on structures of a later design. However, it was not uncommon to find these were separate sheds belonging to the original

Carnforth now acts as a base for West Coast Trains. These massive 'Cenotaph' coaling towers were once common on the former LMS and LNER lines. IAN TAYLOR AND LICENSED FOR REUSE UNDER THIS CREATIVE COMMONS LICENCE

The interior of a standard 'Churchward Shed' at Didcot, seen in a posed shot taken shortly after it opened in the 1930s, with the integral offices and stores built onto the left-hand wall. This is a useful image for anyone intending to model the inspection pits. COURTESY GREAT WESTERN TRUST

companies that had subsequently been absorbed into one complex at the grouping.

Infrastructure and ancillary buildings: The MPD would have numerous storage sidings for loco-motives, additional roads for incoming and outgoing coal and ash, sidings for wagons and vans conveying spare parts or items for repair, more watering points and much more complex point-work to enable flex-ibility of movement. With its larger loco allocation and expanded facilities, it would employ numbers of men on both the running and shed staff side. That in turn would create the need for more offices, stores, mess-rooms, toilets and cycle-racks. Road vehicles were rarely, if ever, glimpsed within the precincts of an MPD.

As in all the previous examples, the back story behind your MPD will determine what it looks like, the size of the site and to which company or region it belongs. There is plenty of research material available and it is of little consequence whether you use it first to inspire your build or come to it later to flesh out and add detail to your own vision.

The most important feature, however, is to keep it looking busy.

OPERATING POTENTIAL

If you intend to do some live running you will need somewhere for your trains to 'hide' offstage before returning. The same, albeit in reverse, will be needed if you intend to show visiting engines arriving for

Loco-hoists, although sometimes located outside, were more usually found in lofty workshops, such as this example at Didcot. It was a better way of working, although it does deny us a modelling opportunity. COURTESY GREAT WESTERN TRUST

A 'cathedral of steam' shot in the unlikely setting of Saltley MPD. Note how the engines are parked tight up against the back wall, ensuring better safety for the enginemen pushing the turntable. BEN BROOKSBANK AND LICENSED FOR REUSE UNDER THIS CREATIVE COMMONS LICENCE

service. These facilities apply equally across all three phases in the life of the MPD or Steam Centre. Simple sector plates or cassettes are quite adequate, but the final phase will need extra-length facilities to store the additional carriage stock.

Without going into too much detail, some, if not all, of the following can add movement to your diorama, though you should remember that you need to consider all the possibilities for each phase:

• Locos arriving for service and departing.
• Locos arriving for coal, disposal or turning, and then on-shed.
• Footplate rides on a designated siding or running line.
• Loco changeovers and servicing for the above.
• Brake van rides with two or three vans coupled together.
• Carriage rides and diners on a longer running line.
• Locos off-shed for static display, turntable demonstrations and so on.
• Locos off-shed for demonstrations and run pasts.

Such a programme or schedule should be more than enough to keep an operator and quite a large locomotive fleet in action. This would certainly make the project suitable for the exhibition hall since it can include everything from small tank engines to mainline express examples. That would involve a lot more variety and activity than could possibly be achieved at a typical terminus occupying the same space.

Even before the eventual run-down of steam by BR, many sheds were often in a continuously dilapidated state. Some were damaged by the ravages of time and weather, while others had been set alight by their occupants. BEN BROOKSBANK AND LICENSED FOR REUSE UNDER THIS CREATIVE COMMONS LICENCE

THE BACK STORY AND THE BACK-SCENE

In the previous chapters there have been frequent mentions of the importance of an appropriate back story to explain the nature of your model as a whole or in part. This project is somewhat more complex and is designed to have the potential to become a layout in its own right. However, in addition to the normal elements of a back story – what it is, where it is, when it is, why it is and so on – there is the further

What is it?	An MPD with a probable allocation of about 20 locomotives
Where is it?	A semi-industrial setting anywhere in the UK
When is it?	Phase 1: mid-1950s
	Phase 2: 1970s preservation
	Phase 3: modern Steam Centre
What is it for?	Phase 1: to supply and service sufficient engines for local and long-distance freights
	Phase 2: to be a base for the collection, restoration and operation of steam-era stock
	Phase 3: to be a fully operating Steam Centre and tourist attraction

practical consideration of justifying the models that need to be included within it. It's a bit like 'the chicken and the egg', since the models must drive the back story rather than the other way round. This may well be familiar to anyone planning a new layout that must include existing elements from a previous venture. The best way to tackle this is to jot down some of the key points and see what they inspire:

From there you can go on to detail the elements that must be included, such as a modern multi-road shed, older multi-road shed, ramped coaling stage, offices and stores, turntable, boiler-washouts, sand furnace and one or more water towers. This gives us enough information to draft a back story, even if it is later revisited.

While some sheds were a hundred years old, others were surprisingly new. Templecombe was built by BR(S) to replace the original wooden structure in 1951, but was closed by BR(W) just fifteen years later. BEN BROOKSBANK AND LICENSED FOR REUSE UNDER THIS CREATIVE COMMONS LICENCE

The half-roundhouse was almost commonplace on continental railways, but never caught on in Britain, even though they were easy to work and considerably cheaper to build than the fully covered type. Many will also house almost as many engines. This is the old LSWR shed at Guildford. BEN BROOKSBANK AND LICENSED FOR REUSE UNDER THIS CREATIVE COMMONS LICENCE

This half-roundhouse at St Blazey on the Western Region managed to survive as a diesel stabling-point and now enjoys listed status. A ready-to-site model has recently been introduced. BEN BROOKSBANK AND LICENSED FOR REUSE UNDER THIS CREATIVE COMMONS LICENCE

THE BACK STORY: PROJECT EXAMPLE

In the mid-nineteenth century Anytown already had a well-developed industry centred on fabrics, woodworking and furniture making. The Anytown and Elsewhere Railway Company was an immediate success and established its engineering facilities in the town. During the 1880s the A&ERC was taken over by one of the emerging major players. The locomotive factory was closed but the adjacent Carriage and Wagon works was further developed to take on all the manufacture and servicing for the new owners. In 1923 it all passed into the control of one of the Big Four. (Which one is 'to be decided', but it will probably be the GWR.). They were happy to keep the C & W works going but found the old four-road shed inadequate for the levels of traffic. Rather than demolish it, they opted to build a second new shed on the site and also built a new coaling stage and offices.

When British Railways took over in 1948 they ceased building new vehicles in the works but maintained it for repairs and refurbishments. That remained the situation until the 1960s when the plant was finally closed. The MPD itself had large allocation of goods engines for both local and long-distance workings; it

also had a few larger mixed-traffic locos for passenger and fast-freight duties. It survived until the end of steam on the region, albeit with a reduced allocation and the gradual closure of its facilities. BR Lettings reluctantly leased what was left to the embryonic Anytown Steam Traction Preservation Society (ASTPS), who immediately began the long process of restoring the site and inviting other groups to join them. It was precarious at first, but Open Days, fund-raising events, legacies and the support of the local councils eventually secured it a significant place in the Association of Railway Preservation Societies (ARPS) and it became a major tourist attraction in the region.

The old works were demolished in the 1990s but this was accompanied by the gift of part of the site which is now occupied by one of the centre's running lines. The focus of the ASTPS is now concentrated on the Great Western and the Southern railways and the centre regularly services and hosts visiting engines from the frequent rail-tours. Its monthly Steam Days are hugely popular.

This is the back story that justifies the shape of the project. In particular it explains the continued presence of the 'old' shed and the looming bulk of the C & W works, which constitute almost all the back-scene. (For a map and the plan, see the Appendices.)

BUILDING THE BACK-SCENE

This may seem a little like putting the proverbial cart before the horse, as common practice suggests it's more normal to add the back-scene after the layout has been completed. Since this particular item, however, is going to be a low-relief building with a physical as well as a visual impact on the layout, it is best to get it finished even before the detailed track planning exercise. Without wishing to sound even remotely emotional, I think that having it place will also help to keep us ever mindful of the back story that is driving the project.

Main walls

It was important to ensure that whatever went at back of the layout fulfilled several different functions. It had to dominate the early phases and this was to be achieved with a semi-flat/low-relief structure that, when removed, would leave space for a new section of track. It also had to tie in visually with the rest of the site. The simple answer was to see what might be achieved by using photocopies of the Bilteezi 'old' shed, which, according to the back story, had been built by the same company at the same time.

The original card was cut into its main components and these were re-assembled as tightly as possible on an A3 sheet. The next, and somewhat harder, step was to juggle them around on an A1 mounting board to ascertain how they could be fitted together to look like one single structure. Some semblance of order was determined in time, but it was necessary to trim most of the sheets to ensure the even and regular spacing of windows and other features, and the removal of plinths from the first and second storeys. When this was done all the components were stuck down with spray adhesive and left to dry under a mountain of books to prevent warping.

Windows

The windows were among the weakest aspects of any Bilteezi kit and since fifty windows would be needed, each with twelve panes, this would be quite a problem to remedy. I had no suitable replacements and I baulked at the alternative of systematically removing every individual pane with a scalpel. I then had a stroke of luck following a bit of reverse-thinking. The use of spray matt varnish to dull down the shine on printed card kits is a common piece of advice, so why not use several coats of carefully applied high gloss varnish to actually put the shine onto the windows? It wasn't a total success and, with 600 panes getting three coats from one my smallest detail-brushes, it certainly wasn't a five-minute job. A slight shine is still visible from the right position, but in any case no one would ever treat factory windows to a weekly once-over with the Windowlene.

Supports and roof

The supports for any low-relief building need to fulfil two roles. On the one hand, they need to 'support' in the quite literal sense of keeping the structure upright and providing additional surfaces that will help to secure it to the layout. Their other task is to maintain the walls in the vertical and give the required pitch to the roof sections. They need to be

cut accurately. These are a mix of foamboard and mounting card. Once they are firmly glued behind the walls, the roof can then be fixed in position. I used 200gsm heavyweight paper as a template and then applied spray adhesive to attach the photocopied slates. These ensured that the factory continued to match the 'old shed', even though the roof had more joins than I would have liked. My advice to anyone intending to try this part of the project is to photocopy the roof while it is still intact: there will still be joins, but fewer than on my version.

Detailing

As has been shown on some of the earlier projects, detailing not only gives extra character and realism, it is also useful to hide any inaccuracies. There isn't much scope on a structure like this, so I limited the additions to buttresses, guttering and drainpipes. Card was used throughout but similar, or better, results could be obtained from the ironwork in an accessory pack. Final weathering required just the modest application of some pastel dust since the print itself already looked the part. (See also the diagrams in the Appendices.)

CONCLUSIONS

As a scenic modeller more usually engaged on rural backgrounds, I approached this job with a degree or two of apprehension. Once the overall plan was determined, however, and the various photocopies tested for fit, the rest was generally plain sailing. The end result may not be an architectural gem but it does provide a low-cost and appropriately dominating backdrop to the shed scene. Above all, it helps to reinforce the back story and will, once demolished, provide the space needed for the extra Phase 3 running line.

The building will not be enough to cover the whole length of the module as the area behind the coal-stage is still blank. This could be filled quite easily with any sheet of commercially available background paper, ideally with an industrial theme. Equally, and for little extra cost, the Carriage & Wagon Works could be doubled in length to form a continuous low-relief or flat structure. This would be perfectly acceptable given the massive size of Victorian factories.

CHAPTER FIVE

BUILDING THE NORTH LIGHT SHED AND COALING STAGE

AN INTRODUCTION TO DOWNLOAD KITS

When constructing a Scalescenes download kit, the company recommends using a simple glue stick to glue copier paper to various thicknesses of card, followed, where necessary, with clear or universal glue to combine the components. The technique may be new to many modellers, so I will take the liberty of passing on a couple of the key points encountered during the project.

GLUE STICKS

Like all readily available off-the-shelf products, these vary in quality and price. They are all relatively cheap, however, and purchasing several different makes and sizes will enable you to do your own product testing when applied to your normal copier paper and some appropriate card. There are, though, two potential problems since the paste glue dries very quickly. If you are not careful it can grab your paper before you are ready, and peeling it off to try again may cause some damage. The other problem is that, since both surfaces are quite absorbent, it is difficult to ensure that you have a secure fixing across the larger areas. This is particularly in evidence when walls, roofs and flooring sheets are involved or when items need to be bent and folded.

In almost every instance you will be gluing paper to paper rather than card to card, as on most pre-printed kits. This is where the second problem mentioned can be a real nuisance: all too often one discovers that the two papers are firmly glued but they have now become separated from the backing cards.

• Test the glues and buy at least two sizes, one for large areas and one for small.

• Wherever possible apply the glue to the card as generously as you can.
• Work quickly and position accurately. If possible, press and smooth down as you stick.
• Double-check for firm fixing before joining the components.
• Keep some PVA or paper glue handy and repair any faults with small quantities on a paintbrush slipped between the separated paper and the card backing.

ABOUT THE PRODUCT

My two existing layouts, not to mention any early commissions, were completed well before the advent of the download kit. It was therefore with a mixture of anticipation and apprehension that I looked at the Scalescenes website. I was impressed and soon wished they had been around in the distant days when I first entered the hobby.

I am anxious not to appear too lavish in my praise, but it is always the case that quality and value for money will out. I decided to go for the north light shed, since this can be built in a variety of arrangements and sizes, and also to include the coaling stage, which was perfect for my vision of the MPD. These downloads are amazingly inexpensive, with most kits costing less than £5. For that modest investment you can print as many sets as you want, making it the ideal solution for those modellers wishing to install a large, multi-road, major shed on their layout.

The files were downloaded to my basic Toshiba laptop and one shed set was printed off on the usual 80gsm paper through my HP Photosmart C4280, which goes back some years. I also, via a memory stick, obtained a second set from a local print shop. With both versions in front of me I honestly cannot tell which set is which. Neither has any trace of the 'sheen' that is so often a drawback with colour print-

 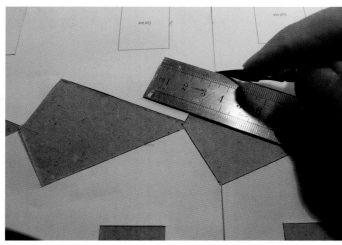

ABOVE LEFT AND RIGHT: *Templates are best glued very firmly to their respective card bases. When cutting out the main walls, seen here, take care to keep the straightedge held tightly against the template and keep the scalpel blade as vertical as possible. You should aim to keep a balance between accuracy and pressure.*

ing. Indeed they are so 'flat' that I decided to dispense with any pre-spraying of the matting varnish.

The artwork on the printed sheets is beautifully done. It is as good, if not better, than most card kits. The nineteen pages are comprehensive in the amount of detailing items supplied, right down to the inclusion of some well-drawn inspection pits. Moreover, the actual design of the kit itself and the clear, well-written instructions that accompany it fully mirror the quality of the artwork.

Is it a kit or indeed a concept that can be tackled by beginners? The answer must be 'yes', provided the modeller gives the project the care and patience that it truly merits. After all, a conscientious beginner will often achieve a superior end result than the so-called expert who may be inclined to rush things.

The tools and glues required are no more elaborate than those needed for the card kits with which we have already dealt. The only significant difference is that reinforcing card now becomes an essential rather than an option. The printed sheets are simply one's usual copier paper and the various elements of the construction process require them to be pre-fixed onto three different thicknesses of card: 'light card – approx. 200gsm', 'medium – approx. 1mm' and 'thick – approx. 2mm'. For those who want to match

these specifications exactly, the website gives contact details for suitable sources. This is useful information since you are likely to have some difficulty fulfilling the exact specification from a high street art shop or out-of-town superstore.

I decided to use whatever I could find among the debris that is my store of cards and papers. This turned out to be heavy quality watercolour card (0.34mm) for this version. I also tried both the back of a writing pad and mounting board (1.3mm) and the back of a block of drawing paper (1.85mm). It all seemed to work, so most modellers should be able to find suitable materials either close to hand or via listed sources. The most important resource is time. Don't rush it. There is a tremendous amount of scalpel work required and precision cuts are essential. The project version for a four-road shed, for example, is four bays long and this means that four outer and four inner walls have to be removed from the printout. Each one requires twenty seven scalpel cuts, making a total of more than two hundred operations – and that is before we tackle the reinforcing walls, glazing, plinths and buttresses. Allow somewhere in the region of one-and-a-half and two hours for this task alone. As I said, this is not a 'quickie'.

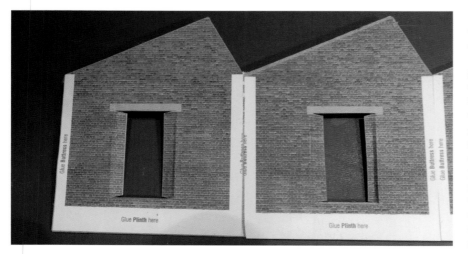

The printouts of the outer walls are glued one bay at a time. The almost instant grab of the glue stick does not allow any time for repositioning or adjustment. Try to place each segment as accurately as you can and accept the fact that any minor problems, as shown, can invariably be disguised behind drainpipes or buttresses.

A blow by blow account of the assembly process would be as tedious in this instance as it would have been in earlier card kit sequences. The instructions laid out by designer John Whiffen are perfectly clear. I followed these more or less to the letter and will simply highlight any specific difficulties or problems as I encountered them.

MAIN WALLS

Remember that I am combining two sheds to provide walls of four bays (four walls to each side) and with a total length of 340mm (85ft to scale). The chosen thick card backing came from the back of the sketch A2 pad and, while it is close to the recommended 2.0mm, it is not high quality – but it certainly is tough. It also lacks the glaze and finish of mounting board, so it is very absorbent and demands plenty of glue stick to give a chance of smooth and even fixing.

If you have not worked with this thickness before you should be prepared to use considerable pressure on your scalpel. For safety's sake, as well as for neatness and precision, make sure you keep the blade as flat as possible and always vertical to the cut. Pressure plus twisting equals snapping!

I decided that I wanted the printed artwork to go directly onto the card. Instead of gluing the templates down completely, I used just enough to hold them securely but so that any possible damage to the card would be minimized when I peeled them off. This bit of the job took the best part of another two hours.

Once this exercise was done I chose the best sides on which to fix the printed wall sections, two to each backing piece. At this point I would emphasize that, wherever possible, you should always apply the glue stick to the card, not to the printed sheets. This is particularly true when using unfinished card as it needs a liberal coating, which means working quickly and using plenty of pressure. Don't attempt to fix each two-bay sheet in one go. The chances are the glue will begin to dry before you achieve accurate positioning.

With the outer layers of relief brickwork in place, now is the time to touch in the considerable number of exposed edges. It's a job for 'best-match' watercolours, a steady hand and a degree of patience. Any smears on the printed surfaces should be swiftly removed with a moist tissue.

Work to one bay at a time and carefully remove any possible creases and bubbles. I used a round pencil (or pen) like a rolling pin, some finger pressure and, with care, the back of the scalpel blade for minor problems. Once the first bay is firmly in place, gently lift the remaining portion, glue the card and then press it back into position. Repeat all this with the second two-bay sheet and ensure that you have a good butt joint to the first one. Don't despair if you find that the last bay is running slightly out of true. Simply use your scalpel to separate it, cutting down the centre of the positioning blank for one of the buttresses. Then glue it as before, but now in its correct position on the backing card with the error falling where it will be concealed by the buttress.

Buttresses

The buttresses themselves are pretty simple, just plain rectangles. You do, however, need a lot of them – five for each inner and outer wall – making twenty in all. I decided to batch cut the whole lot and so prepared the thick backing card to their required height and then, this time, glued the templates into place.

It was then just a question of slicing them all off ready for use. Once again, though, remember that it takes lots of pressure and a vertical blade to cut that thick card. Although the instructions imply that the inner wall should also have its 2mm backing card, I thought this might be excessive even though the finished product would be only one scale foot in depth. The actual printed walls are shown as alternative rows of headers and stretchers, which is known as English bond and was commonly used by all the railway companies. This produces a non-cavity wall approximately nine inches thick, so it seemed justifiable to substitute thinner and easier to work mounting board. It also seemed logical to use it as a substitute for everything (two layers of roughly 1.4mm mounting board, plus the acetate and the two sheets of 80gsm, would be close to the 3mm or 9in that our scale required).

Finishing the walls

Completing the walls is a lengthy process. It took just over twenty hours of concentrated modelling to get from the first cuts to finally gluing the pair of subassemblies and adding the numerous details. It's worth stating that, while their all-round quality and low cost make Scalescenes hard to beat, the modeller who has limited time to spend on the hobby should perhaps look elsewhere. There are a few tips that might be worth passing on:

Windowsills: These are relatively small scraps of paper and need to be positioned accurately and fixed securely. A glue stick will do the job but I found it cumbersome and not that efficient. The problem is that such small components tend to dry before you have them exactly in place or they 'grab' too quickly, which is just as bad. My usual method for these is to

The buttresses are best tackled as a batch-job. Remove all the templates from the various sheets and reassemble them onto the appropriate card. Keep them tightly together and, if possible, aligned top (or bottom) to a machine-cut edge, which will help to save time by reducing the number of scalpel cuts.

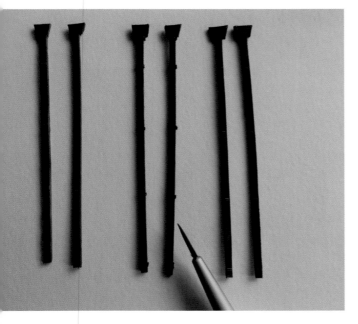

The drainpipes and hoppers are fiddly little items and extra care should be taken when cutting them out and mounting them. They should always be painted before assembly and can be improved by the addition of address label strips to represent the brackets, as here on the centre pair.

use small quantities of either craft PVA or paper glue brushed onto the front-facing part of the sill. This allows a little more positioning time before the final push through to secure the inside.

Drainpipes/trunking: These should be treated as batch jobs, making sure they are firmly glued to the medium card. The scalpel blade must be as new as possible as they are narrow, delicate and need a very precise cut. The end products are good as card representations. Paint or colour the exposed edges before fixing. Plastic accessory kits are an alternative source, but these come at a price. The trunking could also come from suitable plastic strip.

Exposed edges: Although the instructions suggest using felt-tip pens, I would advise caution. These pens are usually in basic primary colours and their inks may dry 'shiny', meaning that the cure could be worse than the illness. As I have previously stated, I prefer

to use watercolours since the shade and strength can be adjusted to give a much more accurate match and they dry matt.

Colour schemes: Drainpipes and other metal-work were often painted in 'house colours'. It might be an idea to use enamels on these and this would further help to differentiate between the printed paper as brick and printed paper as metal.

Glazing: Scalescenes produces some excellent and imaginative artwork for the windows and the actual north lights, each one capturing the essence of 'stained glass' in a non-ecclesiastical context.

I am a little uneasy, however, about the actual printing on OHP acetates. The trouble is that this is a very thin material usually referred to as 'film'. It is barely three-hundredths of an inch thick (0.09mm). It is therefore quite prone to bowing when installed and somehow lacks the requisite solid appearance of real glass set in iron frames. By way of compari-son, it is exactly half the thickness of the Truescenes glazing sheets and only a third the thickness of that contained in the Metcalf kits. This is probably something we have to live with, however, since even commercial copiers can only cope with OHP stock and suitable replacements do not seem available. It is worth noting, however, that Brassmasters offers some correct etches, if you are prepared to invest some extra cash and time.

Lintels and columns: This lengthy four-road structure is wholly reliant upon the four roof assemblies and their lintels to maintain the correct width and to impart a degree of solidity to the shed. The lintels and the two outer columns are also essential to keep the walls vertical. It therefore follows that these subassemblies must be carefully cut out and glued to ensure that they are sufficiently robust to fulfil the role. I chose to use mounting board throughout as the 'thick card'. As already mentioned, this is marginally less than the recom-mended 2mm thickness required, but it scores heavily in its consistent quality and ease of use. The difference, once all the layers are glued together, is just a few millimetres and this does not appear in anyway inadequate to the task. More tips may be found in the accompanying illustrations.

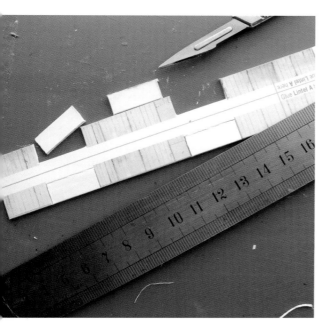
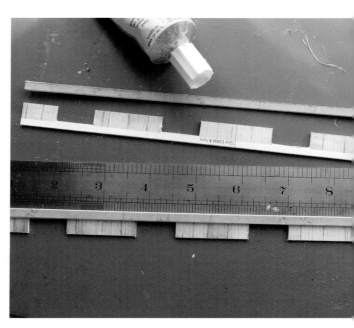

ABOVE LEFT AND RIGHT: *The lintels are easier to handle if they are left as a pair. Always use a steel rule wherever possible; accurate cutting is essential if the final assembly is to go smoothly. The outer strip of the lintels is best fixed with clear glue, which allows a few extra seconds for any careful repositioning.*

Whenever you need to bend and fold, always use the steel rule and the back of the scalpel blade, score lightly but firmly, and do not cut or tear the printed surface. This is a good example of how the previous score lines enable the wrappers to be accurately folded into neat channels ready to accept the multi-laminates of the actual columns.

When making up the lintel/column subassembly, a useful trick is to keep everything properly square on the cutting mat. Clip the lintel to the long side and then use the short side to glue the outer/first column exactly vertical. As the glue will take a few minutes to set it should be clipped in place. The provided spacing templates and the grid can be used to fix the three inner columns. Leave the second outer one until the rest are firmly fixed and then repeat the first operation. Store the front and back subassemblies somewhere safe as they remain vulnerable to damage.

ALTERNATIVE ASSEMBLY SEQUENCE

When I had assembled the two walls and was about to continue assembling kit according to the fifty-four illustrated sequential steps on the instructions, I paused for thought. The shed was going to be a big structure, some 14in long (350mm) by close to 10in wide (250mm), which would be a pretty unwieldy item for my model bench. I also felt that it would be a difficult shape to manoeuvre when fixing all the other internal and external details. For a structure lacking any full-strength gable ends and that was no more than heavyweight walls (each 75 grams) hanging from much lighter roof sections, it would also require a considerable amount of handling.

I therefore decided to continue following the instruction sequence but producing everything as a series of more manageable individual subassemblies. These could easily be put to one side until the whole lot were combined into the final build. This would minimize the amount of handling to which the carcass would be subjected and thus reduce the inevitable strain on the various joints. On reflection that simply mirrored the flat pack or pre-assembled method used in today's building industry.

Those modellers who are making the basic single kit for their layouts should have no such qualms and can simply follow the instruction sheets, but anyone building a four-road, four-bay example, or larger, would do well to consider this alternative method.

ROOFS

Without any good quality 1mm card to hand, I used the nearest thickness from the backs of A4 pads as an alternative. I have to admit to encountering a problem here. The instructions (items 13/14) seem to imply gluing the whole pre-scored outer sheet to the roof, bending it and then fixing the interior. I tried this several times with little success. In the end, using the walls to ascertain where the ridge-line would be, I cut and almost scored through the actual roof-template in order to ensure a clean, sharp bend. I then cut the outer sheet in two along the score line and carefully glued each half into position. Even this is tricky as these are large expanses for the glue stick

to adequately cover and to remain sticky during the essential positioning. As it was, it had to be lifted and re-stuck several times before it was right. The same procedure was then carried out on the underside.

After all that it soon became apparent that the card covered templates now had a tendency to warp as the glue dried. All four roofs were therefore quickly set aside and pressed flat beneath a pile of my heaviest books. If I were doing the project again I would fall back on my normal method for building large north light roofs. This uses mounting board throughout as the templates and entails cutting each 'side' of the roof as a separate item neatly at the ridge. Mounting board has a lesser tendency to warp and it also gives more strength to what is, particularly in cases like this project, a sort of upside-down foundation beneath which the walls and other features are hung.

Smoke troughs and vents

These are among the trickiest of all the subassemblies within the kit. The vent sides (normally referred to as 'troughs' in railway parlance) are all identical in

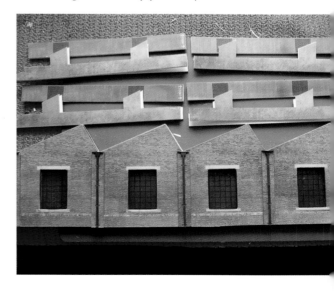

The main components for the smoke troughs have been prepared ready for assembly. Don't forget that you will need extra downloads to make the required four sets. It's useful to keep a finished wall close at hand: the troughs will only fit one way and it's all too easy to get it wrong.

This illustrates what can happen when you ignore your own advice. I have stressed the advisability of always fixing any printed sheets to the white side of the mounting board, leaving the grey or black side for interiors. If I had remembered this simple rule I would not have had to paint the insides of the troughs. Apart from that they can now be put to one side awaiting installation.

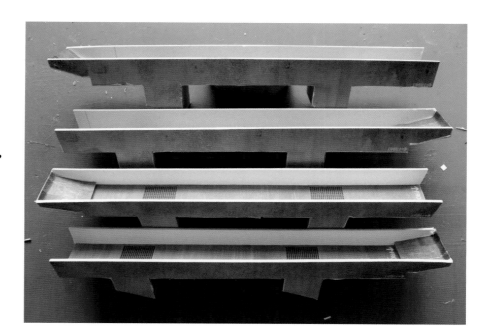

profile, but that does not mean that they are in any way interchangeable. Far from it, you need to exercise considerable caution when assembling all the seven components that make up each unit. There are guidance comments in the instructions and identifiers on the prints themselves, but it is still important to offer them up to be sure.

This is particularly true in cases such as here, where one is almost working upside down. The tops of the subassembly, the actual vents, are the fixing points to the underside of the roof. It is worthwhile placing the building on the bench (or a section of wall if your build sequence is following mine), but even that is no substitute for a thoughtful and careful approach – as I found out the hard way.

There are points that are here worth mentioning. Always make sure that the printed sheets are glued to the white side of the mounting board, which is more suitable for this job. The second is a word of warning to those making the four-track, double-length structure featured in this project. Combining two kits is fine for the building as a whole, but it won't give you sufficient troughs, vents, inspection pits or other details to enable you to fix full-length complete sets over the tracks. You need at least two more sets of the appropriate sheets to obtain the large number

of pre-prints and backing templates required. Since these are well scattered, and since no extra costs are involved, it is probably just as easy to print off two more complete sets. The surplus items will always make useful additions to your bits box.

As for colouring the edges prior to building, once again I prefer to leave this task until all the subassemblies are complete. Then use watercolour and pastel dust to achieve the correct colour matches and an even end result. If you have used the card correctly the black or dark grey underside may save having to paint the inside of the trough.

Roof supports and trusses

These are among the more difficult items to cut out since they include a number of internal angles and are somewhat delicate. The four-road, four-bay structure in the project needed six assembled sets or downloads, each made up of laminations on 1mm (medium) card. This would have produced girders of 2mm thickness and their supporting pillars of 4mm. I took two different approaches, largely driven by a lack of accurate medium card. I did one batch using single-sheet mounting board (about 1.5mm), which reduced the thickness and strength by about 25 per cent. It was no more than adequate and, with the

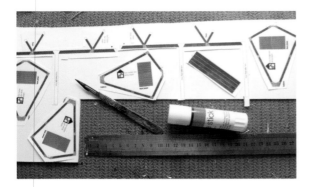

All the components for the roof trusses have been roughly cut from the sheets and regrouped as economically as possible on some board offcuts.

The individual items can then be separated with kitchen scissors to make them easier to handle. This is an opportune time to double-check that they are securely glued across their entire area, keeping the paper glue handy to remedy any problems.

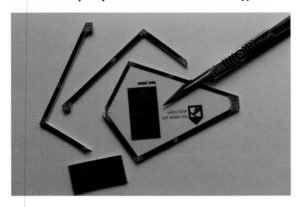

When making the final separations before assembly, try to avoid cutting into the corners of any angled pieces. If you make the slightest slip you'll end up with two components instead of one. It may seem trivial but such a mistake will jeopardize the strength of the final job.

RIGHT: *The assemblies are posed to show how you can match the printed sheets when touching in with watercolour. The other 'shiny' column demonstrates that it is better to use this technique than to rely on felt-tip pens.*

A pair of girders, trusses and columns ready for installation. Constructing them on the workbench was easier and helped to ensure that they were as square and robust as the design would allow.

ironwork barely visible from ground level and only glimpsed through the north light, it proved acceptable but flimsy. For the second batch I went the other way, using mounting board again but as a 'two-up' lamination. This effectively increased size and strength by about 40 per cent and proved an ideal solution. The new assemblies were neat, robust and did not look too heavy; this further reinforced my personal view regarding the much wider use of this convenient and inexpensive card.

Rooftop vents and smoke chimneys

While much of this interior detail is rarely, if ever, wholly visible during normal viewing, the same cannot be said of the rooftop vents or smoke chimneys, if you prefer. The project required no fewer than sixteen of these and the additional print-outs were duly produced. As the accompanying illustrations show, the preparation and assembly of these items is well suited to a batch process. With the potential for so many individual components on my small worktop, I chose to make up eight at a time. I find that this technique saves time by reducing the number of cuts needed, even allowing for some preliminary work. It also helps to ensure consistency and to avoid mistakes by keeping the whole production run constantly in view.

The following comments may help in both the planning and execution of these items:

Adhesives: I would certainly keep with using ordinary PVA carefully applied with a small brush. This allows for the subtle repositioning necessary to get the best results. The side sheets can be done with a glue stick.

Wraparounds: For these you should definitely use PVA, sticking first the sides and also the short tabs on the vent tops, followed by the remaining long sides. Press and smooth them all down with the back of your scalpel.

Assembly: If you are using mounting board, which is thinner than the recommended 2mm card, this will require an extra backing piece inserted between the two halves. When joining the sets of outers and inners, it is vital to keep all the bases aligned in order to obtain the neatest match in the vertical plane. It sounds complicated but it simply means holding all of the components firmly down on a level surface, such as a cutting mat, and then pressing a steel rule into the angle made by the front of the vent. This may, and probably will, lead to some irregularities at the top and at the back of the vent. Trim these as best you can with your sharpest blade. The only critical bit is to ensure that the two tops are level and square to support the vent top itself.

It is never easy trying to get the valley gutters to sit neatly in place. This is another instance where I opt to use paper-glue, applied generously to the underside. Position the gutter using the back of a scalpel blade and then hold it in place by simply laying a couple of steel rules on top of it.

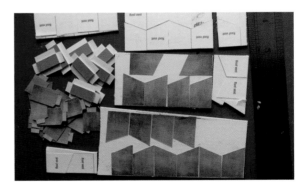

The smoke chimneys are a perfect candidate for batch production. Cut out all the relevant parts and have your glue close at hand.

The various matching halves of the inners are laid out ready for use. Work on the chimney caps is already underway.

If you are using mounting board, you will need at least one extra piece to bring the assembly to its correct thickness (width). When dealing with the small fold-overs I choose to fix the shorter tabs first, as this somehow results in a neater job. The best result come from applying paper glue with a small brush and then smoothing the tabs and pressing down with a scalpel.

One of the key tasks with all card modelling is to touch in the exposed edges. If any are left they will completely spoil the hard work that has gone into the build. White bits draw the eye no matter where the structure is sited on the layout. This is so unnecessary when all it takes is a few minutes with the watercolours.

Time: You should remember that even these simple units can eat up the hours. The sixteen vents required for the project involved about 800 cuts of card, paper or both. The time taken, spread over three days of modelling, from selecting the sheets to completing them ready for installation was more than sixteen hours.

Inspection pits and hard-standing: These have not been included in the main assembly process. The pits may be featured beneath the proposed ash shelter, where they might be better seen (for construction tips and any comments, see Chapter 6). For the existing structure the hard-standing and shed floors will be built into the layout, and dummy pits will also be included at that stage.

CONCLUSIONS

The Scalescenes range provides some excellent additions to the kit market. They are not quick to build but the end products are accurate, attractive and well worth the extra time and effort involved. Don't rush them and allow considerably more hours than

that demanded by the traditional card kits, such as those by Superquick and Metcalf. Have several packs of blades to hand before you start and change them more frequently, as it is essential that they are fully sharp. If you are contemplating combining kits, plan ahead by taking advantage of the free downloads that provide more than enough of each item. Before you

A final job is to examine the building in a good light for any areas where the gluing is less than perfect. Once again the remedy lies in paper-glue and the smallest paintbrush (or even a cocktail stick).

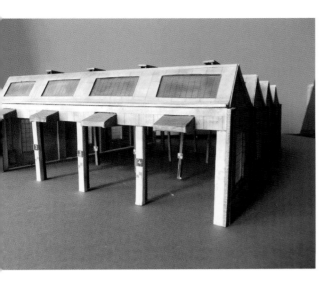

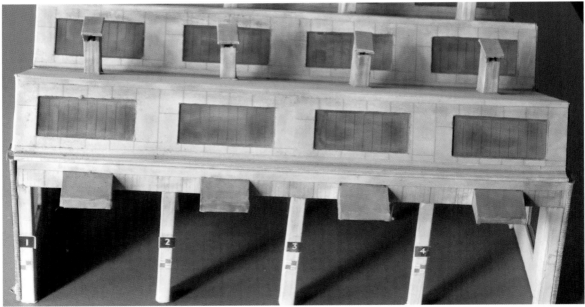

ABOVE AND OVERLEAF: *The north light shed is now ready to take its place on the layout. It has made up into a large, handsome and realistic structure with a light and airy interior. The notices for 'restricted clearance' were provided among the downloads. I have also used the 'road numbers', although I could find little evidence for these in real life, probably either because they were quickly learned or because most sheds would have had their own slang names for them. The only problem I could see was the difficulty of keeping the columns looking absolutely vertical from every angle. This is not unique to this Scalescenes kit, but is common to all similar constructions. If the shed is being built for permanent installation, then the obvious answer is to glue the base of each column to the baseboard. This will need a glue that will permit some initial adjustments and a palette knife or similar to reach inside and tweak the columns into position. It won't be easy but it can be done. If the shed needs to be removable, then an arrangement of spigots and tubes might make a workable solution. What is most pleasing, however, is the ease with which the kits can be combined, effectively allowing the modeller to build any multi-road and multi-bay shed for an initial payment of less than £5.*

start, remember that the bigger the project, then the more space it will take up; the use of subassemblies will help. Don't be afraid to experiment, as this is one case where trial and error comes free.

The use of 2mm and 1mm card for the key structural components makes for a very robust model. The heavier material, however, is not the easiest to source nor is it particularly easy to work. If I were to build another extended four-road shed I would probably take the chance to use mounting board throughout. Indeed, where the roof is concerned, I would certainly always upgrade to this card. The roof is, after all, the 'foundation' of the structure since there are no floors or ceilings. I would also

model the two sections of each north light, as I do when scratch-building, as separate items joining at the ridge. I find this easier and more accurate than the bend and stick principle.

None of these comments imply any criticisms of the Scalescenes offering. It is outstanding value for money and provides the modeller with the sort of challenges upon which we should all thrive. I must repeat, though, don't rush it. The project exercise took well over 100 hours of modelling time. One last tip is to have two scalpels in use, one for the majority of the heavy, blunting, basic cuts, the other kept ultra-sharp and exclusively for the tricky bits of detail work.

ADDING A COALING STAGE

Even in the earliest days of the steam railway it was soon apparent that large numbers of locomotives would require extremely large quantities of coal. Common sense showed that while this could, if necessary, be simply shovelled up from a heap in the yard, this was slow, inefficient and labour-intensive. How much better it would be if the coal heaps were raised at least to the floor level of the delivering wagon. Even this still involved the hard work of shovelling it up into the tender or bunker. The obvious answer would be to raise the 'heap' still further to a height where it could be tipped more or less directly down to the waiting engines.

The simple coaling platform would become a raised structure served by an inclined ramp, up which the loaded coal wagons could be shunted, their contents unloaded into tubs and then tipped down into the tenders. It could never be described as a particularly sophisticated answer, but it worked and with but few alterations would continue to serve the railways until the end of steam.

Over the course of time all the various companies introduced their own individual styles and, in true Victorian enthusiasm, produced some elaborate designs. One of the most innovative ideas was the use of these brick- or stone-built structures as a convenient base upon which to site the depot's main water supply. This soon became almost standard practice with tanks containing tens of thousands of gallons perched on top of the stage. These not only provided a reserve against shortages, but more importantly ensured that the vital water pressure was kept constant.

In its simplest form a stage would have just one chute accessed across a steel floor by steerable tubs usually holding about 15cwt of coal. An inclined ramp with curved stops at the end enabled the tubs to be pushed out over the waiting tenders and their contents tipped down into them. Such a stage could be operated by just two coalmen, who could service their shed's full allocation of engines. Larger sheds had larger stages with two or even three chutes and a proportionally increased number of coalmen.

The job was one the dirtiest on the steam railway but it was still quite sought-after. Coalmen were, on the Great Western at least, the only employees to be paid at piecework rates – the more tonnage they shifted, the more money they earned. Woe betide the driver who failed to line up properly beneath the chute and caused a delay. Woe to the shed pilot who was late replenishing their supply of full wagons. Many a young fireman was also subjected to the coalman's

ABOVE LEFT AND RIGHT: *Here is something to aim for. Didcot's coaling stage and water tank are a very close match for the Scalescenes kit. The pre-war photograph includes the disposal road and ash pit with the ash road alongside. The second image was taken in the early days of the Great Western Society, with the remains of the wartime ash shelter still in the background.* COURTESY GREAT WESTERN TRUST

rich vocabulary and his accuracy with a suitably sized lump of coal. One other benefit enjoyed by these individuals, and jealously guarded, was the supply of constant hot water in their rest-room located in the ground-floor space beneath the stage.

MODERNIZATION

The technological advances in steel and concrete construction, together with the increasing size of locomotive tenders, brought about the introduction of entirely new methods of coaling made possible by the monumental 'cenotaph' coaling plants. These giant towers more or less removed the job of coalman from the depot. Now, thanks to the added advantages of electric and hydraulic power, the delivering coal wagons were simply shunted onto a lift, raised to the top of the tower and tipped straight into the tenders. A similar mechanized installation was also introduced to cope with the ever-growing problem of ash disposal. Many depots soon boasted both of these labour-saving plants.

Although they were undoubtedly a huge step forward, they were by no means installed everywhere. For a start they needed a not inconsiderable capital investment and this could only be justified at the larger sheds and MPDs. They were also designed to handle the harder types of coal, which meant they were more applicable to the LMS and LNER than elsewhere. The Great Western, while it certainly had some very large sheds, also had a locomotive fleet specifically designed to work best with the softer grades of Welsh steam coal. This contributed to the GWR retaining its ramped coaling stages up to and beyond its transition into BR (W).

In the model world there are card-kit examples of all of these structures, but our needs for the MPD project are best served by the traditional ramped version.

MODELLING THE COALING STAGE

The coaling stage download from Scalescenes makes up into a large, handsome and realistic structure. It is definitely not quick to build and repays the extra effort needed to get the best results. That said, the average modeller should be able to go from download to installation in about three weeks. Those with perhaps a bit more leisure time, and some extra experience, should have the finished model on the layout in a fortnight. The instructions and advice are both clear and comprehensive, a typical example of Scalescenes thoroughness. The recommended build sequence is more than adequate for the task, though I did depart from it in places and for the reasons given on the previous kit. We all have our own ways of working but do, in any case, follow all the step-by-step procedures on the many subassemblies.

The glues used were cheap glue sticks and Everbuild Stick 2 All Purpose Clear Adhesive. The latter was new to me, costs about £1 for a 30ml tube and turned out to be a winner. Once the nozzle was squeezed to limit the flow it never oozed or leaked throughout the exercise. The usual problem of stringing was minimal and what little occurred was barely a cobweb. It also gave a valuable couple of seconds for adjustments, yet set firmly in about three or four minutes. I am always reluctant to make recommendations, but this is one of the best glues of this type I have encountered.

Will it fit?

To return to the stage itself, it is a hefty piece of architecture and so needs a generously laid out yard to do it justice. The frontage, excluding the ladder to the tank, is 190mm and the depth is 160mm ($7\frac{1}{2}$ x $6\frac{1}{2}$in). The actual coaling road should be a further 20–25mm out from the base. To this must then be added sufficient space for the ramped approach and for the full-wagon storage on the far side. On the layout, the dimensions for these will depend upon the gradient used and how many full wagons are to be held. The gradient must reflect the number of wagons to be propelled upwards and the ability of the chosen shed-pilot loco to manage the task. This is a decision that can only be taken by each modeller since questions of available space and loco capability are specific to the individual layout. I have opted for a version based on my Sherborne shed on 'Wessex Lines', where an A1X Terrier can manage two loaded wagons, but I have eased the slope to make it more visually attractive.

A modelling opportunity

The ramp and the extension are useful to the modeller in that they offer at least a modicum of opportunity for some scenic work. Few readers will probably have seen these features outside of the photo albums, so some brief generalizations may be of assistance. Most examples would have been built at the same time as the shed itself and the actual stage. They would normally be constructed of rubble and soil excavated during the preparation for the shed or brought in from the nearest convenient point on the mainline. They would need retaining walls at the base to hold the loose tippings in place. These walls were constructed from the same brick or stone as used on all the other buildings, and were usually six to eight feet in height. The slopes to the embankments would probably correspond to the rules of the company's Civil Engineer, but forty-five degrees would seem to be reasonably realistic and easy to model.

PLANNING THE DIMENSIONS

On the project, the footprint of the ramp and the extension were derived by a mix of offering up, drawing and measuring. The completed model of the stage was placed on the track plan in its intended position, revealing the probable space available on either side. The width of the entrance was measured together with its height above ground level (40mm and 50mm respectively). The width would be that of ramp's trackbed and this was drawn on the scrap pad at 50mm above the horizontal ground line, with the required 45-degree angles plotted down on either side of the trackbed. The one on the yard side was cut short at a point exactly 24mm above ground level, which represented the position of a 6ft retaining wall, which was the height of the piece of artwork I wanted to use.

The other angle was cut to the point at which it would meet the edge of the layout board. This exercise showed that the width of the ramp/extension footprint was exactly 100mm. Give or take a millimetre or two, the lengths of the ramp and extension could then be taken straight off the track plan and used as the base to draw on the elevation and determine the gradient. The extension on the far side

of the stage could be modelled as level track, and a further, short wagon-length of level track was plotted in front of the entrance to avoid too abrupt a transition. This was sufficient information to be able to draw the footprint on the track plan and to eventually construct the two elements.

Flexibility has been defined as the 'fourth dimension of planning'. I have always tried to take advantage of this ability to capitalize on previously unforeseen ideas rather than sticking rigidly to the original plans. As it happened this all worked out rather well; the new plot revealed a useful extra space between the retaining wall and the coal road that was just wide enough to include a new siding from the edge of the board up to the access steps to the stage.. This new storage line (350mm long) could 'prototypically' be used to hold four or five incoming loaded coal wagons or, if one was available, the depot's breakdown crane and tool van.

It is probably worth mentioning as an afterthought that the ramp and extension need not necessarily be built on an embankment. Where space was tight these were often built on an inclined plane of brick or stone arches. If this option were used on the project, and there are kits and ready-builds available, it would provide sufficient room for a second siding, enabling both the crane and the coal wagons to be conveniently positioned.

ASSEMBLING THE COALING STAGE

There is little need for further comment about this Scalescenes product except to remind readers that it is a quite ambitious kit and one that is destined to be the most prominent feature on the layout. The front of the building, in particular, is full of character and merits the very best of your modelling skills. Don't be too dismayed, however, if errors do occur, since repeat downloads of any sheet, or even of the full kit, are free within its already low purchase price (£4.99 in mid-2015).

Preparation

There are nine pages of well-detailed, fully illustrated instructions covering the ninety-seven assembly steps recommended by designer, John Whiffen. The kit itself consists of another eighteen pages, eleven of which will become card-mounted bases or templates. The remainder are the pre-printed covering sheets and the window glazing. The combined package, which together comes to just under 200 individual components, might seem daunting to the beginner and even to an old hand like me. You can be reassured, however, that after reading the instructions a few times, while at the same time identifying the many parts, everything will come clear.

The first step is to ensure that you have all the tools and materials required close to hand before you start. A handy check-list is provided, from which I would emphasize glue sticks, clear glue, plenty of spare blades, a square and six- and twelve-inch steel rulers. Above all have ready access to all the necessary card in the optimum thicknesses for the various bases. As we discovered when building the shed earlier, the recommended thicknesses are not easy to track down on the average high street. Without repeating the various arguments, I opted for mounting board for the heavy jobs, the backs of scrap pads for the medium, and 200gsm drawing paper for the thin jobs. This seemed to present no difficulties except in those instances where extra packing was necessary; these will be highlighted as they are encountered.

Alternative approaches

It is quite acceptable to glue the complete A4 sheets to their appropriate cards and then separate each component as required. I personally find this to be a rather wasteful procedure, with the added downsides that it is difficult to ensure that the quick-drying glue stick has properly secured the entire sheet and that the cutting out of smaller parts is not easy from these larger pieces. My own approach is to separate all the components first, cutting just a few millimetres outside the actual markings. These are then regrouped as economically as possible on their respective cards and carefully glued down before being accurately cut to the proper marks. In order to locate them quickly as the assembly progresses and prevent them being lost in the chaos of my workbench, they are placed in labelled envelopes according to their eventual roles in the assembly process.

Scalescenes kits certainly give you plenty of parts for your money. Here are the constituent parts for the coaling stage; the heap of detritus to the right shows just how much cutting-out was required. Despite their low cost these are definitely not quick to build and may can contain about 200 parts.

This is very much like a production line and will ultimately result in more than 100 components. It is, to say the least, a somewhat tedious process but do not rush it. These pieces are the internal jigsaw upon which the whole structure depends for both its appearance and its strength. Care and accuracy are essential if it is all to fit together easily and correctly.

Important reminders

When you finally get round to the assembly, remember to have some simple paper glue and a fine brush close to hand. You will be fixing paper to paper and this is your last chance to make sure that all the templates and bases really are secured across their full area. It is then no more complicated than simply following the instructions and, since we have already covered the various step-by-step procedures when building the shed, to do the same again would be tedious. Here, though, are a few points that may deserve special mention:

Test and fit: The whole kit is based on the eventual combining of laminated sections. Some of these will include several layers and accurate alignments are essential to ensure that the adjacent sections fit together firmly and squarely. It is almost inevitable that small errors will have occurred at some point when cutting or gluing. By testing the fit before joining the sections, you can judge whether extra trimming and tweaking is required.

Windowsills: These four small pieces of pre-printed detail can often create problems quite disproportionate to their size. They are very visible from all angles and any misalignment can ruin the all-important front aspect. My advice is to carefully score the back of each sill exactly along the line between the outer 'concrete' and the fold-in flap. Make sure all four are scored precisely the same, then fix them to the outer wall using the brick courses as a guide to keep them perfectly horizontal and in line with each other. Then push the small flap through the window and secure it. This may seem to be time consuming, but it's vital for the best results.

Access steps: These require quite a complicated subassembly and it is all too easy to get it wrong. I chose to sort out the lower flight of steps and the landing first, followed by the two outer walls and then the inner pair. This left the top flight and final fixing until last. The two flights themselves are tedious and there are no possible short cuts. Follow the instructions but, since we are using card that is thinner than specified, you will need to add several extra 'bases' beneath the steps to get them to finish at the correct heights. I found that five pieces were sufficient and fixed them to steps A, C, E, H and L. (It occurred to me that it might be possible to solve the problem by finding correctly sized balsa strip (2mm) at your model shop.) You may find things are a bit tight when it comes to putting it all together and adding the final engineer's blue capping bricks. The important thing is to get it to look right from the front and to conceal any errors at the back, or at the base where they can be hidden with ballast.

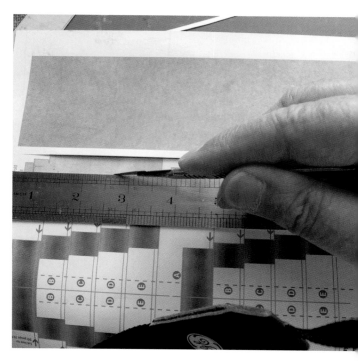

Among the very few tricky elements in the kit are the two flights of steps that lead to the stage itself. This is another instance where my decision to use mounting board didn't help, as additional packing pieces will be necessary to restore the required height. It is also essential to keep the cutting precise and the two flights absolutely square.

Water tank: After several trial runs I decided to change the build sequence from that described in the instructions (from item 56 onwards) and to assemble the bases A, B and C on the workbench. This would ensure that the overlaps were more precise and would avoid undue handling of the main structure. I also made changes to the tank itself. I noticed that the curvature of the two B supports was marginally low at their joins to the central A cross-member, but it was correct at the fixing points to the outer tank sides. To solve the problem I added some strips of 200gsm paper across the joins, which had the added benefit of making an additional surface area available on which to glue the tank top. I then fitted the front side first to ensure that the all-important front aspect was as near perfect as I could manage, with any less than satisfactory joins being confined to the rear of the tank.

The only other problem I encountered was the profiling of the tank lid. It was necessary to add some extra packing of 200gsm art paper to achieve the correct curvature. Note that the change in the building sequence, described in the text, is evident here as the front of the tank is already in place.

Tank roof: It is vital to get the curvature of the tank top absolutely right. The scoring of the template is critical since the eventual curve must be smooth and consistent across the whole area. Make sure that every cut exactly follows the printed lines and, above all, that they are to the same depth. Any discrepancies will cause the template to curve in uneven steps or twists. Do plenty of test bends before gluing the tank top-sheet very securely. Working on the bench will now enable you to accurately position and fix the roof to the tank and hold things in place with elastic bands: this would not have been possible with the tank built onto the main structure.

Adding the details: The last item on the agenda is the ladder up to the inspection hatch and the safety rails at the top. These are cited as 'optional', but I would suggest they are essential, not only for the sense of realism but also since they make attractive and very visible details. The safety rails can be made from the thinnest plastic rod (Evergreen 0.2mm) and the ladder is best sourced from the signal accessory pack from Ratio. You will need to carefully join several sections in order to obtain the correct length as the inspection hatch is some 40ft up. This is a very

delicate item and is best left off until the stage is firmly sited on the layout; paint it first with matt black and matt white for the lower half-dozen rungs.

Buttresses: These are another area where the mounting board templates need some extra thickening. They should be multi-layer laminates of 2mm card and to make up the difference the larger central buttress at the rear will need two extra pieces and the corner buttresses will need one extra. However it is possible to avoid this task by simply trimming off the excess pre-print overlays from the corner examples and living with the rear one, which is unlikely to be seen.

CONSTRUCTING THE RAMP

Basic landscaping

This is a relatively straightforward piece of scenic work and is done in exactly the same way as any cutting or embankment on your existing layouts. If you have no such features, or have yet to construct them, then this is one of several methods that you may wish to try. Much of the basic calculation was done earlier when plotting the ramp and extension

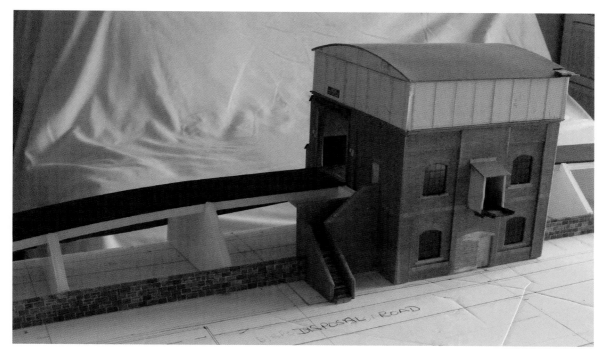

Once the stage is finished it can be offered up on the layout, flanked by the two elements of the ramp. At this point the subassembly of the access steps has still not been secured permanently; it is important to get this to fit snugly between the ramp and the stage and also correctly aligned with the doorway. Note that the stone retaining wall compares favourably with the one at Didcot.

footprints; this information can now be put to good use. The drawing made for the ramp profile at the entrance is the starting point. Select a suitably sized piece of 7mm foamboard and mark and cut five sections to match that drawing. Three of these will serve as the formers for the extension and the other two will be the upper section of the ramp. One of these will need to be reduced in width to fit immediately below the entrance and thus behind the access stairs, the second will represent the top of the incline at an appropriate distance from the entrance. All that then remains is to cut a further three sections to the same profile, but progressively reducing the height of the sloping sides to produce the planned gradient.

Completing the ramp

Once all the sections are ready they will need a slot approximately 8mm deep cut out at the top to accept the eventual trackbed. This is yet another piece of 7mm foamboard cut to the width of the slot,

covered with the customary play foam and then separated into two lengths, as per the plan, to make the incline and the extension. Assemble these two sets of cross-members, adding the print-covered 6ft walls to one side and simple bracing card to the other. Cut a good supply of roughly half-inch strips of drawing paper to create the latticework for the sloping banks and then clad with the material of your choice. From here it is a simple exercise of joining the three sub-assemblies together (ramp, stage and extension) and making sure that they are level and properly square.

Track laying

The track is best formed from a single one-yard length of flexible track; as usual I chose PECO Code100. There are no fixed rules on how you should approach the job, but this is the method I use. Thread the piece from right to left through the stage, starting from the end of the extension. Don't attempt to fix it yet but make sure it starts (or ends)

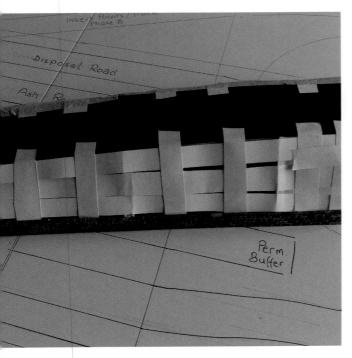

The simple latticework is in place and some strips of thickish drawing paper are quite adequate for these small sections. These two elements are being worked up away from the main module. This is a lot easier and less stressful than trying to do the jobs in situ at the back of the layout.

The paper towelling that forms the surface has been glued in place and smoothed down. The stiffening coats of matt black emulsion are being applied. Two or three generous coats will be sufficient to give a reasonably stable and solid landscape on which to work.

exactly where the stop-block will be and then mark the piece approximately one wagon-length out from the entrance off the ramp. Withdraw the piece and very carefully bend the track downwards to match the slope of the ramp. This is quite a tricky operation as you are asking the track to do something for which it was not designed. Be patient, work a little at a time and keep offering it up until you achieve an acceptable result. The piece is likely to remain 'stressed', so it is likely that a liberal coat of PVA and numerous track-pins will be needed to keep it in place. On the section across the stage itself it is only possible to use glue and you may wish to add a more robust adhesive in this area.

Weathering and finishing

When you are satisfied that all the glues have dried and that this fairly large item is now ready to be installed, you can then indulge in an hour or so to finish it off. Paint the section of track first. It is likely to appear very rusty and in poor condition. The ballast too will be nondescript and most of it will be coated with coal dust. The banks themselves will be far removed from the grassy slopes of the rural branch line. They will also have their fair share of coal dust and areas of exposed or displaced loose ballast. Any vegetation will be sparse and little more than weeds and thistles, and even that could be scorched by the rain of cinders from the overworked shed pilot. It is obviously better to do this 'off-layout' as this will enable you to experiment with paints, pastels and scatters to get the optimum results. This would be far more difficult with the stage fixed firmly at the very back of the layout and thus hard to reach. The accompanying photographs should clarify all these processes.

After about an hour the paint should be dry enough for you to start applying the scatters. You need to remember that the soil here is likely to be half coal dust and half cinders, neither of which will support much vegetation. Stick to a mixture of dull greens, ideally varying the textures as you go. For small areas like this I tend to brush on paper-glue rather than use spray adhesive: it's slower but less messy. Larger weeds like thistles, docks and dandelions can be added last and any bald patches could be covered with loose ballast or coal dust.

The finished assembly can be put to one side until all the tracks are down and the main ballasting exercise can be continued in order to disguise the base of the structure.

CONCLUSIONS

Despite my initial misgivings, I can foresee a great future for download kits. Without any tooling, printing, packaging or distribution costs, they can be made available to the modeller for a fraction of the price of a comparable card kit. From a technical point of view they are well thought-out and go together with little more effort than their card counterparts. The overall standard of the artwork is excellent, as are the amount of detail and degree of realism. If they have any downside it is simply that they are not for the modeller in a hurry, but that in itself may be an advantage for the many others who are more than prepared to invest extra hours to achieve such distinctive and handsome additions to their layouts.

CHAPTER SIX

ANCILLARY STRUCTURES

THE 'OLD SHED'

As the original structure was built at the same time as the Carriage & Wagon Works, this is an integral part of the MPD back story. Its more recent owners have continued to find a use for it as the depot has always retained a relatively large allocation of motive power. This was quite a common occurrence even into the mid-1950s where pre-grouping structures had been augmented by newer buildings rather than being replaced by them. That is exactly the situation here and the 'old shed' still provides useful accommodation, albeit only for the smaller goods engines and the numerous 0-6-0 tanks. (In terms of the project, it was needed to justify the use of the oldest kit on the market and to demonstrate its adaptability as well as its capability to hold its own among contemporary products.)

BUILDING THE BILTEEZI SHED

This is about as basic as kits can get, being no more than a printed design on a sheet of lightweight card. The artwork, however, like everything in the Bilteezi range, is full of character and printed with outstanding precision using commendably matt inks. These designs were first marketed by C. Vacey-Ash in 1947 during the dark days of Austerity and they introduced an exciting new world of kit-built structures. Prior to their arrival, the only way to have realistic buildings inside and outside the fence was to resort to scratch-building. I well remember my own first efforts in 1956, constructing this same kit and the wayside station for a Hornby Dublo layout in an 8 x 6ft garden shed built from scratch by my dad. Despite all that has happened since, the Bilteezi sheets are still with us.

Essential reinforcing

For those not previously familiar with these kits, the biggest difference is their complete lack of any relief detail. The finished product is completely flat with all the doors, windows and other features simply reproduced as part of the exquisitely printed artwork. The card used is very thin, about the same weight as a postcard, and this means that backing sheets are essential. My own choice is to remain with mounting board and to reinforce not just the walls, but also the equally large roof sections. This ultimately leads to a square and robust finished building. If it is used carefully then it will also offer some scope to introduce modest relief features, not least of which are some replacement windows.

Tailoring the kit

The requirements of the project prevented me from building the kit in its intended form. The space available was insufficient to accommodate the full-length shed and, in any case, I wanted to model a four-road version. This would then represent the earlier facilities provided by the original company and before the building of the north light new shed. The side walls were therefore cut in two just beyond the third window and the spare portions carefully stored. Separating the kit in this way would also make it easier to install replacement glazing.

At this point I should confess that I was not working with the original kit but rather with a series of commercial photocopies printed on a similar light card. I needed an extensive supply of shed walls for the Carriage & Wagon Works that would eventually become the scenic background according to the hypothetical back story. Somehow, though, I managed to lose the originals! The new copies were glossier and the card proved more difficult to cut and bend,

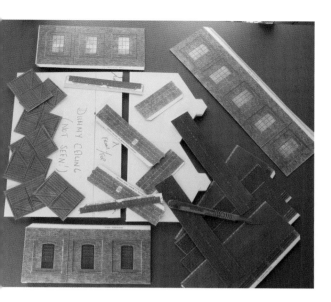

The kit of bits for the project version of the venerable Bilteezi shed. It will be constructed as a four-road type but with the length reduced to fit the available space. One full-length side is shown for comparison.

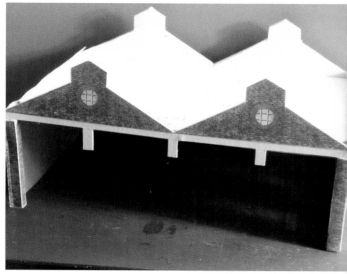

Construction is under way and this illustration shows the role of the 5mm foamboard in the false ceiling and the dummy rear wall. They combine together to improve the building's strength and stability, and also provide a solid surface for the ends of the four roof sections.

making life trickier than it would have been. With more than fifty Bilteezi kits on my loft layout, I would definitely advise caution and making a series of test runs before you resort to the copier.

The large square window surrounds were cut out and removed, then the window apertures themselves were taken out. Some suitable glazing was found among the Truetexture industrial windows sheet using the black-framed side. These were initially too short, so the bottoms of the frames were trimmed off and extra sets of lower panes and frames were cut from elsewhere on the sheet and cemented into place. These various 'bodges' are almost invisible at normal viewing distance. The final step was to add a little relief by gluing the surrounds behind the reinforcing board. Some touching in with the water-colours was required to disguise the joins and the addition of single-row strips of engineer's blue brick paper completed the sills.

In my opinion a sheet of engineer's blue is an essential resource for every kit or scratch-builder. While it may be encountered only rarely

in domestic architecture, it was widely used by all the railway companies and other industrial build-ers. It was not just seen as a decorative material but its durability made it an excellent choice within bridge-works, for platform edging and even for such extensive projects as the vast retaining walls at High Wycombe. The main advantages for the modeller are that it makes a convincing way of disguising all those less than perfect joins and bends as well as being a 'prototypical' means of adding decorative touches to doorways, windows, plinths and quoins.

Additional reinforcing

The proportions of the shed make for some problems regarding its stability. Although it is not a particularly difficult exercise, it did take some thought to determine the best way of arriving at a properly robust end result. As already mentioned, mounting board would be the reinforcing medium, but I then opted for 5mm foamboard to make a false ceiling and the new rear gable end wall. This

The shed is now nearing completion and seems to have acquired its proper character in its new configuration. The two nearside roof sections have been modelled in removable form. This is necessary since in Phase 2 they will have to be 'distressed' and may even disappear in Phase 3. The front three columns, each made up of a laminate of four pieces of mounting board covered with a wrapper of brick paper, are being threaded onto downward-facing projections from the lintel. That conspicuous main girder is simply a strip of the charcoal coloured board. The four sets of doors are also ready for fixing but will be among the last items on the schedule.

provided the necessary strength for the shell and also provided the added benefit of thicker edges for fixing the walls and roof. The actual build process was quite simple and matt varnish effectively killed the unwanted shine.

The two trickiest areas were at the front of the shed, namely the large girder that formed the lintel and the three supporting pillars. In its original form these items were the usual very simple 'fold and glue' components. None of my several attempts, both with and without additional reinforcement, was wholly satisfactory. In the end I resorted to mounting board, making the pillars from several laminations covered with wrappers of spare brick-work, while the lintel was just a suitable length of board applied directly with its charcoal-coloured backing facing outwards.

Extra detailing

This venerable old kit was going to be sited only a few inches away from Scalescene's recent north light version and it would need some discreet embellishments to bring it up to par. I didn't want to lose its essential character so I simply added soffits and barge-boards, a strip of ridge tiles to the louvres, some guttering in the valleys, guttering and downpipes. I finally made smoke hoods to fit above the four tracks. All the fabrications used the same 200gsm paper seen in the earlier projects. The finished shed may not be an architectural showpiece but it fits the overall plan and doesn't look out of place.

CONCLUSIONS

It is not easy to calculate the actual build-time. A considerable number of hours were spent

The barge-boards and soffits are in place, as is the purely decorative strip above the lintel. The front of the building seemed to be lacking in detail, especially when compared with the Scalescenes 'new' shed just a few inches away. Some smoke-hoods, quickly knocked up from heavyweight paper and assembled using clear glue, have been left unpainted for the photograph.

When trying to predict the time needed to assemble any card kit it is advisable to include a realistic allowance for painting all the exposed edges. If one also intends to add more details and extras, as in this instance with the Bilteezi shed, then still more time will need to be allotted. These tasks actually took precisely three hours.

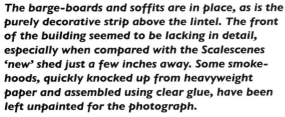

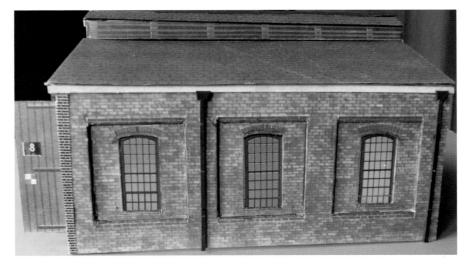

The shed is now fully detailed and ready for installation on the layout. The doors, new windows and drainpipes are fixed and the smoke hoods have been painted. Nothing has been done to the interior since, even without any engines posed in the entrances, this is largely invisible.

examining the options for the conversion and during the usual trial and error tests. More time was then used up adding the extra details. The Bilteezi kit, on its own or with others, makes a good starting point for a multi-road straight shed. It is not expensive and its lightweight card is easy to work and to adapt. It does demand additional reinforcing throughout, however, which makes it almost a form of scratch-building in reverse. In this instance the 'carcass' fits inside the covering, instead of the covering fitting outside the carcass. If anyone wants to have a go at building the project version, however, about thirty hours should be enough from start to installation.

THE NECESSARY FACILITIES

These are an essential part of any MPD. The bigger the site is, then the more locomotives that will be allocated and, hence, the more men and facilities that will be needed. Most sheds large enough to justify the term MPD would operate around the clock, 365 days of the year. There were no set ratios for the various grades and types of men required, but a rule of thumb breakdown can be calculated from little more than simple logic. It is largely a question of working back from the number, type and probable rosters of the allocated locos. From the modeller's perspective that means our own collection of engines, either present or intended.

Most of them will require at least two sets of men; many, like the local pilots and the overnight heavy-goods engines, will have three sets of engine-men. They will all work shifts and they are all coming and going at different times during the day and night. There will also be 'spare sets of men' called for duty in case of absenteeism or special workings. All these men would require mess-rooms where they could relax, get up to date with the latest traffic notices or just chat. There would be primitive cooking facilities for breakfasts and suppers and to keep the obliga-tory tea-urn on the go There would also, of course, be the necessary toilets and wash-sinks.

ESTIMATING THE REQUIREMENTS

Given that even a smaller sized MPD might hold thirty locomotives, this would mean anywhere from around sixty sets of men to perhaps eighty or more. To this 'running side' must be added two or three foremen, a clerk or two and the usual army of cleaners, perhaps a score or more. Nor does it end there, since to these one must be added all the various grades that make up the shed staff: once again a foreman or maybe two to supervise the work of the clerks, ash-men, coalmen, boiler-wash-ers, fire-droppers, fire-lighters, labourers, store-men, tube-cleaners; plus all the 'shop-grades' like fitters, smiths, turners and welders.

If your MPD houses thirty locomotives it could have a total complement of about 180 men, although in the real world they would not all be on site at any one time. Enginemen would be coming and going throughout the day, in addition to those already on some of the footplates or preparing or disposing of their engines. Most, but not all, of the shed staff would be around all day, even if not necessarily in view. Nonetheless, for the modeller who enjoys figure painting and subsequently posing their 'huminiatures' into realistic cameos, the MPD is a good place to practise this art. For the moment, it would not be unreasonable to see a dozen sets of enginemen and between a dozen and twenty shed staff, the latter of these mostly in civvies or standard overalls and shop-coats. (For further discussion of engine allocations and staffing issues, see Chapter 4.)

ACCOMMODATION AND FACILITIES

All this motley crew must have somewhere to work and somewhere to rest, in addition to the facilities already described for the loco-men. The minimum requirement should cover the following:

- Foreman's Office (running side)
- Foreman's Office (shed staff)
- Shedmaster's Office (possibly)
- Charge-hands' Office(s) (cleaners, fitters and so on)
- Enginemen's mess-room
- Cleaners' mess-room
- Stores/Store Office/issuing counter
- Lamp room
- Shed staff mess-room
- Staff toilets/washroom
- Fitters' workshop
- Boilermen's workshop
- Forge

All of that will take up to a considerable amount of floor space, either concentrated in one block or dispersed around the site. Given the enormous number of the original companies, the 'Big Four' and the BR regions, it is not surprising that there was no set answer as to how these facilities would be accommodated. Indeed there was little in the way of a common approach until quite late in the life of the railways. The real emergence of standardization only followed the Loans and Guarantees Act of 1929, which enabled each company of the 'Big Four', if it so chose, to set about rebuilding and modernizing its sheds and MPDs.

The Great Western Railway certainly took up the opportunity with considerable relish with the so-called 'Churchward Sheds', in their many shapes and sizes, quickly replacing many older and often ramshackle installations. These new sheds are immediately recognizable as they have many design and building features in common, notably the inclusion of most, if not all, of the listed facilities as an integral part of the main shed structure. They were usually built along one wall of the shed and were only accessible from the interior walkway. Other companies had their own answers, but the built-in solution remained the easiest, quickest and most cost-effective.

CURRENT LACK OF KITS

When viewed from the modeller's perspective, however, there is a problem in that little is to be had in the availability of suitable kits. I am unaware of anything that is both realistic and affordable. The only proper answer at the time of writing lies in the portfolio of Timber Tracks who offer a laser-cut, early two-road Churchward shed, correct in every detail, but at £163 it costs rather more than a Scalescenes creation for under £5!

In order to maintain a sense of 'realism' it is necessary to resort to 'kit-bashing' or scratch-building to reproduce these vital facilities within our project. The north light shed as modelled does not take readily to being adapted to include a built-in office block, at least not in this version.

BUILDING THE OFFICES AND STORES

I should make it clear from the outset that this is an exercise in kit recycling carried to extreme lengths. There were four major factors to be considered. The MPD certainly needed these facilities, but only one site was available so it had to be 'built to fit'. I was also interested to see what, if anything, could

be done from the bits box rather than undertaking a full scratch-build. Lastly the building would have to be both 'distressed' for Phase 2 and then 'rebuilt' for Phase 3. This was a demanding requirement, but I hope the results will show what can be achieved on a limited budget.

PLANNING

This is a simple exercise involving nothing more than tracing the site space straight off the project board and getting a rough idea of the building's eventual size and shape. Since it was destined for a triangular corner site at the front of the layout, it needed to be a roughly L- shaped block, leaving room for the planned sand furnace as a permanent feature.

The next step was to work through all the bits left over from previous builds. This yielded a lot of ancient Superquick island platform sections. The most suitable of these were laid on the tracing and

This kit of bits, which may be useful for the offices and stores block, has been put together from oddments in the bits box and includes numerous sections of Superquick, some very old Airfix canopies, replacement brick papers from Scalescenes and Howard Scenics, and various pieces of glazing material. Also in the photograph are the quickly sketched floor plan and the very simple toolkit. Some semi-finished portions may also be seen, revealing the mounting board strips used for joining and bracing the hotchpotch of components.

rearranged until a reasonable structure emerged. The use of these consistently sized sections made it easier to then envisage what the ultimate Phase 3 Steam Centre version would look like. Some parts would possibly go completely and others might be repositioned. The discovery of some completed, but long forgotten, Airfix canopies inspired further possible ideas for the final version.

It is worth pointing out that all these oddments can be cheaply acquired from among the semi-scrap and spares boxes at any toy fair. It's always worth buying this sort of junk for a few pence to create your own bits box against similar opportunities.

BUILDING THE OFFICE BLOCK

Some preparatory work was needed, notably the selection of suitable windows, which again came from the bits box. The Superquick kit's shiny walls were then covered with some spare brick print-outs from the Scalescenes shed. This both covered all the

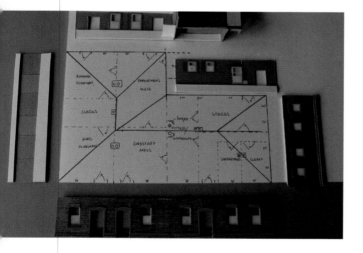

This shows the floor plan and the eventual floor/foundation. The various offices and other facilities, together with the likely positions of their fireplaces and chimneys, are marked in red. The bold green lines indicate the ridges of the 'L' shaped roof. The next stage, here omitted for clarity, would be to plot the best positions for the internal bracing and roof supports. This is an entirely hypothetical construction and the internal 'walls' are plotted to fit in with the existing doors and windows of the Superquick parts.

inevitable joins and ensured that these two adjacent buildings were better visually matched. These various steps were exactly the same as those described in the earlier chapters. Both tasks were also carried out at the same time as the Superquick sections were being fixed to pre-cut reinforcing inner walls of mounting board.

The outer walls of any L-shaped structures, six in all, have very little stability when they are joined up. It is always desirable to cut out a false floor from mounting board or foamboard and to include this as part of the assembly process. Additional corner strengtheners, if needed, can be taken from carefully cut angles, the punched-out window segments or ¼in square balsa.

We now have an open but roofless 'box' and it is necessary to remedy that situation. The best answer is to make a scale drawing, plotting the exact elevations of all the walls onto a plain sheet of paper. Remember that only hipped roofs will be possible since there are no gable ends available for your building. There are no hard and fast architectural rules for the precise slopes that should be used. With a soft pencil, which is easy to erase, and a set square, draw in a selection of pitches and decide which looks best. It may sound a bit hit and miss, and it probably is, but all that matters is whether it looks right. From your plan, and from the arrangements of doors and windows in the original walls, plot the various rooms and decide where the chimneys will protrude through the roof.

Draw it in more firmly and measure or calculate the exact roof shapes required and also the dimensions of the internal formers upon which the roof will rest. It is best to model the largest segment of the 'L' shape as a continuous item, adding the shorter section to it as a separate exercise. The illustrations should make this clear. The internal walls and roof formers must be carefully cut from mounting board or foamboard to be an exact fit within the outer walls. The roof must commence in line with the wall tops. Using your carefully drawn plans, ensure that you position some of these formers exactly where the pitch changes direction. Any additional ones can go wherever convenient.

The building is now well advanced with the bracing and roof supports all in place. The mounting board roofs are cut out and the foamboard chimney stacks are also under construction.

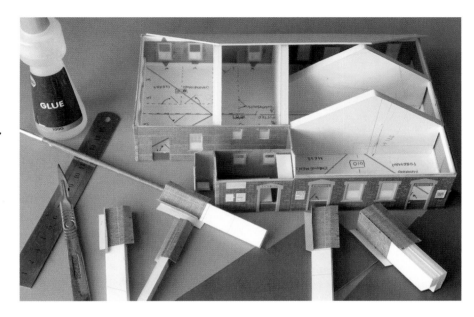

Roofs

Attention can now be given to the roofs themselves. No matter how skilled you are at drawing and measuring, it is always worthwhile to do some tests with templates cut from thick paper or thin card. You will ultimately be joining six roof sections to the two L-shaped ridge-lines, and that is easier to describe than it is to achieve. It is far better to use these quick templates to check your calculations than to find that those carefully cut final versions don't fit.

When you have got things right, it is a good idea to fix the roof paper before cutting out the apertures for the chimney stacks. Remember these will mostly be central on the ridge-line, so half of the hole must be cut from each roof piece. As a general rule adjacent offices will have their fireplaces back to back and share a common stack, albeit with separate flues and chimney pots. All the offices will have them as will any staffed stores. Only the toilets, washrooms and simple storerooms would be without. I prefer to use mounting board for the roof with the eaves actually resting on top of the walls. Always chamfer the underside to ensure a neat, snug fit. At the top it's best to let one half rest on top the other in order to give a clean sharp ridge-line. When cutting the card, make sure that the first half is shorter by the width of the card. The illustration should show this quite clearly.

Finally add your ridge tiles, lead flashing, gutters and downpipes as in the previous exercises. Should you wish you can then label some or all of the doors with the appropriate signs.

Chimney stacks

The illustration shows the rather idiosyncratic floor plan and the arrangement of the various offices. It also plots the possible location of the fireplaces and hence the chimney stacks. Not surprisingly for a building of this size, five or six stacks, including a larger one for the workshop's forges, would be about average.

Chimney stacks have already been discussed in Chapter 3, but the remarks there bear repeating. These are among the most tiresome and fiddly items to model, but unfortunately they also happen to be one of the most important features on any building. If one accepts that layouts are mostly viewed from a higher level, chimney stacks will inevitably be among the most visible items within the whole scene. I have lost count of the times I have thrown hours of work into the waste-paper bin. All too often the accepted method of folding the stacks from thinnish card simply does not work for me. It can also sometimes be difficult to find exactly the right thicknesses of balsa wood, or similar material, to provide a central solid core.

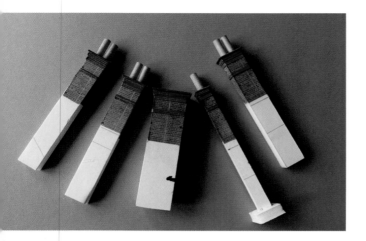

The finished chimney stacks are ready to be installed. They will be glued to the appropriate roof supports central to the ridge-line; their relative heights above the ridge is best judged by eye and the stacks will be adjusted by increasing or removing packing pieces from their bases before final gluing. The single-flue version will be glued to the actual roof itself. The chimney pots are simply cut from plastic tube, but as they are a bit oversized it would better if they were replaced with some of the many white-metal castings obtainable from the trade.

For this part of the project I hit upon an idea I hadn't tried before. There was a pile of foamboard offcuts on the bench left over from making the floor and roof supports. I measured them and found that they were nearer to 7mm thick than the stated 5mm. In scale terms that was slightly under 2ft, perhaps a bit narrow but not obviously so. A few judicious slices with the scalpel produced twin-flue stacks 14mm across and the single-flue versions 7mm square. These were easy to fabricate and equally receptive to gluing on the brick paper, using the spare buttress brick-prints from the Scalescenes sheets to ensure commonality.

The decorative relief brickwork came from scrap pieces of a Howard Scenics sheet (the version printed on thin card). These were cut into sets of five courses, three courses and two courses, which were duly applied to the top of each stack. The essential capping-stones came from the pressed-out portions of the Superquick windows. The complete job took

some time, but it proved the viability of the idea and it is one I gladly pass on as being adaptable to most, if not all, building projects. Including the time taken to touch in the exposed edges, the five stacks took about eight hours. Apart from a few less than square initial cuts, however, nothing had to be rejected and for me that was real progress.

FINAL ASSEMBLY

There isn't much to add at this point since, like most 'kit-bashing' projects, the design and the build phases are almost combined. As each problem arises so the solutions are duly thought out and the answers are simply added at that stage. I suppose in some ways it's not unlike the methods used by our rural ancestors when building their cottages with whatever was to hand, which in turn shaped the finished building without either a plan or an architect in sight. The only points worth mentioning are that certain sections of the roof were not fixed down, in case I wanted to get access for the dilapidations due in the second phase. I also made provision to be able to change the notices that would reflect those different phases.

The roof sections are now being fixed in place. Those with chimney apertures have had their tile-paper cladding stuck down prior to cutting out. The final tasks will be the ridge-tiles, valley gutters and the lead flashings around the stacks.

The finished result comes with a word of advice: if you intend to embark on any large customizing or scratch-building exercise, always ensure that you have enough of everything to complete the task. To my immense chagrin I neglected this and managed to run out of Superquick D5 roof-paper. I thought it would be simple to get another pack as it's a standard sheet, but found that the print design had been completely changed.

The front of the offices has been treated as if it were facing onto a street or approach road. Poster-boards have been fixed to the walls; in the Phase I steam era they would carry vacancy details, while the preservationists use them commercially or for period travel posters.

The inner wall would also display different signage to suit the three different stages in the life of the shed.

STATIONARY BOILER

The steam locomotive was undoubtedly a robust and relatively simple piece of engineering. In principle at least the construction and operation of the smallest tank engine differed little from that of the largest express Pacifics. Both derived their power from water heated to produce steam to drive pistons. Most people will know only too well from their kettles how the process of boiling water inevitably leads to the build-up of residual deposits of calcium and metallic salts.

Steam locomotives suffer in the same way and, depending upon the purity (or otherwise) of the water supply, their boilers become choked and inefficient. They therefore need regular cleaning, which can be a weekly exercise in hard water areas. In shed parlance, this is logically enough referred to as a 'boiler washout' and the larger MPDs would have a number of men specifically allocated to this task.

The key to the operation was the stationary boiler, which nearly always comprised the boiler and firebox of a scrapped and usually pretty ancient locomotive. In many cases this was almost built into the workshops area with only the smokebox protruding through the wall. There are examples, however, where the locomotive was more recognizable and located outside the shed, sometimes with rudimentary protection for those who had to maintain its fire seven days a week. There were even examples of nearly intact locomotives being withdrawn to carry out this humble duty in their final days before scrapping.

Our hypothetical shed allocation of thirty or more locomotives, each requiring a weekly washout, would mean dealing with five or six every day. Naturally enough, following the shed's pecking order, dirty jobs like firing the stationary boiler and clearing its firebox and smokebox will cascade down to the lowest of the low: the cleaners. Many a would-be engineman had his first firing experience on the stationary boiler, which could also provide a convenient place for a smoke away from the vigilant eyes of the charge-hand. Even the stationary boiler can be yet another excuse for a cameo of your 'huminiatures'.

MODELLING THE STATIONARY BOILER

In most instances the available kits that can combine to make the MPD are not sufficiently adaptable to permit the inclusion of a built-in boiler. Those on the project are no exception, so the installation must be external and free-standing. There are few readily accessible visual references to these features so the modeller is more or less free to fall back on the usual 'prototype for everything' argument. There is unlimited choice in respect of how much or how little gets built, but the basics are the boiler itself, some form of mounting, coal and ash heaps and a site adjacent to a shed road for the visiting engines. Protection, if that's the word, can be as elaborate, rudimentary or non-existent as you choose. A complete 'engine-house' in the same style as the other buildings would be just as appropriate as a few sheets of rusty tin replacing a long-since removed loco cab.

The boiler

In order to make it visually attractive, I have used an almost complete locomotive, minus its wheels and traction gear, mounted on a brick plinth. The shovel-

The stationary boiler is shown here prior to assembly and any weathering. The loco, which cost 50p at a toy fair, is in its near-complete state but has been repainted in matt black and has an extension chimney in place. The shelter was literally knocked together from whatever spare bits could be found and will look better once it has been weathered and some extra details included.

ling platform and coal heap have a protective shelter of tin sheets and an asbestos roof. Although in this project the boiler is free-standing, the same design could be positioned quite appropriately flush against a shed wall.

The whole appearance was determined by what I could find in the bits box. For the record, I used the following components:

Boiler: complete Italian (Lima) 4F (50p at a toy fair)
Plinth: plastic brickwork from a 1970s continental station kit
Tin sheet and girders: ex-Bilteezi coaling stage left over from a 1980s shed on 'Wessex Lines'
Asbestos roof: ex-Faller sheet 1970s
Flue and chimney: plastic drinking straw
Steps: unknown source

This 'mini-kit' was reinforced and supported on a mounting board carcass.

Construction

The construction was simplicity itself. Little was done to the loco body apart from removing the

This rarely modelled, but ever-present, facility is now ready to be sited on the layout. Once it is in position the immediate area should be weathered to include coal dust at one end and ash all around the smokebox. There should also be considerable evidence of water and puddles extending across to the adjacent track. Fire-irons and lengths of hosepipe (suitably painted layout wire) would add further authenticity.

moulded handrails and the provision of the tall flue. The only tricky bit was cutting the card former so that it covered the front of the cab and was flush to the firebox. This was done by trial and error. The dimensions of the coaling platform were determined by the amount of brickwork, tin sheet, roofing and girders I could amass. The design was no more complicated than finding the best way of fitting it together into what I hoped was a fairly realistic shelter. It's not an architectural gem, but I think it looks the part and it may also serve its real-life purpose of persuading readers to attempt something similar.

BUILDING THE TURNTABLE AND WATER TANK

TURNTABLE

The current Dapol turntable has been around since the days of BR steam. Originally a Rosebud/Kitmaster product, it was then marketed under the Airfix banner and eventually reissued as part of the Dapol range. In its long history it must have graced thousands of layouts and it continues to be popular, despite the presence of newer and more sophisticated alternatives. The design is not based on any particular prototype and is simply an interpretation of the basic 'over-girder' version. It bears a passing resemblance to the style favoured by the old GWR, but the handrails are wrong and the overhang (needed to accommodate the larger engines) is definitely not a real-world feature.

All that aside, it is a good-looking model of a 75ft turntable, hundreds of which were built by various contractors for the Big Four companies. This makes it ideal for the project, which is equally non-partisan in its location. We will build it to be operable by hand and non-mechanized, even though there are kits that can make it fully capable of remote operation. Although the assembly process is quite straightforward, it does need some extra care if it is to rotate realistically. This is especially so when it is expected to support a large and heavy engine. It is, after all, only a relatively inexpensive plastic kit that was aimed as much at the toy market as the modeller.

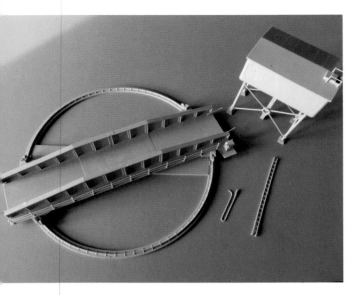

The two completed models are still unpainted and the more delicate details await fitting. Even in this raw state, however, the substituted micro-rod handrails look far superior to the recommended cotton version.

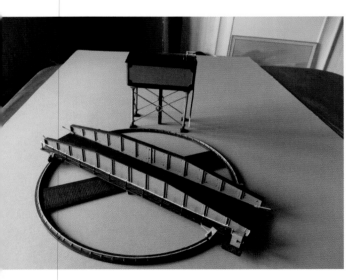

Both of the models have been finished in BR Wagon Grey (Precision P126) and matt black. Two coats were needed to get a decent overall result. The handrails and stanchions were treated to matt black and matt white, largely for effect; all-over black or even a metallic black would have been equally suitable. When these items are revisited in phase 3 they will have been repainted in GWR colours.

The instruction sheet of twelve illustrated assembly steps is more than adequate. In particular, I would underline the advice to paint some of the components before or during the build. Many areas are very difficult to get at when the model is complete. Other than that there are very few potential pitfalls, but the following comments may be useful:

- Before you begin, check all the parts for any warping and carefully straighten any that need attention, if necessary warming it by holding it in the steam from a kettle.
- Carefully remove any flash with a scalpel and check for any discernible misalignments that may have occurred in the moulding process. Double-check for these as you build each subassembly, paying special attention to key areas such as the tops of the girders.
- Use the point of a scalpel to clean or enlarge the holes into which the small pegs on the next component should be an easy but snug fit. This is particularly necessary on the four pairs of holes designed to retain the all-important carrier wheels. These items are not exactly precision-tooled, and it is vital that the wheels are as true and as free-running as you can make them, given their obvious limitations.
- Take care when fixing the girder subassemblies to the floor of the table. The riveted sides must be on the outside so that they 'click' neatly into the recesses. If they don't, you will probably find they are the wrong way round.
- The components that make up the inverted U-shaped pipework of the vacuum take-off are barely 1mm in diameter and they have to be butt joined. I would recommend doing this as a separate exercise on the workbench, ideally on a piece of glass. Ensure that they are firmly cemented together and true in all aspects; they are best left off the rest of the kit until the final assembly and painting are completed. They remain very delicate and are all too easily snapped.
- The instructions suggest that nylon thread is used to represent the guard rails on the walkway. I tried this many years ago on my first kit and finished up with

This is the repainted business end of the turntable showing the winding-gear and the vacuum take-off. The pairs of pushing-handles have been discarded as, in normal practice, one would not expect to encounter all three; there would be only one of the man-powered options, either the handles or the winding-gear, not both. Be careful with the vacuum take-off, as it's tricky to assemble and is all too easy to break. I managed to snap mine four times before the project was over.

broken stanchions and sagging rails. A better solution is to substitute some 0.25mm plastic rod. This is much easier and quicker to fix, and the end result is a far more realistic representation of the steel rails.

There are no instructions for the colour scheme on the finished kit, presumably to allow the modeller to reproduce the scheme used on their chosen region. This may not be easy, however, since coloured photos of turntables in the steam era are rare. In order to keep things 'non-regional' on the project, I opted for BR wagon grey with matt black detailing. 'Sleeper grime' was used on the walkway and the usual rail colour for the track. A similar matching colour scheme was then used for the water tank.

It should be noted that in Phase3 the turntable and the water tank will receive a repaint into GWR colours, based on the information provided in the HMRS Livery Register and the preserved example at Didcot.

WATER TANK

This Dapol kit is another veteran dating from the steam era. Like the other items in the range, it is a general-purpose tank that could be found on any railway and would be equally at home on an industrial site or military installation. Their purpose was the same as that attributed to the larger tank on the coaling stage, providing a small emergency supply and maintaining an adequate water pressure across the site. The capacity of the tank is not quoted, but the actual dimensions and a bit of basic maths suggest that it held 20,000 gallons. Its place in the project's back story is that it was erected to serve the original shed and survived the various changes of ownership. It is an easy kit to assemble and its accompanying instructions are quite adequate.

The initial extra tips given in respect of the turntable apply equally to this model. I would also add the following:

• Take special care when assembling the two pairs of tie-bars (Items 1 and 2). These will eventually be

The turntable has been installed in its well, which was carved out of the surface, using the actual model as a template. As usual the only tool required was the simple scalpel, such is the ease of working with foamboard or play foam modules. Note that the well has two levels: the deeper one is for the track and the shallower upper layer accommodates the turntable deck.

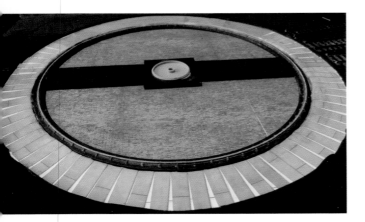

The base of the well has been covered with brick paper and the upper level has hand-cut paving slabs.

joined to the main legs (Item 5) and any mistakes will be instantly obvious. I would advise the sparing use of tube poly-cement rather than the liquid poly, since it allows a valuable few minutes for readjustment, if necessary. Note that the small fixing lugs on the outer ends of the tie-bars face differently on the short and long sides.

- The ladder is a weak link visually, since it is far too chunky and over-scale, with the rungs placed the equivalent of nearly 2ft apart. It should really be replaced with something more accurate, but if you can live with the incorrect rung spacing there is an alternative, albeit a rather tedious one. Use the flat of a sharp scalpel blade and patiently scrape away half the plastic until the whole thing looks more delicate.

- As with the turntable, there are no instructions on painting the kit and appropriate references are hard to find, since tanks like this were much too common. They could be all-over cream, grey, green or even black. To keep things consistent on the project, I opted to use the same grey and black finish as on the turntable. Also as with the turntable, the water tank will be repainted into GWR colours during Phase 3.

All things considered, this remains a justifiably popular kit that is relatively easy to construct. It is suitable for any shed installation from the smallest to the largest: larger MPDs might have two or three clustered together, reflecting the shed's expansion over the years.

ASH SHELTERS

At the start of the Second World War the entire nation, civilians and industries alike, was instructed to carry out blackout precautions. Streetlights and station lights were reduced to a bare minimum and even the few that remained were shrouded. Vehicle headlights were reduced to hooded slits and factory, shop and house windows were masked by heavy black curtains. These restrictions were enforced with a stringency that led many people to believe they were in greater danger from accidents than from stray enemy bombs.

The railways understood that they were potential targets, no matter where they were located. Carriage lighting was reduced to a single bulb in each compartment and pull-down blinds covered all the windows. Locomotive cabs had their side windows plated over and the whole expanse between cab and tender could be quickly encased in a canvas sheet. The meagre lighting at engine sheds and MPDs was still further reduced, but one problem remained, namely 'fire-dropping'.

Anyone who has watched this operation at a Steam Centre's night event will know that it is a convincing display of pyrotechnics. Sparks, hot coals and ash, and the glow from the open firebox door illuminate the whole area. Amplify that single demonstration by twenty, thirty or perhaps forty or more locomotives on the disposal roads throughout the night and it is

Didcot's 'Hall' illuminates the night-sky at a special Photographers' Evening in the mid-1970s.

easy to imagine that it would make a tempting target. The resultant glow would be easily visible to any pilot miles away and several thousand feet up.

Something had to be done quickly. The answer was to build a simple barn-like structure to cover the disposal pits and the adjacent ash road. Ash shelters came in shapes and sizes to meet the specific requirements of each particular shed. They were built as quickly and cheaply as local resources would allow. The Great Western had a sort of standard design that measured 100 x 30ft (30 x 9m), which was sufficient for most small to medium-sized sheds and could cope with two large tender-engines at the same time. It had a brick-built base with walls about 8ft high; this supported metal or timber uprights with an asbestos curtain screen immediately below the eaves. In some cases, but by no means all, there was a gap of about 5ft between the top of the wall and the screen; whether intentional or not, this allowed some of the dust and sulphurous smoke to escape. The roofs were usually corrugated iron topped by a full-length, semicircular galvanized vent.

Didcot's dilapidated ash shelter lasted into the period when the depot was acquired by the Great Western Society. This was the only photograph that could be found in the archives. The loss of the asbestos gable end, however, means that the delicate steel trusses are sufficiently clear for anyone wishing to include them on the model.

Ash shelters did their job and many remained in use for several years after the end hostilities. The threat from the air may have disappeared, but the shed staff were quick to appreciate that these primitive structures provided a degree of protection from the elements and made a dirty and unpleasant task a little more tolerable

MODELLING THE ASH SHELTER

This will have to be another exercise in scratch-building as I have been unable to find any commercial product that even remotely resembles this very basic structure. Its very simplicity, however, makes it a relatively easy task that should present few difficulties to anyone who has progressed through the previous projects or has already tackled similar jobs on their own layouts.

Choosing a prototype

The prototype was sourced from the introduction to E. Lyons's *An Historical Survey of Great Western Engine Sheds*, 1947 (Oxford Publishing Co., 1974). The drawing is based on the example located at Didcot MPD. This makes it an ideal subject for the project, since it lasted well into the preservation era under the auspices of The Great Western Society.

Didcot's example was slightly larger than the standard GWR design (see above), measuring 125 x 32ft (38 x 9.7m). Anyone wanting to attempt an even more ambitious version should look at Banbury, a few miles to the north, which had two shelters. The first was almost identical to Didcot's, but the second was large enough to span three roads. Their construction was similar, except that at Banbury the asbestos cladding completely enclosed the side walls. The project here could easily be adapted to combine any of these variations.

Will it fit?

Turning to the build itself, the first step is to check how large a footprint the layout can accommodate. In terms of width this is predetermined since it must span the two relevant tracks, which on the model dictates a minimum of 28ft (112mm). The length, however, will present a problem since Didcot's 125ft would equate to 600mm, which is far too long for the shed; even half of that would be squeeze. It would also entail reducing the eight 12ft 6in bays on the plan to just six. There are no problems, though, with the scale height and all the necessary construction materials are easy to obtain. I always prefer to do this initial planning phase while starting to decide the various materials that might be needed. This approach certainly paid dividends on this occasion.

Materials

The supporting brick wall, which is 8ft (32mm) tall, could come from mounting board covered on both sides with Howard Scenics brick paper. This would underline its newness against the existing older brickwork of the adjacent coaling stage. The asbestos-screens, which are 5ft deep, could be sourced from the appropriate download from Model Railway Scenery, laminated either side of a sheet of 200gsm drawing paper to provide extra strength without undue thick-ness. The corrugated iron roof could come from the same source, but with a base of thin card. The usual material for thin card is the back of a scrap pad, but unfortunately these are always A4 (295mm), which is

This is the scratch-build kit of parts for the shelter with some of the pre-printed cladding already fixed. The book is E. Lyons's An Historical Survey of Great Western Engine Sheds, 1947 (Oxford Publishing Co., 1974), which provided the basic details for the construction.

5mm short for the current plan. It would seem to make little or no visible difference, however, if the whole structure was shortened by that small amount, reducing the length of each bay by a mere 1mm.

According to the original drawing, the roof and the screens were supported on the uprights that divided the bays. They were shown as being 6in square timber. Since I had nothing suitable to hand, however, I opted to go for 6in (2mm) 'L' girder, using my supply of Evergreen plastic. Since it was obvious that the end result would be very flimsy, some form of base or false ceiling would be necessary. The presence of the tracks and ash pits ruled out any kind of base, so the sensible answer was to repeat the exercise already proven on the Bilteezi shed. A false ceiling of 7mm foamboard would provide all the required stability and could be hidden behind the screens and gable ends.

Preparing the 'kit'

The 'kit of bits' and assembly processes were now determined.

All the components were given pre-printed sheets cut to fit. A few minor amendments were made to the plan: the two brick walls were left at their original 300mm length and some additional foamboard for bracing and reinforcing was cut and shaped to fit behind the gable ends.

Putting it together

Assembly was relatively straightforward using the glue stick to fix the pre-printed sheets and clear or universal glue to join the various components and subassemblies. The only words of advice needed are that construction is easier if it is carried out upside down. The false ceiling, gable ends, roof strengtheners/profiles and the rear roof section should be completed first. Leave the front roof section until later to make handling easier. When it comes to papering the walls, remember to add small strips to cover the four exposed ends. This may seem more tiresome than simply wrapping paper around the whole job, but it gives a better end result. The fourteen girders need to be painted in the matt black of structural steelwork. Not only is this best done before fixing, it is easier if it is done before the strips are cut to size. This can be left until they are *in situ*, but you

False ceiling	1 x 7mm foamboard 295 x 112mm (74 x 28ft)
Brick walls	2 x mounting board 295 x 32mm (74 x 8ft)
Roof sections	2 x A4 scrap pad 295 x 66mm (74 x 16ft 6in)
	(width obtained by drawing and measurement)
Girders	14 x 2mm L-section plastic 72mm (18ft)
Gable ends	2 x shaped scrap pad 112 x 44mm (28 x 11ft)

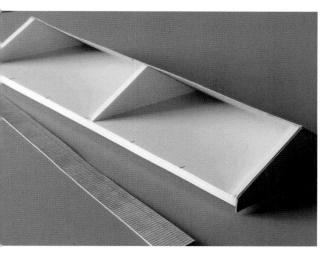

Without some significant strengthening the shelter would have been too flimsy and difficult to build. The use of 7mm foamboard to make the false ceiling, roof supports and gable ends provided the necessary solution.

will then need a very fine brush, a steady hand and two and a half hours to spare, as I discovered.

Turning our attention to the walls, fix the painted uprights at the correct intervals. Once these are secure, glue the asbestos screens along the tops. The rear wall can be added first but don't forget to 'nick' the foamboard ceiling to accept the flanges of the 'L' girders. Carry out any internal weathering that you wish and then repeat the process with the front wall. Check that everything is properly square and vertical, correcting any faults with additional fillets of card. Finally you can now fix the front roof section in place and weather the whole roof area. There is no need to overdo the pastel dust as this particular downloaded sheet is well finished.

Full-length smoke vent

All that now remains is the tricky problem of the half-curved, full-length smoke vent. There is little to help us in the original drawings, with no dimensions and nothing about its construction. After studying all the available photographs, I decided that the material is probably galvanized iron, which is almost rust-proof and is the same as that used for livestock drinking troughs and cold tanks in older properties. Here it would be used in overlapping 10ft lengths and curved to 30–36in diameter.

These half-round shapes are among the most difficult to recreate in model form. Despite searching everywhere I have been unable to find a suitably sized and shaped section in either brass or plastic, although this doesn't mean that there is no such thing. In the end I had to resort to the traditional method of wrapping thickish 250gsm drawing paper around a correctly sized core, in this case an Evergreen plastic tube (11.1mm or $^{7}/_{16}$in diameter). The circumference of the vent was calculated to require a strip of paper at least 17.5mm wide. The actual piece was made

The coats of enamel have now dried and left the shell sufficiently rigid to remove it from the plastic-tube former. It can now be cut and trimmed to its proper size and fixed to the roof. Don't forget to add the distance-pieces of 2mm 'L' girder to the underside.

The finished ash shelter is now ready to be sited. The semi-open sides of this Didcot version make an ideal model since it allows at least a glimpse of what is going on inside.

This is the usual modeller's-eye view of the ash shelter with its tin roof showing obvious signs of weathering and rust. The downloaded sheets from Model Railway Scenery are of excellent quality in respect of colour and revealed no evidence of shine. My only observation is that the size of individual tin sheets seems rather larger than I would have expected, scaling out at more than 12 x 5ft (3.6 x 1.6m).

slightly oversize and, with one side as the machine-cut edge, the second side was carefully ruled to the final width. The paper was then tightly wrapped around the tube, secured with elastic bands and treated to several coats of liquid glue, followed by an equal number of matt black enamel.

While this was being allowed to dry, I located a plain grey printout from the Scalescenes shed and cut it into the required 10ft lengths (40 x 17.5mm). Simulated joints and rivets were added to one end of each strip with a fine black pen. Once the job was ready the strips were glued in place along the vent, each one overlapping the previous by the length of the drawn joint.

The completed vent was now ready to be installed, but it had to stand clear of the roof by several scale inches in order for the smoke and steam to escape. Once again the L-shaped strip came in handy. It was cut into a series of small distance pieces and duly glued to the underside of the vent about 1mm in from the edge. The flanges were then glued to the roof itself, taking particular care to keep the vent aligned to the ridge and equidistant on both sides.

Conclusions

The final task alone needs to be spread over several hours, due to drying times required, but it is worth the extra effort since the vent and roof detail are the most consistently viewed parts of the whole building.

The actual ash shelters were nothing to look at and the model is unlikely to be hailed as a fine example of creative art, but it is an unusual feature with a story to tell about shed life during the Second World War and the drab years that followed. Now that the basic design and relevant measurements have been established, the average modeller should be able to reproduce a shelter in a couple of evenings.

CREATING THE YARD

This is the point when we discover whether our initial thoughts, plans, sketches and carefully constructed buildings will all combine into a visually satisfying whole. For those who are aiming for an operating layout, it must also be capable of being worked in a properly 'railway-like' manner. The project has been designed to fit within the rather artificial constraints of two A1 boards, while at the same time providing a suitable setting for all the many structures that have been demonstrated. This is an unlikely scenario for the majority of modellers, who are best advised to cherry-pick those elements that they judge to be relevant to their own situation.

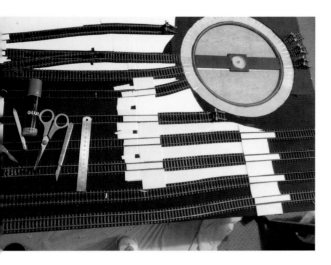

The shed layout with the track in place and the strips of play foam inserted where necessary. The first layers bring the surface up to sleeper height and the second, shown in white for clarity, take it to rail height. The few items needed for the job are shown and the whole exercise shouldn't take more than a couple of hours. Note that, where it represents the concrete areas around the sheds, it only extends a short way inside and the rest is out of view.

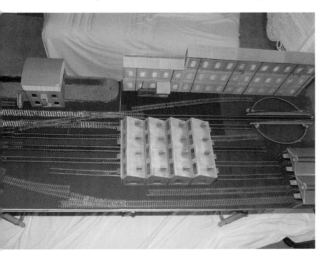

It was obviously a lot easier to complete the ballasting before all these buildings were installed. Some extra work was then needed to properly bed them in. No work has been done to construct the ash pit and inspection pits as these are all hidden inside the buildings. Should you wish them to be outside, the Scalescenes shed includes some excellent artwork.

Chapter 3, which deals with the yard aspects for the larger two-road sheds, contains all the necessary information regarding surface levels, finishes, colours and detailing. These apply equally on this MPD project, but there is a much bigger area to consider. The main points for the operators to bear in mind are that the clearances are frequently inadequate and the arrangements shown are wholly dependent upon offstage access roads. I would suggest that the layout should be built with at least an extra 3in of width (6in would be even better). Details of the available access will be influenced by your choice of points and by either the rest of your layout or by the cassettes or traverser installed, if the model is to be a stand-alone version.

- Don't be afraid to rearrange the tracks and point-work to get the optimum balance between storage roads and ease of movement between the various facilities.
- Remember that single and double slips, together with three-way points, can save plenty of space. They are not cheap but they are worth seeking out second-hand at toy fairs, although you should make sure they still work.
- Try to avoid short-radius points except in locations that are restricted to your smaller tank engines.
- Use simple play foam to establish your levels: it's cheap, easy to source and very easy to work.
- Experiment with colours and finishes and try to find some good images to inspire your palette.
- Don't forget the junk and debris. The closer you have set your model to the mid-1960s the more of this there will be. Accessory packs are an obvious source, as are loco detailing parts.

Provided everything has indeed gone to plan, you should now be able to look at your finished MPD with a degree of pride. We have come a long way from that first Alphagraphix single-road shed. All that now remains is to bring it to life with engines and people, and see how it can be changed in the next decades of its back story.

CHAPTER SEVEN

THE MPD IN THE STEAM ERA

This is the point at which life might have been easier if we had been modelling a particular MPD rather than a hypothetical example. We could simply have referred back to our research data and extracted all the information about allocations, staffing and duties. If our research had been sufficiently thorough, it might even have been possible to tie that down to a specific date or at least a precise year. As it is, we must rely on the back story to produce a credible version of the likely activities and the typical motive power that would have been needed. The advantage of this, though, is that we can choose the engines that we would like or already have in our collections. The details of the back story may need to be tweaked, but that is always an essential part of what is commonly known as 'modeller's licence'.

TRAFFIC DEMANDS

GOODS WORKINGS

The back story would seem to indicate that our particular 'Anytown' is a modestly industrialized centre, with local traditions in the areas of furniture and fabrics. It still has the old Carriage & Wagon Works generating traffic. No doubt many other factories are busily producing items for the burgeoning national economy. This would all add up to considerable goods traffic based on the principle of 'raw materials in and finished products out'. One could therefore expect to find a number of local goods depots and goods yards, as well as a fairly large yard needed by the C & W works. Additional freight traffic would come

A reminder of a typical scene on shed in the steam era. This is Didcot in the early years of British Railways and therefore quite appropriate to start this chapter.

This is our own MPD in its steam-era phase and showing a fairly typical allocation of engines. There is an obvious bias towards the GWR/BR (W) with a couple of Southern locos also on shed. In order to maintain the back story, most of the stud comprises freight and mixed-traffic types. The Hall, which is clearly the shed's pride and joy, would be rostered for specific turns such as express-parcels and semi-fast passenger runs.

ABOVE LEFT AND RIGHT: *These aerial views show just how much stock could be accommodated in such a relatively small area. Under normal operating conditions one would not have so many locos jostling for space. During the morning peak they would be going off-shed in their required sequence, leaving the yard almost empty save for those on later turns or in for maintenance or a boiler washout. Remember that the track plan has been compressed to fit within the confines of two A1 boards; it is still operationally viable but needs an extra 3in of width to maintain the correct clearances.*

from the normal urban demands for domestic and industrial coal, and the local gasworks would need its regular supply of coking coal. Last, but by no means least, would be the incoming loads of consumer-led items from foodstuffs to durables.

PASSENGER WORKINGS

Passenger traffic would fall into two distinct categories: inbound commuters coming from the outlying areas and outbound commuters heading for the nearest city; and longer-distance traffic of inter-regional trains and those destined for the capital. It would not be in any way far-fetched to suggest that some of these workings would originate from our own station, while others might require an engine change.

PLANNING THE ALLOCATION

We have therefore established a need for a wide variety of engine types within the allocation of about thirty locos. The various yards will all need their own shunters (more properly known as yard pilots). The station itself will require a pilot to both attach and detach vehicles and act as a replacement for any engine that has failed on a through service. The regular trip-workings between the yards, together with the local pick-up goods trains, will create a further demand for smaller freight engines. When it comes to the heavier and longer-haul trains, something more substantial will be needed.

The passenger side is equally diverse in its requirements , ranging from the smaller and quicker 'suburban-tanks', through the mixed-traffic locomotives, to at least a couple of moderately powerful express-passenger engines.

MEETING THE DEMANDS

This is not the place to suggest exactly which classes and locos you should buy. By now you should have chosen a geographic area and the appropriate company or BR region, as well as knowing exactly

ABOVE LEFT AND RIGHT: *Two more semi-aerial views of the shed complex. The first is taken from the roof of the north light 'new shed' looking towards the offices and the access roads, the second looks the other way towards the Carriage & Wagon Works and the turntable.*

what is already lurking in your stock box. We will now go one step further, however, and try to match the implied demands by establishing the probable 'links' that our MPD would operate. Don't forget that the career progression for all enginemen was only achieved by working through the ranks from fireman up to driver. It was all about experience, route knowledge and seniority: 'fast-track' training courses were far in the future.

Links

There is nothing very scientific about what follows. It's little more than an exercise in balancing logic and numbers, but the results appear to be fairly realistic when compared with real-life examples in the archives. There are seven links to cover the shed's duties, needing an interesting cross-section of motive power to handle them. No attempt has been made to quote any classes as every region will have its own type for each requirement.

That gives an allocation of twenty-eight engines, which is just about as many as one could squeeze into the space available on the project. Not all of

The design of the coaling stage and the relative siting of the disposal road and ash shelter will leave room for an extra siding. In this shot it is duly occupied by the depot's breakdown crane. The A1x 'Terrier' is using the ramp as head-shunt to marshal the outgoing coal empties on the offstage yards.

No 1	Shed link	Shed pilot and C & W pilot	two 0-6-0Ts and one spare
No 2	Goods link	Yard pilots and trip freights	three 0-6-0Ts and one spare
No 3	Goods link	Pick-up goods and local goods	two 0-6-0Ts
No 4	Goods link	Through freights	two 2-6-0s, two 2-8-0s and one spare
No 5	Passenger link	Station pilot and stopping-passenger	four 2-6-2Ts and one 2-6-0
No 6	Passenger link	Semi-fast inter-regionals and express-parcels	four 4-6-0 M/T and one spare
No 7	Passenger link ('Top-link')	Mainline duties	four 4-6-0 passenger

these would be on-shed at any one time. It would also be more than acceptable practice to introduce a few veteran locos, spending their last days at some branch-line sub-shed and returning for minor repairs or their weekly boiler wash-outs. At the other end of the scale will be visiting 'foreign' engines, express and heavy-freight, coming on-shed for turning and servicing before taking their return workings back home.

At the far end of the shed yard a visiting H15 has been coaled and turned and is about to go off-shed to pick up its return working. This is one of the author's more bizarre episodes in 'kit bashing': the boiler and footplate are mostly from an Airfix 'Schools', some fittings are brass and white-metal, other parts are scratch-built, the chassis and power unit are from a Bachmann B1 spares pack and the tender is ex-Lord Nelson. No two H15s seemed alike and many were altered during their lifetimes, so mine just sits on the end of that hybrid class.

Even in the early 1950s young men still wanted to work on the railways. This little bunch of ex-National Service squaddies have swapped their denims for the more glamorous uniform of the Teddy Boys. First impressions count and the Shed-master and his staff may not be too impressed! The Teddy Boys are by Langley and the others by Airfix/Dapol.

The general area in front of the 'old shed' is usually home to the smaller engines in the allocation.

Mix and match

If one assumes that the MPD is a stand-alone layout fed from an appropriate bank of storage sidings, sector-plates or cassettes, the possible movements are almost endless. The variety of different classes that could be displayed during a session, at home or on the exhibition circuit, is equally vast. In real life the Shedmaster would go out of his way to reduce the number of classes as far as he could, but such niceties need not restrict the modeller. While the Shedmaster and his Running Foreman would doubtless prefer their nine 0-6-0 tanks to all be the same, the modeller can happily supply all nine from different classes, with different power ratings and, to a degree, even from different eras.

HUMINIATURES

This is always going to be a controversial subject guaranteed to produce heated debate. I cannot recall exactly when layouts began to appear almost devoid of human life, but it is a fairly recent phenomenon. Nor can I understand why this should be, unless most commercially available figures fail to match the increasingly high standards of locomotives, rolling stock and infrastructure. There is no doubt that the UK market is poorly served in this respect, with nothing like the immense choice of accurately sculpted figures readily available to our European colleagues. It is small wonder, then, that their layouts are always well populated, while ours have an almost post-nuclear air of abandonment.

REALISTIC STAFFING

When it comes to archive photographs of steam sheds, the sceptics can quickly point to a real-life lack of human activity. This is as undeniable as there is a simple explanation: most amateur photographers could only gain access to the sheds on a Sunday, and

Under normal circumstances the boiler washouts would be located adjacent to, or even be integral to, one of the main buildings. Since the layout plan ruled it out, this seemed the best alternative site. It was also conveniently served by its own 'wash-out siding', which would fit well into the changes planned for the later phases.

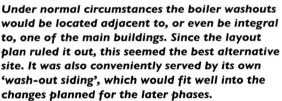

RIGHT: *The boiler washout staff are in for a busy shift with two engines already queuing for attention. These two small tank engines have come for their regular weekly service. The small dock tank will return to its branch sub-shed later in the day. (The relaxing enginemen are from Mike's Models and Dapol.) The second engine is GWR 5 Portishead, which is the resident shed pilot and normally does the same job on the author's loft layout. The actual Portishead started life on the London, Brighton and South Coast Railway (LB&SCR) and was sold to the Weston, Clevedon and Portishead Light Railway in 1925 before being absorbed by the Great Western. I simply had to have this little A1x as I saw the real one in Swindon works in the early 1950s.*

The Castle has just been coaled and is making its way down the disposal road to wait for the turntable. Queuing was always a problem on busy sheds, especially at the end of the day. It would not be too difficult to envisage, or indeed model, a procession of returning engines on the shed approach queuing first to drop their fires, the shuffling forward to the coaling stage and then awaiting their turn on the table. If the turntable was only hand-operated then delays would be inevitable: the engine would need to be perfectly balanced and then pushed slowly through an almost 180-degree turn. The shed foreman would have his work cut out to keep things moving.

A typical morning scene as the engines wait to go off-shed for their various duties. They will probably take a quick top-up from the water cranes conveniently sited between the tracks. No doubt the crews will be enjoying their first cup of tea and a Woodbine, the fireman will have turned on the pep-pipe to hose down the coal and then washed the footplate clear of dust. If the coal is particularly dusty and they are rostered to have some tender-first running, he may well ease forward and use the bag on the water-crane to drench the whole load.

The elderly Pannier has clearly been failed by its driver, much to the displeasure of the Running Foreman. The spark arrester suggests it was due for the morning shunt over at the Carriage & Wagon Works, so the fitters have been called out to get it moving as quicklu as possible.

ABOVE LEFT AND RIGHT: *The cleaners are putting the finishing touches to* **Lady Margaret Hall**, *affectionately known to everyone as 'Maggie'. These would-be footplate men are toiling under the watchful eyes of the senior lad and one of the charge-hands. (The cleaners are by Langley, the charge-hand was an Airfix passenger and the senior lad an Airfix USAF ground crew.)*

then usually with an official tour. These were naturally timed for periods when the place was at its quietest and the attendant risks were minimal. (I know this to be true from visits to Swindon's running shed, which entailed a twenty-mile Sunday cycle-ride each way for the privilege.) The other reason is equally obvious in that, whenever visits took place, the objective was to get photos of the engines without wasting any of the expensive film on intruding persons. Autobiographies give a far more accurate impression of shed life as it was lived at the time.

It would, however, be easy to justify a score or more figures on the project MPD engaged on their daily tasks, appropriately divided as they were in real life with the footplate staff on one side (more properly referred to as the 'running side') and the shed staff and special grades on the other. The former would be doing exactly as has been described in the earlier chapters, except there would be more of them. The important thing to remember is to position them as realistically as their poses will allow.

Unfortunately the choice of poses is rather limited since only three main suppliers cover this period: Dapol, Langley and Monty's Models. The trick, if there is one, is to separate those in the same pose and spread them around the site. If they can appear to be doing something different each time, then so much the better. For example the same figure of a driver simply 'standing', might be reading the noticeboard, examining the cylinders on his engine, chatting to a foreman or fitter or just arriving with his bike. As long as each 'cameo' is remote from the others, their similarity will be less obvious.

Another view of the shed yard as the various crews go about their business, some probably going to sign off at the end of their shift, while others are heading for their engines or collecting their full set of 'irons'.

As the Castle moves up the yard the elderly Earl inches forward to get beneath the chute. If the driver is a bit slow off the mark he can expect to be shouted at by the coalman ready poised with his tub of Welsh coal. 'Coalmen' and 'patience' were words rarely heard together on a busy shed.

The loaded coal wagons were always parked on the level, or very gently sloped, track on the far side of the stage. As they were unloaded they were simply heaved out onto the ramp to roll down into the waiting sidings. The next full one would then be pushed or pinch-barred on the stage.

ABOVE LEFT AND RIGHT: *Some more views across the yard. If your shed is going to be operable, always make sure that your nicely posed figures don't get in the way of engine movements. Accidents were all too common in the days of steam, but that is one aspect that we don't want to replicate in miniature.*

Many of the footplate crews will, of course, be permanent fixtures on their respective engines, as no one wants to see empty cabs when they are actually running. This will use up most of the figures in more energetic poses that may be more difficult to deploy in relaxed roles. It is always worthwhile searching for other figures, even from non-railway kits, that might be painted and posed to augment the meagre selection currently available.

All these remarks apply equally to the shed staff and the specialist grades, such as fitters, boilermen and welders. There is a slightly better choice here as Langley, in particular, offers a number of sets with workers engaged on specific tasks. Of these the most useful are obviously the cleaners, the welding sets and the soldiers in fatigues. Remember that industrial clothing was still some way in the future and ex-army or government surplus was as common on the railway as it was on the land. Shed staff in the general labouring jobs would also wear life-expired 'civvies' and this is well represented in the Dapol sets. In that context it's worth looking for RAF wartime ground-crew (wearing the 'fore and aft' forage caps) and any military figures wearing berets. I wish I could include some of the exquisite little HO personnel from Preiser, but, while their civilians are acceptable on the platforms,

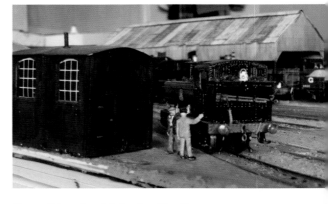

One of toughest jobs for the fireman was topping up the sanders. These are as important to the enginemen as coal and water. Usually it meant picking one's way across the yard to the furnace, filling the bucket with dry sand, staggering back and then heaving it, head-height, up onto the footplate before climbing up and emptying it into the hopper. Often when rails were icy or wet in winter the fireman, or some equally unfortunate labourer, might need to do this a dozen times just to get one engine ready for the road. No wonder European and US engines had their sand hoppers on top of the boilers where it was kept dry and could be topped up mechanically. Here the driver of the tank loco has saved his fireman the job and taken the engine over to the sand furnace.

Enginemen coming on duty scan one of the boards for any special traffic notices while the Running-foreman chats to other crews on their way home. It's worth remembering that car ownership was a luxury throughout the 1950s and even senior top-link enginemen used the humble bicycle as their main method of transport.

Two more views from the operator's eye-level showing what were doubtless known in shed-parlance as 'front yard' and 'back yard'. Note how the bulk of the old Carriage & Wagon Works dominates the background in the second photo, exactly as on the original plan.

their railway figures are not only too small, they are also far too 'continental' in appearance.

The accompanying fully captioned illustrations will, I hope, show some of the more obvious cameos and groupings that can be achieved using a mix of figures. Inevitably many items have been duplicated into different roles and I'm sure that readers will have many more imaginative versions for their own layouts.

MPD POTENTIAL

The steam-era MPD can offer enormous potential, especially for the modeller who is strapped for space. It imposes few demands for scenic work and it need not be seen solely as an adjunct to a larger layout with its attendant running lines. Above all, it is an unrivalled showcase for an extensive collection of locomotives that may come from any region. It may be set at any time from before the 'Big Four' to the end of steam and the dawn of the diesels. Its overall shape (or footprint, if you prefer) is infinitely vari-

The fitters are busy working on the elderly LMS 3F. The welding set is one the many specialist kits available from Langley, which also offers an arc-welding set that may be interesting if your shed has a breaker's line. One of the foremen is chatting to the engineman off the 4F that will probably have to take over from its smaller relative.

Another view showing part of the allocation posed in front of the imposing 'new' north light shed. It's easy to envisage how even more of these Scalescenes kits could be combined into a truly impressive multi-road version, although you would need the extra space and trackwork to accommodate and operate it.

It was never easy to keep a steam shed neat and tidy, but the labourers did their best and doubtless enjoyed a chat while they worked, perhaps asking one of the enginemen going off duty to put a couple of bob on the outsider in the two-thirty at Newbury. (The labourers are by Langley and the rest are Airfix/Dapol.)

able from 'short and fat' to 'long and thin'. If you have room for it, then 'fan-shaped' is ideal.

An MPD can suit the needs of the non-operating collector who merely seeks an interesting and realistic diorama in which to display his array of motive power, and yet it can also provide an operator with hours of challenging fun moving engines on- and off-shed. Indeed, if one then adds in the appropriate timetable for the various duties and the implications of dealing with visiting locomotives, the tasks facing the model shed-master should be more than sufficient to occupy even the most enthusiastic operator managing thirty or forty engines chipped for DCC and preparing for computerization.

The cleaners have now turned their attention to the recently ex-works 2-8-0. In our 1950s setting the Great Western 'mid-chrome-green' would have been replaced by BR's more sombre unlined black, but it would still be pristine and shiny, at least for a week or two.

One final view of the shed shows the appealing elevation of these north light buildings that is so distinctive. The two engines on the 'back roads' give a better idea of the shed's overall size.

CHAPTER EIGHT

THE MPD IN PRESERVATION: THE EARLY DAYS

Anyone visiting one of today's preserved lines or steam centres would be hard put to imagine how they looked in the early days of the steam preservation movement close to fifty years ago. Those were the days before health and safety regulations, risk assessments and bureaucracy took a dominant position. It wasn't exactly laissez-faire: prospective visitors were expected to watch out for themselves and to recognize that they were entering a semi-industrial and largely unregulated environment without a yellow jacket to be seen.

These were places where a handful of deeply committed individuals were striving against the odds to preserve our industrial heritage. With hindsight it is difficult to say which was in shortest supply: experience, equipment or cash.

Nonetheless, they regularly opened their doors to fellow enthusiasts and to the more adventurous, or just plain curious, family parties. Aside from the grime and potential hazards, they were certainly exciting places to visit. Without wishing to take anything from the contemporary scene, their very informality was part of their attraction and I'm sure it did much to recruit many new volunteers, both young and old. For the modeller they offer a real challenge as there is a lack of reference materials and the only sources available might be the first editions of the various society guides and handbooks. If one were fortunate enough to have encountered them at first hand, however, one's own memories and personal photographs would make the perfect starting point.

There will be a lot of tarpaulins in this chapter, but you will need to make your own. The 4mm range by Roger Smith offers examples of the familiar black 'wagon-sheets' as branded for the Big Four companies and for the original pre-grouping railways, but none of them meet our needs. Fortunately they are easy to make from thin paper, kitchen film or even kitchen foil. Batch production is the answer. Simply tape the chosen material to a piece of card or the cutting mat, and then get to work with enamels or acrylics. Aim for suitably washed-out greens and rusty browns. Details of the owners or hire companies can be added with a white gel pen.

REWORKING THE PROJECT

For the project I have taken our already modelled MPD and rolled it forward in time to a few years after closure by BR. The various structures will still appear but they are now more dilapidated and are possibly even damaged or part dismantled. Most of the trackwork could still be in place, but the odd lifted siding and the rapid advance of nature would be much in evidence. The key features would, of course, be the accumulation of items assembled on site by the various work groups, ranging from active locos and stock still in ticket to the hulks recently rescued from the locomotive scrapyards at Barry in South Wales and scrapped vintage carriages and wagons. Some of these will be being worked on, even though we are modelling a public open day. Some will be parked awaiting attention and may be covered by the ubiquitous sheets of mostly green or brown tarpaulins.

There will undoubtedly be some locomotives and rolling stock that have been restored, even if only cosmetically, and these would be rolled out for viewing, perhaps even for 'cabbing'. By this point many of the first generation of diesels had been withdrawn and a few shabby specimens could even add an extra dimension to the scene.

These events were intended to raise funds and as such they could well include car boot sales and market stall displays by the resident groups. Others might have memorabilia on display in carriages or vans, while any located in the shed's offices would be reliant on hand-painted signage. Catering could be in a retired buffet car or housed in the shed, and the ice-cream concession would be operating from the customary Bedford van.

OPERATING ATTRACTIONS

The main visitor attractions would be footplate rides up and down the yard or brake van rides for the less adventurous. These features might be accessed from temporary platforms, part of the coaling stage or by simple steps. Remember that informality is the key and even the hallowed footplates might be crowded with family groups. Naturally any signage would likely be hand painted and safety barriers, if they existed

at all, would be road pins and blue rope. If you can manage it, some of the exhibits might be marked off with the familiar red and white safety tapes.

VOLUNTEERS AND VISITORS

Your back story will have determined where the shed is located and the space now available for a car park, vintage bus services or a pathway from an adjacent BR station.

That brings us to the 'huminiatures' and here we need to differentiate between the resident work groups going about their business and the visiting public. Both of these can come from any of the often expensive, pre-painted accessory packs or from your own treatment of unpainted plastic or white metal figures. The main thing to remember is to avoid 'high visibility' styles and try to recreate the colours and styles of the late 1960s and early 1970s.

AROUND THE SITE

In terms of stock almost anything might be included, even if it couldn't actually move. The early steam centres were rarely focused on preserving the artefacts of just one company or region. Indeed it would not be out of place to have at least one genuinely foreign loco on display. The company most likely to provide the working steam element would probably be the old LMS, which was the last region to withdraw steam, so Black Fives and 8Fs were early acquisitions. Industrials too were popular in this early period and would be seen in the livery of their previous owners or repainted into the colours of their preservation group.

The site area is the two A1 foamboards and simply adapts the existing MPD layout to suit its new role. Much of the detail is hypothetical, but that doesn't mean we should abandon our goal of achieving a 'railway-like' atmosphere and 'prototypical' appearance. My own reference points were frequent visits to 'Steamtown' at Carnforth, the early days of the GWS at Didcot and the yard at Bridgnorth on the Severn Valley Railway. This project, however, is very much about 'inspiration' and the ways to pack a lot of activity and modelling into a relatively small area. Since it is free

These first glimpses of the new phase in the life of our MPD captures some of the atmosphere of the early years of the preservationists. In the late 1960s and early 1970s Carnforth's Steamtown and the GWS at Didcot were starting to attract steam enthusiasts and families looking for somewhere different to visit. Much of the infrastructure remained intact, even though often somewhat the worse for wear. There was little evidence of rules and regulations, being more like adventure playgrounds for kids of all ages. The former buffet car seen near the coaling stage is now doing the same job as an on-site facility.

of constraints, one can easily justify visits from the ever-popular Thomas alongside a gloriously restored A4 or pristine Castle, perhaps backed by a row of rusting Black Fives and Bulleids.

DISTRESSING THE SITE

As you will recall from the back story recounted in Chapter 4, this project is currently in Phase Two of a cycle of three. Our final exercise will be to bring the 'Steam Centre' up to the present day. That poses a modelling dilemma, since any evidence of dereliction that we carry out in the current phase must be reversible on the final part of the project. This was one of reasons for selecting certain kits and the use of some recycled items. Such constraints do not apply on your own layout, as I think it most unlikely that you would wish to model all three periods. Your choice of shed or sheds is entirely your own.

Although the depot may have passed almost immediately from BR to its new private owners, that does not necessarily imply that it was handed over in good order. Those sheds that survived up to and beyond the steam era were, all too often, in a very neglected state. Most had received no maintenance for many years and, together with the absence of any shed labourers, had become almost no-go areas from a safety standpoint.

Many of the new owners found themselves repairing buildings rather than restoring locomotives. The weather would have continued to take its toll and acts of vandalism – corporate as well as individual – would be much in evidence. The following lists are not comprehensive, nor are all the suggestions modelled on the finished layout, but they may give some idea of what you might wish to portray:

- Damaged roofs, from a few missing slates to whole sections exposed to the rafters. Hasty repairs with asbestos or tin sheets would be obvious. In other places tarpaulins would be there to protect leaks.
- Damaged doors and rotting woodwork.
- Broken or missing windows and frames, and boarded-up offices and stores.

The younger members of the family would often entertain themselves, while the head of the household was happy to be reunited with his early years, probably getting a lot closer to real live steam than ever before.

- Heaps of debris and general detritus simply shoved away from more public areas.
- Puddles of mucky water from blocked drains, pitted roadways and burst pipes.
- Broken gutters and missing downpipes.
- Damaged walls and sites where equipment had simply been torn out.
- Deeply rutted entrances and roadways.
- Broken and missing fences.
- Rusting, distorted or lifted sidings and abandoned turntable pits.

Any of the above could be modelled in its most raw state and other items can show signs of the repairs being undertaken. To model this with any accuracy will mean having to remove sections carefully from the pristine kits and then scratch-building the new elements for the damaged version. Most of this requires imagination and ingenuity rather than any advanced model-making skills. Those who have dabbled in military modelling may have a head start since 'damage is damage', whether caused by military intervention or plain neglect.

CREATING DAMAGE

The biggest and most obvious areas to suffer would be the roofs and any attendant features, such as chimneys and smoke vents. Initially you need to determine just how much damage you want to model: too much and the damage will become an unwanted focus for attention; too little and it's probably not worth the effort. I decided to use the Bilteezi shed and to opt for two main areas of damage with one of them partially covered by tarpaulin. I then added a few missing and slipped slates. Concentrating all the damage on just one side implies that this was the side facing the prevailing wind. In order to make these tasks a bit easier, and given that the shed has its reinforcing fixed ceiling, the two roof sections were modelled as detachable.

The exposed damage involved cutting out an irregular area to show how the slates had been torn away in strips and groups until they encountered their more securely fixed neighbours. The next task is making up the revealed ribs and any visible por-

tions of the main roof trusses. I plead absolutely no architectural knowledge here and merely created the trusses and laths using various balsa and card strips to knock up something that looked right.

Tarpaulins

Turning our attention to the 'repair' jobs with the tarpaulins, there is obviously no need to cut out the whole area. I suggest that only one corner is dealt with to reveal just some odd laths and one rib. I would avoid using the railway-type wagon sheets but instead make up your own sheet representing about 20ft square (50 x 50mm). I have tried several materials for this and tend to opt for either a thin plastic sandwich bag, sheets of toilet tissue or even baking foil. They all need to be pre-painted with suitable green or reddish-brown matt enamel. Fix the pieces of sheet, cut larger than you need, to a piece of scrap card, pulled tight and secured with masking tape. Paint the whole area to give a uniform coating then cut out the squares you need with a scalpel. Use the same method for toilet tissue but substitute heavily applied watercolour for the enamel.

The intervening period before the site was leased to the preservation society has not been kind to the offices and stores block. Parts of it may still be in use but a large portion of the roof obviously needs attention and the frontage has been secured against vandals. At the moment it's a lower priority than the much more exciting task of breathing new life into rusting steam locos.

ABOVE AND BELOW: *The preservation movement in the UK started much earlier than in the rest of Europe, where steam was still operating on an everyday basis in many countries, even on main lines, until well into the 1970s. A number of societies purchased engines in reasonable condition and shipped them to their new homes to augment the meagre selection of types already present. Industrial steam lingered on for a few more years and became the mainstay of steam workings on the emerging preserved lines. Some of these were actually ex-BR engines (although none are featured in this project, some research will reveal several suitable r-t-r models). Here a French 'Nord Pacific' stands in for a similar attraction at Steamtown in the early 1970s. Most of the figures in these scenes are either Langley or Dapol. The visiting school party recalls the days before jeans and anoraks became acceptable wear on official outings. The ex-GWR King has been cosmetically restored into the experimental Caledonian blue favoured by Swindon in the first years of British Railways.*

In the real world the tarpaulins would be secured by ropes from all four corners, with a couple more along the top and bottom sides, Cut some lengths of black or brown cotton, longer than needed, and secure them with a small blob of clear glue to the sheet. Next glue the sheet to the roof, leaving the portion over the revealed damaged corner unfixed. Depending upon your choice of kit you will have either chimney-style smoke vents or the long louvred type along the ridge. Secure the top cotton ropes to these and trim any excess, making sure that the ropes are taut. The lower ropes would hang below the eaves and simply be weighted by tying all of them around a heavy baulk of timber or securing them to individual weights. You only need to do one corner and the two side ropes. The loose corner can now be bent back and glued, suggesting that its rope had broken and it's flapping in the wind.

More roof damage

With the roof held right way up, nick out a few slates at random, removing some completely and leaving others as wholly or partially slipped.

If you wish to go further, you can consider damage to any smoke chimneys or louvred vents. This will depend entirely on your choice of kit and how these features are assembled. Confine any such damage to ripped-off or dislodged woodwork and don't overdo it. Your roof is then ready to be positioned according to the kit's instruction sheet, or the whole building put back if you are modifying an existing structure.

STRUCTURAL DAMAGE

Once again we want to suggest misuse and lack of maintenance rather than an *ad-hoc* demolition job. Look at the more vulnerable features first and the most obvious of these will be the guttering and downpipes, barge-boards and soffits, windows and doorways. Of these the most likely to be repaired or patched up will be the windows and doors, particularly those that might otherwise encourage illegal entry or further damage.

Doors can always be shown boarded up with timbers nailed across the frame. In other cases they might be bricked up with new or different brick-work. Damage to the main shed doors is less likely

since these are pretty massive affairs. Nonetheless one door could be left on the ground with a suitably posed worker repairing broken hinges.

Broken windows can be modelled in several ways. In kit form they will invariably comprise pre-printed acetate sheet representing the glazing set within the traditional cast-iron frames. Those frames will not show any signs of damage, so whatever you do to the panes must be carefully executed in order to leave the iron-work intact. For this you will need an ultra-sharp scalpel, good eyesight and a steady hand. Any repaired panes would be lower down the window in a position where it is more likely that someone has tried to fix them. You could replace the original clear glazing with frosted glass. Carefully and lightly roughen the inside of the panes and paint them with matt white enamel or acrylic. Some panes may have been boarded up with a sheet of plywood or even stout card. In this case, carefully remove the whole pane and glue a small piece of pre-printed card behind the frame, it is a tricky task it but can be done.

Another option might be to replace the whole window. This would only apply to the smaller and probably wood-framed windows to offices, toilets or stores. This is another 'bits box' exercise to find a suitable replacement. If you are successful, then fix it in place. But don't leave it at that. Carefully cut out the original window, removing all the excess acetate from outside the frames. Remove a pane or two and damage others, then prop it against the wall as if it had just been taken out.

Guttering, downpipes etc

These are always vulnerable and any damage is easy to model. Sections of guttering can be completely removed or, better yet, shown dangling from one end. Downpipes may be missing a bottom section or have a middle section disconnected and bent to one side. In all these cases some suggestion of staining and damp on the walls would be appropriate; a noticeable puddle on the ground would not be out of place.

Barge-boards and soffits

These can be either completely missing or broken and dangling. If you have a length of ladder handy, then some intrepid soul could be on top trying to fix things.

The major attraction for both families and the camera-laden enthusiasts is the prospect of working steam. Our centre has not yet restored any coaches, nor has it much in the way of operating lines. Brake van rides were easy to run, popular and a good source of income. Redundant vans, which were cheap to acquire and often in good running order, offered a different and perhaps more exciting trip than a normal coach. The service is being run as a 'push-pull' with an engine at each end. Ex-Great Western dock tank 1368 still sports its warning bell on the footplate, a reminder of its days on Weymouth quayside. Portishead, the little A1x 'Terrier' at the other end, was previously here as the shed-pilot in the steam era. The passengers, a mix of anyone who could be squeezed onto one of the verandahs, are a mix from Dapol, Preiser, Langley and Atlas.

GENERAL DECAY AND DAMAGE

Once again your choice of kit and use of accessories will determine what might have happened and, more importantly, how you might model it. The list of possibilities is bounded only by your imagination, but not everything can actually be achieved to produce a realistic result. Here are a few suggestions based upon our original list.

Broken fences

If your site is bordered by metal spear fencing, then missing spears, half-fallen panels or spears bent open by trespassing spotters are all possibilities. Brick walls might be part collapsed or part rebuilt with particular damage around any entrance gate. (BR contractors' lorry drivers may not have been too careful.) Original gates could be shown laid aside and broken, while a replacement might be a recycled level crossing gate.

Damaged buildings

These would probably be confined to the corners or 'awkward spots'. Sites like this were rarely cleared by the railway system they had once served. Much more likely was the use of BR's own heavy lorries or those of a conveniently located contractor. Clipping the corner, flattening a lamp post or deeply rutting the gateway and the site in general were all par for the course.

Rubbish tip

The new occupants would find plenty of use for their borrowed JCBs. Old sidings might need clearing and heaps of ash and clinker would have to go. Everything without any value would have to on the heap: rotten sleepers, broken furniture, sinks and toilets, bricks, slates, smashed concrete, hardcore from realigned roadways, spent ballast and the more obvious scrap metal from the restoration projects. The simplest way of reproducing this is to create the core from a lump of filler or plasticine and simply pile on the 'scrap' from plastic or white-metal kits, adding any oddments that, from a distance, might look like something else. A convenient place to dump the rubbish, pending its removal off-site, could be the abandoned turntable well.

The other popular attraction is the rare chance to experience life on the footplate. Very few of us ever enjoyed such a treat in the days when the railways had a proper job to do and rules to follow. For the lucky few the opportunity to relive the excitement and now to share it was a real highlight. In this view, with an ex-Great Western Mogul doing the honours, the driver is explaining the controls while his youthful fireman has a protective arm around a young blonde.

RESTORATION PROJECTS

The most obvious of the several ways in which these can be represented is to feature one of your current locomotives or items of rolling stock. Fortunately it is not necessary to break it up first. Place it on your allocated piece of track and cover it with tarpaulins, leaving just the wheels and perhaps the cab visible. If it is to be a loco, then choose one with a detachable tender. If you wish to portray an early stage of restoration or perhaps something just rusting away in the same state of advanced decay as when it left the scrapyard, try looking for something in poor condition at your local toy fair or car boot sale. Instead of wistfully examining all the expensive beauties on the tables, duck underneath and rummage in the 'everything for 50p' box.

For a project like this almost anything relating to locos and rolling stock can serve a purpose. If it's halfway recognizable, then buy it: badly built or broken Airfix kits, obsolete mechanisms, 'distressed' loco bodies, ancient coaches and vans without bogies vans, scrap tenders and so on. Even horrible plastic wheel-sets and cylinder blocks shouldn't be overlooked. You might get some strange looks when you offer a couple of pounds for a job lot, but the potential gain is well worth the embarrassment (the restoration locos shown in the photos set me back the princely sum of £1.50).

If you wish to add a touch of accuracy to your cameos, browse the list of spares from the current r-t-r manufacturers and check those outlets specializing in brass or white-metal detailing accessories. These items conspicuously displayed beside your sheeted hulk will help to underline what you are implying has been hidden beneath the tarpaulin.

WORKS IN PROGRESS

You will find that you need a lot of tarpaulins, so when you are making the one for the roof discussed above, make a dozen at the same time. It is also worthwhile including some working platforms. These can easily be made from trestles of plastic rod topped by a walkway of balsa wood or hardwood planks. While you are at it, a few ladders and stepladders are easy to make from the appropriate plastic strip.

Even on an open day the weekend volunteers are busy with the seemingly endless task of restoring their precious 'Barry Hulks' to mainline runners. The members of the Resurrect a Saint Society (RSS) are busy pre-empting the present team at Didcot and have made good progress on the boiler and footplate of their 29xx.

The site once occupied by the stationary boiler is now home to the group tackling the ex-GWR 2-6-2 tank. Perhaps they are hoping that one day it will be able to return to Devon, where their colleagues are working on what is now the South Devon Railway.

This group has set themselves quite a task: a 'Big Lizzie' is exactly that. Once the pride of the old LMS, Princess Royal Pacifics reigned supreme on the West Coast main line. It will be a few years, however, before she is able to swop the rust preventing primer for lustrous Crimson Lake.

The former 'back yard' is now host to yet more groups. Some are content to work on rolling stock, while others have rescued another Manor from the locomotive scrapyard at Barry in South Wales. If they are eventually successful, theirs will be one of several that would later find work on the tourist railways.

One interesting cameo might be to splash out on a die-cast low-loader and pose a boiler, a complete locomotive or a tender as recently arrived or even arriving. By adding a mobile crane and some fine-scale chain, the cameo can become an action scene including a suitably impressed audience being shepherded to safety by one of the team. There is no subject with a wider range of modelling opportunities than a 'steam centre' during the early days of preservation.

HUMINIATURES

This is the area where expense and time are inescapable: to do justice to the scene we need a lot of people and they should represent all ages, sexes and classes. This is a very subjective area where each modeller will have his or her distinct attitude to model figures. Taken to extremes some modellers will try to avoid them completely, while others go no further than buying a couple of ready-to-plant pre-painted packs. Most of us aim, with varying success, for the middle ground and use figures to both justify the existence of our towns and stations and to create interesting cameos to study when the trains aren't running.

There are also marked differences on how we treat our figures, from factory-painted versions to those hand painted in enamels or acrylics. My own attempts are different again since I always paint in watercolours, except for military subjects where uniform colouring is a pre-requisite. Since the final choice of source and finish is up to you, it is important to know what is required to produce the desired end result.

These far-sighted individuals are confident that goods trains, which were far more numerous than passenger services on the real railway, might one day be a popular part of the museum railway scene.

'VOLUNTEERS AND PRESSED MEN'

To begin with we can split our total list into two groups. The various club and society volunteers would mostly be males in their late teens and upwards. If the society had a small display or trade stand, however, this would almost certainly be staffed by wives and girlfriends. Not all the restoration projects would see work in progress. Those that were being worked on could be represented by a variety of tasks carried out by anything from a single volunteer to a well-organized party. If the subject of their attentions was fully sheeted then the jobs might involve work on the exposed wheels or perhaps removing or replacing the heavy connecting rods.

Much will depend on the actual 'attitude' of the available figures and how they might be posed to best suggest what they are doing. It is quite possible to conduct some modest surgery on plastic figures, but it is not an easy task to then recapture a lifelike attitude. Avoid it if you can.

Other volunteers might be seen taking money at the entrance, showing groups or individuals around, and acting as stewards at the main attrac-

tions, such as the footplate rides, brake van rides or special displays in carriages or larger vans. Finally you must have footplate crews for the working locos or demonstrations in the cabs of static engines. A total of about thirty such figures would seem realistic, but if you can dream up additional work opportunities then there is no limit to their numbers.

PUBLIC VISITORS

We must now turn our attention to the visiting public and the aspect of marketing known as 'audience profile'. It's not too scientific: simply use common sense and imagination coupled with the availability of the actual figures. Start, if you can, by drawing on your own experience of visiting a steam centre or similar attraction and recall the various groups and individuals you encountered: single males individually or in pairs; males in small organized parties; couples with or without children; older couples alone or perhaps with grandchildren; uniformed school or scout groups. If the centre is really fortunate, a whole coach party might be queuing to enter.

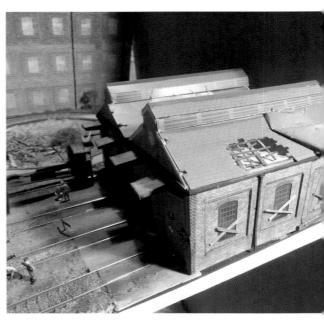

ABOVE LEFT AND RIGHT: *This view demonstrates why the Bilteezi 'old shed' was originally assembled with parts of its roof detachable. The weather has clearly taken its toll and the building is now in a dangerous state. There is a preservation order in place and the site-team have done their best to prevent any further deterioration. Note the ropes trying to secure the large tarpaulins against the winter gales.*

Make it busy

In order to give the desired impression it may be necessary to amass and pose at least thirty or forty figures. In model railway terms this is undoubtedly a large but still justifiable number. As you select your figures, simultaneously imagine where and how they will fit into the final scene. Do not be afraid of combining specialist individual white-metal figures with your plastic ones.

The figures from Monty's Models are the most accurately sculpted and posed. Those from Langley are somewhat cheaper and offer greater variety, even though they are slightly less realistic in appearance. It is also possible to add figures from the accessory packs offered by r-t-r manufacturers such as Bachmann and Master Models. Do not overlook the outstanding products in HO scale from Preiser and Noch. They are smaller, being 1:87 scale as opposed to 1:76, but their sculpting, moulded quality and poses are second to none. In any case not all humans are the same size.

Cameos and consistency

Individual and cameo groupings should reflect what is going on your site at that moment frozen in time. Some may be enjoying the attractions and interacting with the volunteers, while others are taking snaps or watching the trains go by. Some might be queuing for rides, ice creams or snacks. Curious enthusiasts might be trying to peer beneath the tarpaulins. There is bound to be a queue for the ladies' loo, because there always is!

The one thing I would urge is that you are consistent with the finish of all your figures, even if that means redoing those from pre-painted packs. The key factor is to always keep the paint jobs absolutely matt. Fabric simply does not exhibit any shine under any conditions. The only exceptions permitted would be motorcyclists in leathers or anyone with shiny waterproofs. One final point that should be mentioned is that very few of those engaged on work parties would wear overalls, as most would simply be in old clothes.

ABOVE AND BELOW: *Tarpaulins could be used for all sorts of purposes.*

CAR PARKS AND VEHICLES

If your space or layout plan permits, the outstanding die-cast scale models currently available will certainly meet most of your needs. Steer clear of any models of vehicles introduced after the date fixed as part of your back story. There might still be a few pre-war vehicles in use and the classic-car enthusiasts would then be growing in numbers. In addition to the off-the-shelf models, there are a number of white-metal kits available to represent popular runabouts by Austin, Morris and Fords or the 1930s MGs and Singers.

A bus, either vintage or contemporary, could well feature somewhere. There are scores available in most hobby shops and even more choice if you include obsolete models on the stands at toy fairs. If you can find examples carrying the liveries of operators local to the area in your back story, then so much the better.

Cars and bikes belonging to the volunteers can be parked within the site and there might be a couple of vans supporting a trade stand or one of the work groups. Finally you could do worse than build a Dapol JCB and perhaps even the mobile crane from their RAF recovery set. These can be employed upon some task or just parked out of the way. It is unlikely that today's mandatory First Aid requirements would be observed, but volunteers from the Red Cross or St John Ambulance might be in attendance, as might a suitable blue and white police panda car.

Rubbish dumps were inevitable in the early days. The resident groups have here found a fresh use for the abandoned turntable well. With a little imagination and access to a healthy bits box, this scene could become a major feature and talking point on an exhibition layout.

ABOVE LEFT AND RIGHT: *Two typical views of Carnforth depot when playing host to visiting engines from the many specials that were running in the mid-1970s. Points worth mentioning include the immense size of the concrete 'Cenotaph' coaling tower, the immaculate finish to the little 'Lanky' 0-6-0 on the passenger shuttles and the number of original buildings that still exist amid the encroaching vegetation. With a bit of tweaking, scenes like this could easily be reproduced from the shelves of your local model shop.*

OPERATIONAL POSSIBILITIES

Unlike our previous projects, which were primarily designed to function only as part of a larger layout, the 'Steam Centre' could become a stand-alone layout in its own right. This is not the place to go into methods of wiring, control systems or the big question of DC versus DCC, but we do need to mention possible movements.

The number of movements available are not huge, but there are probably enough to satisfy most operators. If you are modelling the layout exactly as in the project then you will need to provide some offstage spurs at the right-hand end and a sector-plate or cassettes to feed the entrance. Typical movements could involve any of the following: footplate rides, brake van rides, engine changes and servicing, special positioning for photos, and the arrival and departure of visiting rail-tour engines. Nothing should appear too grand or too complicated. You should simply make the best use of your available trackwork, exactly as those early enthusiasts would have done.

CHAPTER NINE

THE MPD IN PRESERVATION: THE STEAM CENTRE

As part of the previous phase of the project we were tasked with adding damage and dereliction to our existing structures (see Chapter 8). Now we have to reverse that process by restoring everything to its former glory and even make and add some more modern-looking additions. The same level of transformation must be carried out across the site as a whole.

It is a fair bet that, while many modellers never enjoyed first-hand experience of the early preservation scene, the reverse will be true of today's attractions. The actual number of 'steam centres', however, is somewhat limited and so the best reference points for most of us will be the preserved railways. The stations and shed yards frequently host society stands and visiting engines, and there

is always the public to observe. This makes them viable alternatives for those who cannot make it to the National Railway Museum, Didcot or Tyseley.

Steam centres are, in many respects, no different from any other major visitor attraction. They are governed by the same rules, regulations and recommendations as are all public venues. If anything they are even more stringently managed, since they must cater for an audience often totally unaccustomed to being in close proximity to the industrial nature of working steam. The risk potential is very great for today's risk-averse society. Unlike aviation events, where the simple maxim that 'people and propellers don't mix' is enforced by stringent rules for pilots and many yards of

Didcot is today the long-term home of the Great Western Society and has earned an international reputation over the course of more than forty years. The ashes of the last British Railways occupants had barely had time to cool when the GWS first occupied the site and it was able to inherit a depot almost in running order. The small brick building to the left of the entrance is a standard type of GWR sand furnace.

Visitors watch the resident diesel on the inclined ramp to the coaling stage on a sultry July afternoon. Comparing these images with those from the steam era in Chapter 5, it is quickly apparent how much nature can contribute towards softening the otherwise industrial atmosphere.

steel barriers, the steam centre is heavily reliant on well-trained stewards, the proper execution of 'Duty of Care' and a degree of common sense on the part of its visitors.

THE NEW ORDER

We have come a long way in the four decades since those early endeavours. The whole site will now be properly fenced and secured. The original buildings, if not demolished, will have been carefully repaired and restored; the running lines are permanently protected and the attractions accessed by proper platforms, which are often constructed like mini-stations. New buildings are in evidence, some new and purpose-built, others painstakingly re-erected often many miles from their original site. Works in progress will probably take the form of carefully managed demonstrations alongside the somewhat formalized shed routines of coaling and taking water. Visitor rides are now provided by steam-hauled trains of beautifully restored carriages and the informality of footplate trips has been replaced by 'driver experience' courses. The rubbish and general detritus is long gone and in its stead are new sidings and running lines, gardens and picnic areas. New features like signalling and 'dummy' level crossings can be seen and many of these will be operated from an authentic rebuilt signal box.

In terms of the more obvious artefacts, the steam centre will probably have become more orientated to the works of a single company or BR region. For example, the Great Western Society at Didcot Railway Centre is internationally renowned as the home of all things Great Western and most of the motive power and the wagons represent part of that company's history. Not all the rescued relics will have been restored; where possible, much of the remainder will be stored away from the main public areas. The exceptions are likely to be more high-profile restoration projects that will be in public view, both for fund raising and as evidence of the sheer hard work undertaken by the various groups.

There will almost certainly be guest locomotives in steam alongside the resident fleet. When the dates conveniently coincide, engines from mainline specials will arrive for servicing. All of this means that locomotives will be moving around the yard and therefore through the public areas; the stewards' yellow jackets will be much in evidence. If a 'special' is on-shed then it is likely to receive plenty of attention. One would expect to see its own passengers swelling the numbers of visitors to the site. There will certainly be carefully stage-managed photo-calls on the turntable or perhaps alongside the centre's own fleet. (Scenes like this are a gift if you like figure-painting, but are best ignored if you don't.) Finally the

The Society has gone to great lengths to establish its Great Western heritage. All the many new buildings reflect the old company's style and its 'light and dark stone' colour schemes are everywhere. This is the waiting shelter on the main running-line. It's gratifying to see how closely our own model from a Metcalf kit will resemble it.

Didcot's running-line was established almost from the outset and has since been upgraded and extended. It has seen a huge variety of motive power, ranging from the Centre's smallest tank engines to the numerous visiting Pacifics. The Southern's T9s were regularly seen on-shed in the old days, having arrived off the services on the Didcot, Newbury & Southampton Railway, before its final closure in 1967.

In recent years there have been significant changes to the site on both the visitor side and for the engineering and restoration departments. All the new buildings have been carefully designed to retain a GWR character while still fulfilling their twenty-first century purpose. Some older features have also been put to good use: these bicycle sheds, for example, now display luggage and other memorabilia.

The great thing about preservation sites from a modeller's perspective is that almost any bits of 4mm 'railwayana' can be used to create an atmospheric background. A row of chimneys like these can easily be sourced from the many specialist suppliers; a few minutes browsing the net will produce plenty of leads.

The combined efforts of Mother Nature and Didcot's landscaping volunteers have transformed derelict industrial areas into pastoral scenes that are perfect for family picnics. In the background is the Centre's second operating line, which perfectly captures the feel of a typical rural branch. Lurking among the foliage is the recently restored steam railmotor, a remarkable piece of Edwardian enterprise bought back to life.

Another reminder of just how closely a Scalescenes coaling stage resembles Didcot's version. The buffer stop in front is at the end of the original ash road. The ramp is highly popular with photographers on open days and could be modelled as such, provided you enjoy painting figures and do not need it to be operational.

facilities, such as museums, galleries, museum shops, catering, toilets and disabled access provision will all be up to date and the whole site will be user-friendly and well-signposted.

MODELLING THE CONTEMPORARY STEAM CENTRE

In order to maintain the theme of the life of our original MPD, we will continue to keep the main elements where they have been. As has been said before, though, every modeller will want to make their own version based upon their own preferences and use the appropriate kits for the structures of their choice. While the following sections will apply the various techniques to our existing work, they are nonetheless intended to be largely inspirational and can therefore be applied equally to your own, quite different, interpretation of a steam centre.

The MPD's office block has been repaired and now proudly announces its new role. Vintage travel posters adorn the noticeboards and the woodwork has had a fresh coat of paint.

ABOVE LEFT AND RIGHT: *These two aerial views reveal that, although the general layout is largely unaltered, there have been some significant changes. The dilapidated ash shelter and the sand furnace were clearly no longer fit for purpose and the old Carriage & Wagon Works has been demolished. The turntable has been reinstated and a new running-line and platform occupies the old works site.*

The thing to remember is that this phase now requires the opposite of 'weathering'. Previously we have always tried to overlay everything, even printed card, with the inevitable consequences resulting from daily wear and tear, from the weather itself, from limited maintenance and from the constant presence of dirty steam locomotives. Now we must recreate an ambience redolent of restoration and of loving care, with only relatively rare appearances by those polluting engines.

COLOUR SCHEMES

Any paintwork will generally be clean and, if not exactly freshly applied, it would show little evidence of age beyond the inevitable fading. This is the one case where enamels or acrylics may be more appropriate than watercolours. Several manufacturers offer accurate renditions of the obvious 'Big Four' and BR regional liveries: Railmatch and Precision are the most obvious choices. If these are not readily

available, it should be possible to get a close match from within the ranges by Humbrol, Revell or Tamiya. Avoid full gloss versions, however, since these can be slow to dry and somehow appear much too garish when used on woodwork. Satin-type coatings are fine for newly painted areas, but otherwise stick to matt finishes and add a degree of matt white to show some evidence of weathering.

The chosen kits have mostly been from Scalescenes, but the same principles will apply whatever the choice. I would suggest tackling some of the preparations for these final paint jobs during the initial assembly, which is far easier than attempting it retrospectively, as demanded by the project. In most cases a light spray of Winsor & Newton Artists' Matt Varnish as a sort of primer will help to dull any shine on the paintwork and ease any subsequent painting.

I suspect that by now readers will have noticed my inclination towards all things Great Western. This gave me a choice between the 'light and dark stone' of

The main public entrance is bordered by the traditional spear-fencing and the much-trodden ballast of the earlier phases has been grassed over and is now a picnic and viewing area. The Centre's open day is attracting a good crowd of all ages, portrayed by a mix of Dapol, Preiser and Langley figures.

These general views across the shed's 'front yard' are what would greet the average visitor. The Mogul is still busy giving footplate rides and the depot is hosting some guest engines as well as servicing others from special tours. A preserved Castle is waiting for its turn at the coaling stage.

*The Mogul passes an impressive line-up of Western Region top-link power, two Kings and a 'Brit',
all sporting their once familiar reporting numbers. These were introduced by the GWR in the 1930s
to assist the signalmen in identifying the oncoming trains. They continued to be used throughout the
1950s, albeit with some changes, and just about survived into the early diesel years on the nose of
Warships and Westerns.*

the old company or the widely known 'chocolate and cream' of the BR era. The useful guides available from the HMRS (Historic Model Rail Society) that cover most if, not all, of the main regions will tell you not only the colours to use but also where to use them.

IMPROVED FACILITIES

The actual construction and assembly follow the standard practices used in earlier chapters, so there is little modification or customization to be undertaken apart from the selective repaints. Indeed the only thing that needs to be considered is the likely change of use for some of the smaller buildings, such as the offices, mess-rooms and stores, which can be reassigned to more public-friendly duties like catering, museums and archive centres, or lecture and meeting rooms. This requires little beyond smart-

ening things up and adding notices. The latter can be computer generated or carefully drawn by hand using drawing inks on thin card.

A colourful feature that can now be added to the buildings is period commercial posters, which previously would have been totally out of place. The old companies and BR itself were prolific producers of advertising materials for their own services. They were also more than happy to offer advertising sites to a huge range of third parties. Fortunately there is an almost inexhaustible supply upon which to draw, ranging from realistically reproduced enamel signs to the later paper versions. While I don't advocate plastering them on every available wall, you can certainly make good use of them, perhaps by mounting them on blank company noticeboards attached to fences or on custom-made hoardings judiciously placed around the site.

The T9 has, hypothetically at least, just arrived as part of a special working and has come on shed for servicing and turning. It could equally, however, be a guest-engine taking a breather off the lunchtime 'diner' on the running-line. That is the great thing about the MPD as a steam centre – whatever you wish to happen can happen. Britain's poster industry has produced some deservedly famous images, many of which linger in the memory long after the brand itself has disappeared. A great many of these are available in model form and are also featured at steam centres and on tourist railways. If the ones you recall aren't represented, you can always paint your own.

KEY TASKS

The actual modelling required can be broken down into four categories: new and re-laid track; new buildings and modified existing ones; increased vegetation and landscaping; and, finally, additional artefacts.

Trackwork: Existing track will need no more than a general tidying up and the installation of any new or additional point-work. New track should be modelled in good condition with reasonably clean and well-tended ballast. Sleepers, where visible, could well be freshly creosoted but the rails themselves are unlikely to look any different from those elsewhere on the layout.

Modified buildings: There are no fixed rules here. Just as in the real world it will depend entirely upon the building that was there to begin with. It is then a question of what was it used for and whether it is still needed in that role or what it might logically become. If an important facility did not previously exist, then what could be built to house it, while still blending into the existing site.

The branch-line platform shelter, mentioned earlier, has received some extra detailing and a repaint into GWR colours. It's a perfect little model for settings like this. The scratch-built platform has two faces: the farther one serves the actual branch line and the nearer one, an extension of the old boiler washout road, is used to display guest engines and gives access to the footplate rides. The ex-GWR diesel railcar has just arrived from its trip down the branch that, according to the back story, runs to the offstage carriage sheds and restoration bays. No doubt the corpulent grandfather would have preferred to stay on the train rather than be dragged across to the play area. Most of the figures on the platform are by Preiser, but a few from Dapol are also seen.

Earlier we referred to alternative uses for shed offices and the building and re-siting of signal boxes or platform shelters. Two good conversions that have been adopted at Didcot involve turning an air-raid shelter into toilets and the bicycle sheds into somewhere to display memorabilia. 'New' structures might here include building a facsimile shed or station solely for museum or commercial use. A further conversion might be to find an alternative use for the lower portion of the coaling stage.

Landscaping and vegetation: Landscaping may involve little more than grassing over the surplus flat areas of the site, perhaps with some flower beds for relief. The earth and rubble banks of the coaling stage could have new grass, flowers, shrubs and maybe the location picked out in whitewashed stone. Any naturally occurring trees and bushes could be allowed

to mature and quick-growing varieties planted. New concrete or slabs would provide safe walkways. Prominent flower beds can be planted in picnic and rest areas. An appropriate addition would be a small vegetable plot by the signal box, replicating a very common practice during the 1940 and '50s.

Artefacts: Loco and wagon wheels are an obvious choice, as are loco chimneys. Rescued running-in boards from long-closed stations or signal boxes would prove popular. Relevant and famous loco nameplates and (GWR only) cast numberplates might adorn the outside of the restaurant, museum or shop. The aim is to capture something that looks commercially attractive and that might also emphasize the site's value as a collection, without actually destroying the echoes of its former role.

City of Truro is paying a welcome visit. The real locomotive enjoyed a brief but glorious return to steam in the early 1960s and was frequently on-shed at Didcot, where it was used on the Didcot, Newbury & Southampton Railway line up to Newbury (the author cycled the 20-mile round trip for the unique chance to travel behind this historic engine). The model is the Airfix kit, but it is much detailed and by running on scale wheels it is able to 'double-head' on 'Wessex Lines'.

EVENTS

The question of locomotives and stock is entirely down to each modeller. It is worth pointing out, however, that model manufacturers, as well as the real-life restorers, have ensured that the modern steam centre in both those worlds can present the widest possible choice of locomotives and stock. The much welcomed building of the LNER Class A1 Peppercorn *Tornado* is an excellent example: forty years earlier this wasn't even a dream. No matter where the model steam centre is located there is always an excuse to bring in a 4mm version of something exotic, if only for servicing.

This batch of images demonstrates the sense of colour and movement that can be achieved with the careful grouping of well-painted figures. If you wish to replicate this, however, it's almost impossible to achieve the effect with British 'huminiatures' as you will have to use Preiser figures to get the necessary variety, character and accuracy.

As for the 'huminiatures' and their modes of travel, you only need to update the scene and repaint or reposition a few individuals. If anything, while the dress code has become more casual, it is probably a lot less colourful, with ubiquitous jeans being everyday wear for both sexes and all ages. You may have to extend your budget a little and investigate the US and Continental figure ranges.

The simple answer to the problem of road vehicles is to restrict them to the offstage public car parks, unless there is a legitimate reason for them to be on-site.

'Running days' have become more civilized in terms of operations. There may still be footplate rides, but now they have usually become pre-booked 'driver experience' sessions. The brake van rides have grown into passenger trains of two or three coaches from any era, properly refurbished and often including a dining car for lunches and teas. A new branch line has been opened, perhaps operated by a steam-hauled auto-coach, a diesel railcar or railbus.

These activities will continue throughout the day and, as in the previous phase, make this version of the MPD into a genuine exhibition attraction.

STEAM CENTRE POTENTIAL

In the earlier phases we indicated that the MPD made a near-perfect diorama for the static display of a locomotive collection, while also satisfying the needs of the modeller who wants an operating layout. This final phase enables us to take things further and look at its true potential as an exhibition concept as well as being a semi-permanent set-up at home.

I'm not going to claim that the project version as it stands would be entirely suitable. It was designed and built purely to illustrate what might be created in such a setting rather than as a fully operating layout. With a bit of tweaking, however, and the advantage of a little more space, the basic approach can be made to work.

INCREASED SPACE

As a reminder, the existing module on its two A1 boards measures 69 x 24in (1,750 x 610mm) and the track plan has been squeezed to make optimal

The small signal box at the end of the platform, no doubt open to visitors, is another Metcalf model that is ideal for this setting. The figures are Dapol and so are positioned slightly away from their HO fellow travellers.

The view looking back from the signal box end reveals the generous dimensions of the new platform. It also shows the potential of using the outer face solely for the branch line, while the inner one is multi-purpose. Note that the new site fencing is adorned with yet more posters.

Two more views across the yard with the T9 posing in front of the coaling stage. Photo-calls like this are regular features of open days. The modeller aiming for a simple, but extensive, non-working diorama can use these as an opportunity to reposition engines or introduce new engines into the picture. Operating modellers, too, can use it as a fresh excuse to run engines to and from specific areas. Popular settings are the coaling stage, the turntable, the water cranes or a prominent position outside the main shed. The second photo offers another glimpse of the poster display. If you cannot find an image of the right size for a road- or railside hoarding, either paint it by hand or use a colour copier to enlarge or reduce your chosen design. The Toad brake van has been repainted in GWR 'engineering stock' black, with lettering by Methfix, for work on the author's main layout.

BELOW RIGHT: The brake van rides on the earlier version have been replaced by something more lavish, in this case some stock from my West Country services. This is easy to reproduce in 4mm scale as the major r-t-r manufacturers invariably have at least one 'diner' in their current range. The use of Pullman stock would be equally suitable or, if all else fails, there are accessory kits to help you convert an ordinary open coach. The Centenary 'diner' in the middle of the rake was produced this way by butchering two brake coaches into one and adding the necessary details and lettering. The two spare ends were rejoined to form a new full-brake.

The traditional line-up of resident and guest engines always pulls the crowds: the more exotic, prestigious or rarely seen the visitor, then the bigger the attraction it will be. The crews are usually on hand to answer questions and make minor adjustments to the line-up for the benefit of photographers. This also happens on the Continent when engines gather for festivals or to haul Plandampf services, when steam is specially allocated to operate main lines and branches in place of the usual diesel or electric power. There they have the advantage that, by displaying them at half-roundhouses, the various engines can be moved out onto the turntable and turned a full 360 degrees for the assembled throng. The reporting numbers referred to earlier are based on a fairly simple system. The first number indicates the train's departure district ('1' is Paddington, for example, and '6' is Cornwall). The next two are the real identifiers: '130' is the 'Cornish Riviera Express' and carries the headboard to prove it, '135' is a second portion travelling either ahead of or after the main train. The Britannia has '605', which is the return up-working from Penzance: this famous train was always known by railwaymen simply as 'The Limited'. In our scale the numbers come in an accessory pack together with a white-metal retaining grid to fix onto the smokebox, although, since I needed about twenty sets, I must admit to using the photocopier. They are made up onto small strips of plasticard and then epoxied onto thin wire hooks to hang from the handrails. The result is not particularly neat but at least they can be swopped between the rostered engines.

visual use of this area. Many clearances are not what they should be and the resulting point-work owes more to what I could recycle than to what would have been desirable on a working layout. My first advice is therefore to revise the plan to give an extra 6in (150mm) of width throughout, and an extra 12 to 15in (300–380mm) at both ends. This still keeps the viewing frontage to a modest 8ft (2,440mm). A concealed set of cassettes, storage sidings or sector-plate would add a further 4ft (1,220mm) at the approach end (left).

The extra width would ensure more appropriate track spacing and also allow the front running line to become an additional road extending past the Bilteezi 'old shed', which could then also be modelled to its correct length. On the far side of layout the 'branch line' could be extended back to run behind the coaling stage. The accompanying diagram in the appendix should help to clarify these changes.

OPERATING AND EXHIBITION SEQUENCES

Although the layout has now become more complex it can still provide almost constant movement even with only one operator at the control panel. It can also be worked perfectly well with analogue DC, although DCC would permit more simultaneous rather than mostly sequential movements. The choice of engines and stock remains wide open and I have simply indicated their types, illustrated by GWR examples. The following schedule could be executed in the course of about a one-hour session, which is more than enough at the average exhibition. It could then be repeated using different stock. The permutations are almost without limit if sufficient stock is available.

Main running line

(1) Regular out-and-back passenger service. Two carriages headed by any engine up to a 4-6-0. Loco

RIGHT AND BELOW RIGHT: *The photographers (by Langley) are ever hopeful of that shot-of-a-lifetime. Perhaps they would do better to turn round and take a close-up of the Castle's impressive brass nameplate: Somerset Light Infantry ... Prince Albert's was appropriately a West Country engine for most of her long working life.*

can be at either end and facing in either direction. This would be a 'push-pull' working. (Pannier, 2-6-2 tank, Mogul, Hall or Manor)

(2) Dining-car service to run once in any sequence. Three appropriate coaches (Pullmans, Centenaries or similar) headed by a larger engine. Train can be halted for 'viewing' at suitable point. (Castle or King)

(3) Demonstration goods train. Short consist of immaculately restored wagons, vans and tanks headed by a suitable freight engine. To run once in any sequence. (28xx, 38xx or heavy tank)

Branch line

Regular shuttle service to be operated by railcar, auto-train or B-set. These can be swopped during or between sequences. (Diesel railcar, 14xx or Pannier)

Shed yard

'Driver experience': To operate on the line nearside of the branch platform and to run as required using the ash road and elsewhere as available. Engine can be anything with larger footplate. (0-6-0, Mogul or 2-6-2T Dean or Collet goods, 61xx or 43xx)

Shed movements: These are at the operator's discretion and could include: an engine for turntable demonstration; repositioning engines for photo-calls; coaling demonstration; duty engines returning for servicing or engine changes.

Visiting engines: These can be from any region and can also include diesels. They will probably require coal, water and turning. They may be posed with resident engines or take out a working on the running line. There may be more than one visitor in; this, too, must be serviced in between sequences.

After such a schedule, the operator will have earned a ten-minute break. This is where good presentation comes to the fore. The front panel, which should mask the offstage arrangements, should contain any relevant information about the layout. It should also display clear but informal courtesy information to keep the visitors and the organizers happy, such as 'Next session 12:30', 'Back in 10 mins' or 'Full sequences commence every hour on the hour'.

Most of the heavy restoration work is now confined to the 'back yard' and to the old shed, which has long since been repaired and re-equipped. This area would not normally be accessible to the public except as part of a guided tour. In the background the N15x Remembrance *is being turned ready to take out one of the railtour specials. As a popular and much-admired engine, she may well be sent back to join the official line-up before departing.*

Most tourist lines and steam centres take great pride in their signals, not just in their correct daily use but as working examples of the old semaphore system. Most of the signals on 'Wessex Lines', as on so many layouts, are from Ratio kits. Good though they undoubtedly are, however, they lack detail and are not always suited to their role. Wherever possible I like to choose interesting examples from the albums and copy them to add that extra bit of authenticity to the scene. Of course, they all have the appropriate guard rails and safety hoops. This odd little item is based on an original from Uxbridge Vine Street.

FINAL CONCLUSIONS

In the course of this book we have travelled from that first little Alphagraphix single-road shed to exploring the potential of the MPD as a stand-alone exhibit on the show circuit. I hope that some light has been shone into the murk that shrouded the steam-era engine shed. Large or small, they offer a proper challenge to the keen modeller, especially as they are a whole lot easier to get wrong than to get right.

*The preservationists' work is never done. Even on open days, little gangs of volunteers will still be busily beavering away. There has been a major change in the twenty-first century in that the headlines are no longer dominated by restoration projects, but rather by frantic appeals for funding nearly complete 'new-builds'. The undoubted triumph of the team behind building **Tornado** has shown what can be achieved with long-term effort and commitment, not to mention a great deal of cash. Some ventures, such as the GWS steam rail-motor and the now almost completed Saint, are historically driven. Others are regionally influenced as well as trying to fill gaps in collections. Still others seem to be exercises in wishful-thinking and I find it hard to know what they will do with their exotic engines, if and when they are ever finished. You can be sure, however, that you can expect to have a 4mm version of whatever emerges, from wherever it's being built, ready to join the shed at your present-day steam centre just a few months later.*

RIGHT AND BELOW RIGHT: *In the meantime, spare a thought for the unsung heroes struggling in all weathers to repair a century-old piece of ironwork on a wagon that may never even leave the yard.*

The range of kits and accessories available seems to grow, if not month by month, then certainly year by year. It has never been easier to get the buildings correct and to develop sheds that are fitting homes for the near-perfect model locos now available on every high street. In those rare cases where there is no suitable kit, I hope a few more modellers may have been persuaded to have a go at scratch-building. Perhaps, too, the sales of autobiographies by the fast-disappearing family of steam footplate-men will show an immediate upturn. Their sheds may have been demolished long ago but their stories and often irrepressible good humour are still there to inspire us. In the unlikely event that modellers become bored or disillusioned with their efforts, a quick glance at any of these books should be enough to revive their enthusiasm for recreating former times faithfully within our miniature worlds.

APPENDICES

APPENDIX 1 (CHAPTER 1)

There are as many different possibilities for laying out track plans at single-road engine sheds as there are choices of buildings. It is always important to ensure that the provision of vital facilities, notably coal and water, is properly relative to the shed's duties and that the setting should be 'railway-like'. The diagrams show just a few of the workable alternatives. Note that the width of the yard doubles when you include a turntable.

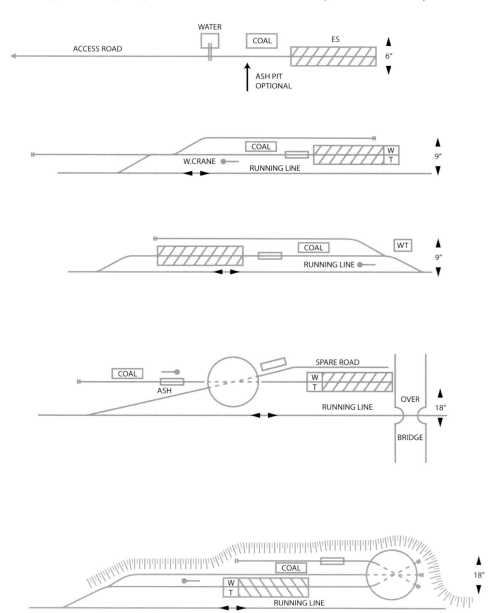

APPENDIX 2 (CHAPTER 2)

The key dimensions shown here were derived from the photo-trip. They should not be viewed as totally accurate but they are the ones that will be used to construct the model. When preparing the drawings and finalizing the artwork I always opted for the higher of the possible figures. If you are short of space, it should be possible to reduce all the dimensions by at least 5 per cent and still retain the shed's essential character.

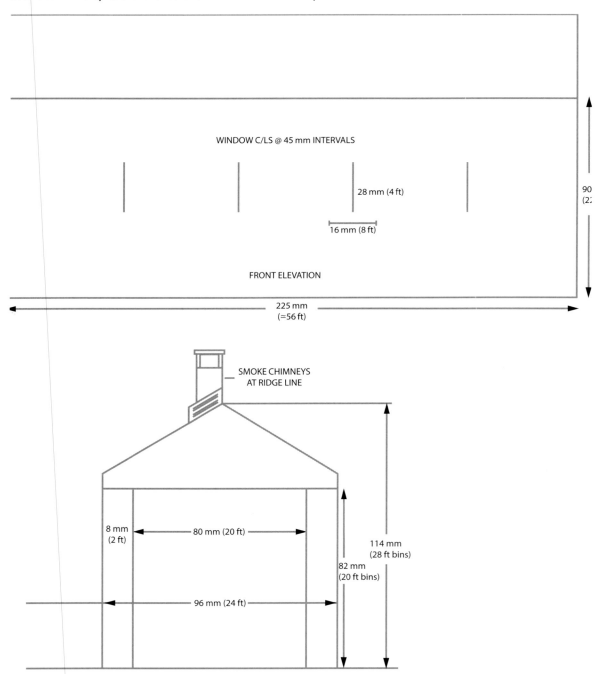

APPENDIX 3 (CHAPTER 3)

These diagrams should help to clarify the back story of this particular project. This type of sketch is an integral part of the planning process. It helps in the selection of the engines that you will need and, subsequently, to roster them onto their appropriate workings. The shed's track plan has been included as modelled, but the ancillary buildings may still be sited to suit your layout. Many depots were located like this and engines were turned using the triangle.

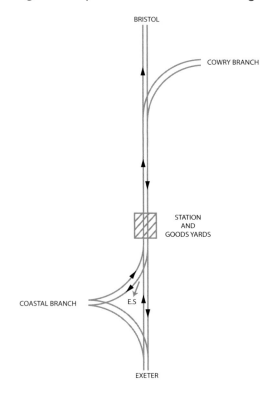

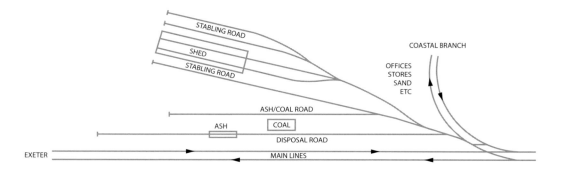

APPENDIX 4 (CHAPTER 4)

There is nothing new in combining several copies of the main walls from a kit to form a background low-relief or even flat structure. Almost any card kit or download can become the starting-point, but you should remember that it is important for railway structures on the project to maintain a consistent architectural style. In the example we used Bilteezi kits for the shed and the back-scene, but the combination of Metcalf/Metcalf or Scalescenes/Scalescenes would be equally effective. The technique is very simple, quick, cheap and ultimately effective. My own methods are described in some detail in Chapter 4. If you can find it, A1 foamboard is a desirable alternative to card for actual backing material.

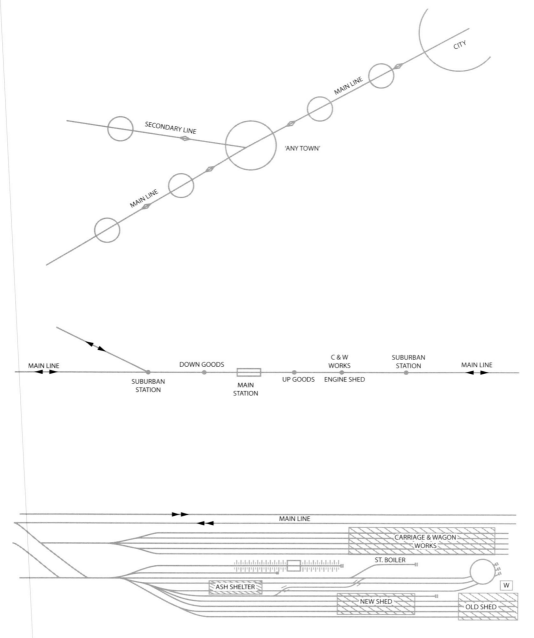

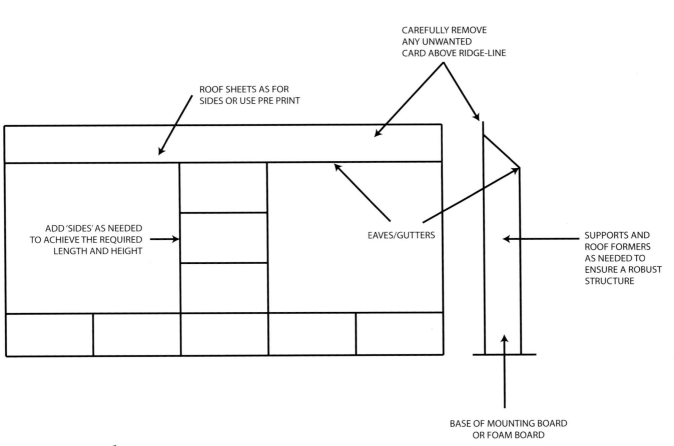

CAREFULLY REMOVE
ANY UNWANTED
CARD ABOVE RIDGE-LINE

ROOF SHEETS AS FOR
SIDES OR USE PRE PRINT

ADD 'SIDES' AS NEEDED
TO ACHIEVE THE REQUIRED
LENGTH AND HEIGHT

EAVES/GUTTERS

SUPPORTS AND
ROOF FORMERS
AS NEEDED TO
ENSURE A ROBUST
STRUCTURE

BASE OF MOUNTING BOARD
OR FOAM BOARD

PRINT OR COPY
MORE THAN ENOUGH
'SIDES' – IN CASE OF DAMAGE

③ TRIM AS NECESSARY AND THEN
FIX WITH SPRAY ADHESIVE

'TRIAL AND ERROR' – PLACE YOUR 'SIDES' ON
THE BOARDS AND SIMPLY JUGGLE THEM
AROUND UNTIL YOU ACHIEVE THE BEST
FIT – AND A REALISTIC FRONTAGE

④ USE BUTTRESSES/DRAIN PIPES
TO DISGUISE THE JOINS

APPENDIX 5 (CHAPTER 7)

This is my personal take on how the project MPD plan might be expanded to maximize its potential as an exhibition layout. (The dotted line encompasses the existing build.) The basic track plan is the same, albeit with proper clearances, and the new or extended lines are shown in red. As drawn, the scenic footprint has increased from 69 x 24in to 108in x 30in: this would make two 4ft 6in' x 2ft 6in modules that can easily be transported in the average estate car. The author's 'East Ilsley' layout, for example, uses foamboard and three-ply to these dimensions and each module weighs only two or three kilograms. I envisage the layout being fed from the left via a bank of cassettes, the number and lengths depending on what is required.

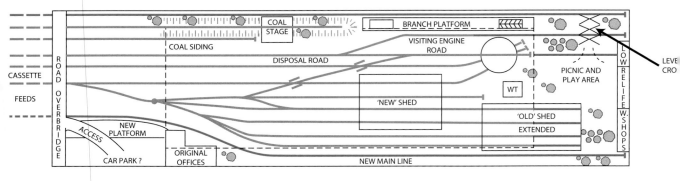

INDEX

RELATED TITLES
FROM CROWOOD

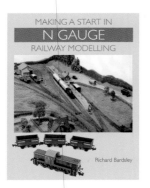

**Making a Start in
N Gauge Railway
Modelling**
RICHARD BARDSLEY
ISBN 978 1 84797 556 0
192pp, 300 illustrations

**Planning, Designing and
Making Railway Layouts
in Small Spaces**
RICHARD BARDSLEY
ISBN 978 1 84797 424 2
144pp, 130 illustrations

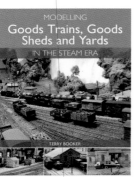

**Modelling Goods Trains,
Goods Sheds and Yards
in the Steam Era**
TERRY BOOKER
ISBN 978 1 78500 068 3
192pp, 250 illustrations

**A Practical Introduction
to Digital Command
Control for Railway
Modellers**
NIGEL BURKIN
ISBN 978 1 84797 020 6
192pp, 400 illustrations

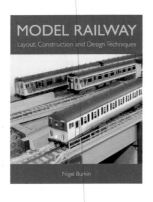

**Model Railway Layout,
Construction and Design
Techniques**
NIGEL BURKIN
ISBN 978 1 84797 181 4
192pp, 340 illustrations

Scenic Modelling
JOHN DE FRAYSSINET
ISBN 978 1 84797 457 0
160pp, 230 illustrations

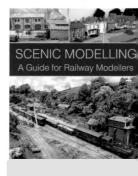

In case of difficulty ordering, please contact the Sales Office:

The Crowood Press
Ramsbury
Wiltshire
SN8 2HR
UK

Tel: 44 (0) 1672 520320
enquiries@crowood.com
www.crowood.com